IF WE'RE TOGETHER,
WHY DO I FEEL SO ALONE?

IF WE'RE TOGETHER, WHY DO I FEEL SO ALONE?

How to Build Intimacy
with an Emotionally
Unavailable Partner

HOLLY PARKER, PhD

NEW AMERICAN LIBRARY

NEW YORK

NEW AMERICAN LIBRARY
Published by Berkley
An imprint of Penguin Random House LLC
375 Hudson Street, New York, New York 10014

Copyright © 2017 by Holly Parker, PhD
Penguin Random House supports copyright. Copyright fuels creativity, encourages diverse
voices, promotes free speech, and creates a vibrant culture. Thank you for buying an
authorized edition of this book and for complying with copyright laws by not reproducing,
scanning, or distributing any part of it in any form without permission. You are supporting
writers and allowing Penguin Random House to continue to publish books for every reader.

New American Library and the NAL colophon are registered trademarks of Penguin Random
House LLC.

Library of Congress Cataloging-in-Publication Data

Names: Parker, Holly (Psychologist), author.
Title: If we're together, why do I feel so alone?: how to build intimacy with an emotionally
unavailable partner/Holly Parker, Ph.D.
Description: New York: NAL, 2017.
Identifiers: LCCN 2016012846 (print) | LCCN 2016021362 (ebook) | ISBN 9780425273487
(paperback) | ISBN 9780698150706 (ebook)
Subjects: LCSH: Intimacy (Psychology) | Couples—Psychology. | Man-woman relationships. |
Interpersonal relations. | BISAC: FAMILY & RELATIONSHIPS/Love & Romance. |
FAMILY & RELATIONSHIPS/Marriage. | FAMILY & RELATIONSHIPS/General.
Classification: LCC BF575.I5 P37 2017 (print) | LCC BF575.I5 (ebook) | DDC 158.2—dc23
LC record available at https://lccn.loc.gov/2016012846

First Edition: January 2017

Printed in the United States of America
1   3   5   7   9   10   8   6   4   2

Cover design by George Long
Book design by Kristin del Rosario

While the author has made every effort to provide accurate telephone numbers, Internet
addresses and other contact information at the time of publication, neither the publisher nor
the author assumes any responsibility for errors, or for changes that occur after publication.
Further, publisher does not have any control over and does not assume any responsibility
for author or third-party Web sites or their content.

This book is for my exquisite husband and best friend,
sweet Guille,
who shows me heaven every single day
and is pure bliss to love.

CONTENTS

INTRODUCTION

Relationships impact almost everything and almost everything impacts relationships. When I say almost everything, I'm not exaggerating. Relationships influence our self-esteem, happiness, physical health, pain tolerance, lifestyle, and career satisfaction. They can fill our lives with joy, security, and energy or be a major player in creating burdensome worry, anxiety, sadness, and a sense of draining defeat. It's not surprising that, as a psychologist, I spend the majority of session time with my patients trying to help heal relationships—the ones my clients have with others, as well as the one they have with themselves.

When individuals or couples come to see me for therapy, one of the most common issues revealed when we discuss their relationships is emotional availability. What is emotional availability? It is the ability and readiness to build an emotional bond with another, and to actively participate in a gratifying and healthful relationship that meets each person's needs. Some people are naturally more emotionally available for connection while others find emotional connectedness to be a real struggle. For those who struggle, opening to connection is a major part of our therapeutic work.

In light of the tremendous influence relationships have in determining a person's quality of life, I feel an intense passion to help people find ways to fill their lives with the healthiest, most rewarding relationships possible. Emotional unavailability is a barrier to meaningful connection and its impact is devastating and far-reaching.

But before going further, I'd like to clear up a common misunderstanding. Contrary to popular myth, emotional unavailability doesn't just belong to the guys. Women can also be unavailable. In my practice and in my life as a whole, I've met incredibly emotionally present men and extremely unavailable women. Although men and women do have their differences, we're actually far more similar than we are different and, in the end, we're all human. And humans, regardless of gender, are unique in how available we are, and in the ways we are available. The same is true for same-sex relationships: Unavailability plagues gay and lesbian relationships just as much as it does heterosexual relationships. Keeping this in mind, if you find the vignettes in this book don't match your gender or orientation, don't worry about it. Just consider the characteristics you're reading about and weigh in on how much the general dynamic fits your own relationship.

Emotional unavailability is a barrier to meaningful connection for anyone, but the good news is that there are techniques to help remove the barriers, or at least move them in the right direction. *If We're Together, Why Do I Feel So Alone?* is a practical guide, one in which each step toward connection lays the foundation for the next one. That's why my recommendation is to follow the chapters in order rather than skip around.

The first step is to identify the ways in which emotional unavailability is present in your relationship and to explore some of the types of unavailability (unavailability can take other forms not mentioned here, but we'll address the issues many people struggle with) and their possible underlying causes. The next step is to take time to consider your situation: You'll be invited to contemplate whether your relationship is one worth fighting for, or whether your relationship is a fundamentally unhealthy one that warrants a self-preserving exit. If you choose to invest your energy into saving your relationship, then in the following chapters you'll learn more about what personally empowering actions you can take to work toward removing the emotional unavailability barriers in your relationship and you'll be given techniques to move forward as a closer couple. If you choose to end the relationship, you'll learn about ways to make meaning out of your experiences and be given suggestions on how to move on.

Regardless of what you choose, self-care is key. The final chapter in *If We're Together, Why Do I Feel So Alone?* offers coping tools to manage the stress of either repairing your relationship or being on your own. I want to emphasize here that I am not implying you are lacking self-care skills. In the act of buying this book, you are clearly seeking solutions in an active and productive way.

As you read this book, I want to invite you to have an open mind and expansive expectations. Why do I say this? First, because it can be really tough to take a long, honest look at your relationship and consider what you can do to improve it if your partner is the one who seems to be undermining it. Second, because I can't guarantee an outcome. We have some power to be a source of influence for people in our life, but none of us can control other beings and "make" them do what we think is best. With this in mind, I suggest you follow the different ways of thinking and the exercises in the chapters that follow, and then be prepared to accept it if your partner still chooses to remain the same.

But *please* don't lose sight of the fact that change is absolutely possible. I wouldn't have written this book if I didn't completely believe relationships can heal and evolve. I am convinced they can—and very often they do.

As you move along your journey of self-discovery and change, you may notice all sorts of feelings coming to the surface. These emotions can be wildly diverse. You might be sizzling with eagerness to implement changes one moment and then hit a wall of self-doubt. Or you might feel a cloud of regret followed by a breeze of happiness. These kinds of contradictory emotions are natural. When we push the envelope, step out of our comfort zones, and do what we know deep in our heart is the right thing to do, it's also common for a cautionary voice to pop up from deep inside, whispering: "Go back to the place you know. Return to the way things were." And you may be tempted to take the easy road and backtrack. Let's be honest: it feels more comfortable to hang out on familiar turf, but only for a short while. In the long run, the only way to change is to move forward.

Regardless of whether your relationship improves, you decide to leave, or you decide to remain in the relationship the way it is, after following my book you'll know you have taken the steps to understand and empower yourself. In my experience, when we examine ourselves and our relationships, invest the time to be aware of our ability to make choices, and take action to enhance our relationships and our lives, we wind up reaping the luminous benefits.

IF WE'RE TOGETHER,
WHY DO I FEEL SO ALONE?

CHAPTER ONE

Recognizing Emotional Unavailability

✣

To be fully seen by somebody, then, and be loved is a
human offering that can border on miraculous.

—FROM *COMMITTED: A SKEPTIC MAKES PEACE WITH MARRIAGE*
BY ELIZABETH GILBERT

It can happen anywhere, anytime. You're sitting across from him
on the train or you click on Match.com; he's a blind date at the
door or the guy on the barstool next to yours; you're working in
the same office or sharing an elevator; he's standing behind you
in line at the bank or walking his dog. Wherever or however it
happens, a connection is made and before long, maybe in an
instant, or in a month or two, a feeling of openhearted desire
blossoms. It permeates your entire being and there's an undeni-
able shift in your world. Your connection to him grows, your
caring deepens, and you fall in love. Beautiful visions of what
could be flit through your mind.

If you're reading this book, I'm going to assume you possess feelings of love for your partner and are still holding on to
some vision of what could be, but what you want—and need—
in your relationship *now* is just not happening. Something has

short-circuited. Maybe you had a twinge early on that things weren't going smoothly. Or perhaps it took a little longer before the neon sign appeared right in front of your eyes blinking "Proceed with Caution!" and you chose to ignore it. There's no point in looking back with regret. Right now this is what you know:

You suspect the man you love is emotionally unavailable. You want to know why he's this way and what you can do to help change the dynamic of your relationship.

But before we start getting into the nitty-gritty of this dynamic and figuring out ways to first identify and then help solve the problem, let's take a quick look at the flip side: emotional availability. Recognizing what a healthy and nurturing partner looks like can help you get a clearer picture of what needs fixing and also aid in setting a goal for the future of your relationship.

When He's Here and Available

In a perfect world, your partner is emotionally available. He's present for you most of the time (no one is on call 24/7), which means your guy tries to stay tuned in to your frequency no matter what you're experiencing, whether you're happy and feeling all is right with the world or you're stressed to the max, feeling defeated, frightened, anxious, or sad. When you have a disagreement, he'll usually join in and try to solve the conflict without shutting down, blaming, or walking away. He's motivated to be positive and caring. In order for all this to happen, he needs to be in touch with his own feelings and be able to talk about them openly. Your emotionally available guy will make an effort to do this. Because he possesses this kind of emotional aptitude, his relationship with you, as well as with others, is for the most part mutually fulfilling.

What's more, when your emotionally available man occasionally misreads what you're feeling, doesn't quite "get it," or trips over his words when attempting to express himself, he'll usually be aware of it and continue to try to figure out how to work through the issue. He aims to be steady and vulnerable. He wants to show you who he is and share what he's feeling. When he reacts in a way that doesn't help a situation (raising his voice, blaming, walking away), it's an infrequent event. He'll usually recognize his negative reaction and come back to the bargaining table, offering an apology. It may not happen right away, but an emotionally connected man generally knows when communication is off. He'll want to put it back on course.

He's also pretty consistent between his tone and his facial expressions, as well as the words that he chooses. When an emotionally available guy tells you he loves you, it sounds like he really means it. You can hear the tenderness underneath his words. When he says he's frustrated, you can detect the edgy truth of that. When he shares that he's down or hurt, you can see and hear his genuine pain. You won't find yourself confused because he's telling you he adores you through gritted teeth.

Will he be Mr. Transparent after the first few dates? Probably not. Getting to know others and allowing others to know us takes time and trust. As long as he's sharing more about himself over time, wants to be honest about who he is, and also wants to learn more about you—that's availability.

He also shows respect to you, your boundaries, and your privacy. What can this look like? He offers advice without necessarily demanding you take it. He doesn't snoop through your belongings or your personal files, email, or telephone. He's ready to give you his perspective but endeavors not to pile it on excessively; and if he overdoes it, he's pretty willing to try to ease up when you point out that he's laying it on too thick. Finally, your emotionally available guy tries to encourage your development and authenticity too.

Before going any further, I'd like to back up for a moment and park on the word "try." This is an important point, because I want to stay real. We're all human, and even if you *hope* your guy will be completely and unequivocally attentive to your needs every single minute, it's an unrealistic expectation. And to be honest, it's also a little creepy. Who would your guy really be if he were constantly fixated on *your* emotional well-being?

In truth, your man could be the most emotionally available dude on the planet and he's still not going to "get it right" 100 percent of the time. He won't be able to understand every single feeling you have. He won't spot each and every fluctuation of your mood. He's not going to be able to detect each inflection in your voice. Even in fairy tales, Prince Charming battles moments of cluelessness. So keep in mind that even the most tuned-in man will disappoint you or inadvertently hurt you. Sometimes he will be distracted. Other times he'll be wrapped up in himself. And there will be times when he's just acting like a jerk. Yeah . . . he's human . . . and so are you.

Stay in the Fairness Zone

Who among us has never missed a clue? Never misread how someone else was feeling? Never wished we had responded a little more constructively? Never disappointed or hurt someone we loved? Not me, and I'm a therapist trained to be especially sensitive and alert to clues. No one can be perfectly fine-tuned to their partner's emotional world. He can't do it—and neither can you.

Yes, it's reasonable to ask your lover to be tuned in to your needs, but keep it *reasonable*. He's not your personal therapist, servant, or parent. If, for example, I'm stressed-out because of a rough meeting, I may need to let off steam in the middle of my workday. But it isn't fair to expect my husband to drive from his work to mine to offer a hug and discuss what's bugging me. And it might not even make sense to phone him, because I know it's difficult for him to take a break during the day. These times, I need to use my own coping skills such as going for a walk out-doors, breathing deeply, listening to calming music, or finding a trusted colleague or friend who is available to listen.

I'd also like to take a second look at the notion of "respect," which I mentioned earlier, and clarify this concept before going further.

Imagine your guy promises you he'll empty the dishwasher when he comes home from work so that you won't have to do it. Then he doesn't end up following through. This is the moment when many good women might be tempted to view this as pur-poseful neglect and ultimately disrespect. "He's broken his promise," you might tell yourself. Or "He doesn't care how I feel." Or "Who does he think I am? His work mule, responsible for cleaning up his messes all the time?" If we label our sweet-heart's fumbles, omissions, or memory lapses as a sign of disre-spect, then we're in for a lifetime of misery. We'll end up seeing disrespect everywhere. Let me be clear. Respect transcends mere oversight or a momentary lack of thoughtfulness. It's a general appreciation for the special gifts, characteristics, and talents that you possess, as well as for your dignity and worthiness.

The bottom line is this: It's up to each of us to meet our own needs and this includes reaching out and asking for help from a variety of people. It also means we have to nurture ourselves and create our own joy and meaning. No one else is responsible for doing this for us, just as no one can be expected to meet every request we make. In a similar vein, no one can literally force us to feel anything (even though it may feel like "he made me furious!"). And remember: This is true for both of you.

I'm going to guess this collection of qualities doesn't describe the man you love, but this also doesn't mean your mate is a terrible person, is trying to purposely wound you or the relationship, or simply doesn't give a damn. Men and women who are emotionally unavailable in relationships are often dealing with personal struggles that get in the way of authentic emotional connection and intimacy. Sometimes they know they put up walls, and other times they don't. For certain individuals, the emotional walls will create chill and distance, whereas for others, walls are built with neediness and the relationship ends up feeling stifling.

But regardless of the kinds of walls you're trying to bring down in your own relationship, emotional unavailability today doesn't mean that your relationship is doomed tomorrow. Dramatic change can and does happen. I've had front-row seats to the power people possess to transform their lives in incredible ways, and there wouldn't be psychologists if people didn't possess that capacity.

If your partner is emotionally unavailable, you may love a man who dismisses the value of your relationship because he's just waiting for you to leave him someday. Or you might be with someone who is always criticizing you and sees the relationship as lacking. These are just a couple of examples, and we'll touch on others a bit later in this chapter.

On the other hand, it's possible to see emotional unavailability where it doesn't exist because you hold well-intentioned but hard-to-attain needs and expectations. For instance, you might expect your lover to share *everything* and be forthcoming with all of his emotions, to know what you need at every moment, or to never experience any moments in which he pulls back a bit and creates a sliver of emotional space.

What if you have these kinds of unrealistic expectations? The good news is that this book will help you reexamine your expectations and give you the tools to pave the way for a truly rewarding connection. Alternatively, if your expectations for an emotionally present partnership are reasonable, and you're with someone who struggles to open up, I still have good news. There are strategies you can follow to communicate your needs and to increase the likelihood that your lover will hear you and want to meet you there. We'll cover these strategies later in the book, but for now, no peeking! You'll need to lay the groundwork for emotional connection first.

In the meantime, if you are in an emotionally closed-off relationship, please don't berate yourself for choosing someone who isn't emotionally available. Be easy on yourself. There are probably very few women who haven't at least once in their lives been in love with someone who is distant, unreachable, defensive, or unattainable. Just think about all those conversations you've had with your friends. How many times have you heard: "He doesn't get me," "I can never give him enough," "He never listens," "I have no idea what's going on inside him," "He gets angry for no reason," or "He can't commit to anything"?

Who Is He?

We'll explore six types of emotional unavailability. But again, let's keep it real. This list won't include every possible behavior by a long shot. In my clinical experience, I've found that people rarely fit into neat little boxes. Because we're human, we're a lot messier. That's why when you go through the descriptions of different types of emotionally unavailable guys, you may find that your partner fits one type perfectly, or you may see him fitting the descriptions of a few different types. He may have some traits of a certain type, yet not all of them. Some descriptions might seem too extreme or others not dramatic enough.

For example, some people in describing their partner might say, "He's cold." For one woman, this could mean her partner is just a little standoffish, while for another, it means she's living with Frosty the Snowman. That's why it's best to consider these categories in terms of a continuum rather than an absolute. It might also help you to look at the different types of unavailability as challenges that are present in your relationship to a greater or lesser degree, as opposed to putting your partner into a strict category of either "Emotionally Available" or "Emotionally Unavailable." Your partner may shut down whenever you express anger toward him (or for that matter, a strong loving emotion), but he may be quite open and receptive when you share your frustrations or sadness over an event in your life, one that doesn't involve him. Some behaviors may go on all the time and others may come and go. As we all know, circumstances change, as do we, and that can certainly have an impact on emotional availability. For instance, you might notice that he withdraws from you after something heavy takes place in his life—a death in his family or loss of a job, for example—but it may not mean his pulling away is consistent or permanent.

Keeping all this in mind, consider the following main types.

The Six Emotionally Unavailable Types

THE ICEBERG

Terrence and Bella have been dating for three years. When Terrence first told Bella that he liked to do "his own thing," she wasn't worried. She respected what she thought was his rugged, independent spirit. Later, she learned that "his own thing" meant keeping his emotional world apart from hers with a barrier of icy indifference.

This is a recent exchange between the couple:

"Okay, Terrence, let me get this straight. You want to take a two-week vacation without me again. Am I right?"

"Yeah."

"Can you tell me why?"

"Oh, no big deal. I just want to take off and do my own thing for a while."

"But we've never even taken a weekend getaway together. And another thing, while we're on it, I'd like to spend more time with you than just one or two evenings a week. It feels like our relationship is stuck in one place. Wouldn't it be great to move it forward?"

Terrence calmly responds: "I'm only saying I want to take a vacation on my own."

Maybe, similar to Terrence, your guy isn't exactly hostile, but he's not Mr. Warm and Cuddly either. There's a lack of warmth cooling off your intimacy and connection. He's playing things close to the vest, keeping his feelings and authentic reactions to himself. If you reach out and ask whether there's something wrong, a shrug and a flat denial may be the modus operandi (e.g., "No, I'm fine"), or perhaps an expression of confusion (e.g., "Why would anything be wrong?"). He could react with irritation or shut you down outright (e.g., "What are you talking about? Everything's fine" or "I don't want to talk about it"). Icebergs tend to avoid discussions about their relationships with their partners and they often expect little benefit from emotional intimacy and closeness with their partners. The misconception that not much good comes from being close to a partner can appear in many guises, like avoiding quality time, changing the topic when subjects get too personal, or dismissing compliments and not returning them. Icebergs' avoidance of connection also applies to deepening their understanding of their partners and they express very little desire to know about their partners' private thoughts and emotions.

Of course, it's not a big deal if this kind of disconnection only happens every once in a while; even the most emotionally available folks pull away a bit and create emotional space sometimes. But if a response that denies or blocks greater intimacy is the go-to strategy for your partner more often than not, then this is a problem.

This kind of behavior might have begun early in his life. Studies show that some children tend to avoid emotional connection and closeness, and manage their emotions in ways that increase distance. In particular, they steer clear of sadness, an emotion that reflects vulnerability and a need for comfort, and frequently express anger in its place, an emotion that conveys power and control and pushes others away. Children who learn that attempts to emotionally connect will probably be fruitless also often learn to build emotional walls. As they grow into middle age, similar distancing tactics continue. When there's a mismatch in the level of warmth that each person brings, it's strongly linked to how satisfying or dissatisfying the relationship feels.

Icebergs are also more likely to minimize how important a relationship is in their lives, as they fear too much emotional intimacy with their mate. To help create more space and disconnection, he'll just pull away. Regrettably, as he pulls away, he separates himself from rewarding closeness and a worthwhile source of support, leaving him less satisfied with the relationship in the end. What does this do to your relationship? You probably won't be surprised to hear that it can be pretty detrimental. If we compare the effects of iciness on relationships versus, let's say, nervously being on guard for impending rejection, iciness creates greater division between partners.

There are usually problems in the Iceberg's bedroom since he may also be uninterested in physical intimacy. You've heard of makeup sex. Folks who don't have issues with intimacy often use a bedroom romp after a conflict to ease tension and increase emotional connection. For the Iceberg, that's not going to happen. In fact, these types are less likely to use sex as a stress-relieving, love-building pleasure play. For him, sex may be more like a chore or merely a physical release. Or he may steer clear of sex after conflict because it's not appealing. And that goes for fun outside the bedroom too.

Studies show Icebergs aren't interested in joining with their partners when exploring novel experiences. Perhaps you've gotten to the point where it doesn't matter whether your partner is with you during leisure activities. You feel alone even when you're together anyway. You're probably not going to see him as a safe harbor of caring, loving support when you need it. Why would you? A brick wall can't offer a warm smile, a soothing hug, or words of encouragement.

If you think you're with an Iceberg, you may be feeling pretty pessimistic right now that the wedge in your relationship could ever close, but don't hang up your hope just yet: Icebergs actually do want to reach out for connection with their partner. This desire just comes with conditions. What are those conditions? If an Iceberg is highly upset *and* he is also in a relationship that feels highly enjoyable, fulfilling, safe, and loving, then he is more likely to seek connection with his partner. On the other hand, if he is feeling bothered but not greatly so, he won't seek connection, but he won't avoid it either. Conversely, if he's extremely upset and also in a relationship that doesn't feel safe, loving, or pleasurable, he'll be likely to pull away even more.

Now, it's at this point that you might be tempted to ring the self-blame bell. Don't do it! Even if your guy keeps a zipped lip when he's distressed and believes that the relationship is not safe and loving, this doesn't mean that it's your fault. It doesn't mean that it's his fault either. The blame game can go on forever, and yet it doesn't get us anywhere. What this does mean is that there is a path toward greater connection. Emotional safety and love can always increase in a relationship, and it's something we'll be working on to potentially melt some of this iceberg.

THE EMOTIONAL SILENCER

Salvatore sighed as he sat across from his new therapist. Gish, his wife of seventeen years, had finally had enough and was threatening to leave him if he didn't get help. This was the impetus that sent her husband to the office. Let's listen in:

"I'm going to be totally honest with you, Doc," Salvatore begins. "You seem very nice, but I have no desire to be here and I don't think I need to be here. I go to work every day. I pay my bills. I have friends. And by the way, I'm not cruel to my wife. But she keeps insisting that I have a problem and she won't stop nagging me. Personally, I think she's the one with the problem, but I love her. So I'm here to save my marriage—not to lie on a couch and have you interpret my dreams."

"Well, I really appreciate your honesty," his psychologist responds. "If you don't mind telling me, what does your wife believe is your problem?"

Salvatore tenses his jaw. "She says that I'm hard to reach. According to her, I'm not good with my feelings. I'm not in touch with them as much as she wants me to be. But look, I don't think that's true. I just don't want to wallow in emotions the way she does. For her it's drama this and drama that. She's sad about this and mad about that. She can feel whatever she wants—just don't drag me into it. You know what I mean?"

The therapist, noticing Salvatore's knee bobbing up and down, asks, "I'm wondering how you're feeling right now, being here and talking with me."

"Why would I be feeling anything? I'm not feeling anything. I'm fine."

"Well, it's just that you're talking about a problem that you don't even think you have. That would be unsettling for a lot of people."

"Look, she wants me to show up, so I'm showing up; it'll make her happy. It's as simple as that. When does this session end?"

Obviously for Salvatore, not soon enough! If your partner

either shuts down when he starts to feel something, or withdraws when others are expressing emotions, including happiness, sadness, and anger, there's a good chance he's what I call an Emotional Silencer. If he finds it difficult to respond to your emotions with empathy, he's probably also unaware of his own feelings. Along the same lines, you might have noticed your mate is also pretty disconnected from his body. For example, before giving a speech in public or doing something else that triggers nerves, you might experience physical sensations like sweaty palms or a racing heart. If I asked you how you were feeling, I bet you would be able to describe your physical reactions in relation to your emotional state. Emotional Silencers are unable to do this, or even if they technically can, they avoid doing it. This lack of internal awareness makes it extremely difficult for him to imagine how you may be feeling. And it's also what makes it so tough for him to respond to you appropriately.

Of course none of us get it "right" all the time. But just trying to understand what's going on can make a big difference. Couples are happier in their relationships when they know their partner is at least making the effort to understand them by asking questions or offering solutions. It makes sense since making an effort to communicate shows he cares. The Emotional Silencer needs work in this area.

THE CRITIC

Chet cringes when he sees the offending food bits lodged deep in the garbage disposal . . . *again*. His mental loop unwinds: "Why can't Quinn do a better job of running the disposal? The sink looks like crap. If only she would run the thing for an extra few minutes. I should have known she was a slob before we moved in together. And by the way, where is she? She said she was going with a friend for lunch and a movie but that was more than four hours ago. Two hours for lunch and two hours for a movie should be plenty of time. She hasn't texted or checked in. Obviously she's as sloppy with time management as she is with housekeeping . . ." And on and on.

You've heard the expression "seeing the world through rose-colored glasses"? The Critic is wearing the opposite pair of specs. He's always looking at the world and interpreting you and what's going on in your relationship with a set of dark lenses.

Let's be clear: we all evaluate the behavior of others. It's human nature. We take our best guesses at what they're thinking and feeling, what their intentions are, and what motivates them to do what they do. But what we often don't realize in our moments of assumptions is that we have choices in the guesses we make. The truth is this: We have a choice about whether to interpret actions in a favorable or an unfavorable light. We can choose to give others the benefit of the doubt.

How does this apply to your relationship with the Critic? Well, you might come home from work a little grumpy and irritable because you've had a hard day. You walk into the other room just to get a breather. While someone tuned in to you might assume you had a rough day and honor your need, or check in with you about what's going on, the Critic is more likely to consider this as just another example of how inconsiderate you are. He might explode with this sort of accusation: "Why aren't you asking about *my* day? Typical!"

Because Critics look for what's wrong, their fault-finding lens can zero in on any aspect of you or the relationship, from gestures of affection that (in their eyes) you failed to provide, the qualities you lack, the opinions you have, or how you express yourself to your clothing style or attractiveness, how you spend your free time, your job, or your ability to take care of the children or household tasks. It's all fair game.

In some cases, the Critic crosses the line into "psychological aggression," a term used to describe actions that can cause emotional damage. Real hurt. If your partner raises his voice and tells you how disappointed and angry he is because you forgot to feed the dog, it probably won't feel great, but it's not psychological aggression either. However, if he calls you names ("egomaniac," "loser," "selfish moron"), gives you the silent treatment to teach you a lesson, or brings up your lapse at a dinner party to humiliate you in front of the group, he's crossed the line into emotional abuse.

Men and women both feel the negative impacts of psychological aggression, but research states their actual experiences differ slightly. Among women, the effect of being verbally demeaned is particularly hurtful and corrosive to their contentedness in the relationship while the form of psychological aggression that is especially damaging to the quality of a relationship for men is a pattern of controlling their behavior and isolating them from contact with others. Why psychological aggression affects men and women differently is unclear; however, what is clear is that men and women on the receiving end of severe emotional aggression react with the same degree of depression and fear of their spouse.

But no matter who is on the receiving end, words really matter; often they don't have an expiration date. I can't tell you how many times clients vividly recount terrible words that another person (especially their romantic companion or spouse) once said to them. Despite the fact that it's been years since the words were uttered, they still feel the hurt as if it were yesterday.

THE DEFENDER

Jenna and Edwin arrive twenty minutes late for their first couples therapy appointment. Their therapist, Dr. Stone, notices that Jenna seems annoyed while Edwin appears exasperated and bewildered.

"I'm sorry we're late, Dr. Stone," Jenna says. "Edwin didn't get back from the office until, like, our appointment time, and then we had to rush right over."

Without looking at her, Edwin comments, "Jenna, I told you, I had a conversation with a colleague and I lost track of time. Would you give me a break? I didn't do it on purpose."

Dr. Stone waves a hand of reassurance. "That's not a problem. It happens to all of us. In fact, for some of us, it happens a lot!"

"That's what's funny, Dr. Stone. Edwin is always punctual for appointments. When he goes to his doctor for his annual checkup or meets friends for dinner, you could set your watch by him. He's always so on the ball. He even gets to the dentist on time!"

"Is that true?" Dr. Stone asks Edwin.

Edwin nods in agreement.

"Well." Dr. Stone gently smiles. "It's not the first time people have preferred a root canal to coming to see me."

Edwin and Jenna laugh and relax a bit.

"In fact, Edwin, I'm wondering if you may feel that way. It would be understandable if this appointment felt different to you than some of your other appointments."

"No, it doesn't feel different to me at all. I just lost track of time—that's it," Edwin said, his tone making it clear that he was done discussing this issue.

"Okay, fair enough. Let's move on. Can I ask what brings you both here today?"

Always on guard, the Defender holds an emotional shield up against a perceived threat whether it's real or imagined. A threat might mean acknowledging he made a mistake and admitting he was wrong, honestly expressing emotions and asking for what he needs, or engaging in a difficult conversation (let's say around sex or money), or it could be listening and staying present while you express anger or any other heightened emotion. Although the defensive shield can help him feel safer, it's an illusion. It generally makes things worse in a relationship because options for open communication and resolution are taken off the table. This is especially true when it comes to conflict. On the flip side, if you feel safe and heard during an argument, there's an atmosphere of trust and connection. But if he is a Defender, he'll likely respond with blame, criticism, anger, and yelling. Not too surprisingly, research shows couples with this issue will be more likely to end their relationship, while those who can argue productively and come to mutually agreed-upon resolutions are more likely to stay together, even if they argue a lot.

The Defender may also fuel a cycle of demand and withdrawal. Frustrated with your Defender, do you find yourself nagging or making demands for behavior change such as asking him to listen more, to be more emotionally open, to apologize, to spend more time together—only to experience him moving further away and withdrawing even more? How frustrating is that? Well, he's not feeling too good about it either. In actuality, partners feel a dip in happiness about their relationship on those days when they hold back from openly communicating with each other. Not arguing can actually be worse for your relationship than arguing!

THE FEARFUL FRAUD

Jamal's voice faltered with anxiety when he thought about sharing a joke with Rae, his girlfriend of one and a half years. "She'll just think I have a stupid sense of humor," he told himself. Even though Jamal is completely head over heels crazy about Rae, he never quite feels comfortable around her. He's always waiting for the other shoe to drop, for the moment when she decides he's not the one for her. Jamal figures it's going to happen as soon as she discovers who he really is.

The iconic comedian Groucho Marx said, "I don't want to belong to any club that will accept me as a member." To put Groucho's expression another way, "I don't have a favorable opinion of myself or see myself as a worthwhile person; no one would accept me if they really got to know me—and I seriously question the judgment of anyone who does accept me." This is pretty much how your Fearful Fraud feels. He's afraid if he shows you who he really is, you won't love him.

To protect the relationship, the Fearful Fraud presents a false front. He creates a mask reflecting what he wants you to see and covers up what he doesn't want you to see. For instance, if he's feeling insecure but thinks you'll find that a turnoff, he'll project confidence and deny what's going on underneath. If he's hurting about a problem in his life but is afraid of letting you in and possibly being judged, he'll remain silent about it.

Differences between the places you like to go, foods you

relish, or leisure activities you enjoy may not be brought to your attention. Also, upset feelings (e.g., sadness, anger, nervousness) toward you or in reaction to anything you said or did and disagreement with your views are unlikely to get airtime. Instead, you'll pick up radio silence. Why? Because to be open and share his deepest thoughts and feelings is to be vulnerable and risk rejection.

On some level we've all done this at one time or another in our lives. When a couple both acknowledge their differences with each other, they chance the possibility that one or both of them will decide that they're not a good match. So even the most emotionally available person gives in to the temptation to hold off from sharing something that would leave them feeling a bit too exposed until they feel more solidly secure within their relationship.

Just as with almost everything we've been discussing so far, the issue with emotional unavailability isn't so much the presence or absence of some reaction or action; it's about the extent and frequency to which it happens. In the case of the Fearful Fraud, masking is habitual and this can be a pretty damaging approach. People who are their real selves are usually their best selves—able to be compassionate, be generous, and feel gratitude. In contrast, if your guy deeply fears rejection on an ongoing basis, then he's not likely to be his best self. He'll spend a good deal of his time being constantly on guard looking for signs of rejection rather than opening and connecting.

Sadly, this kind of defensive behavior frequently backfires and leads to the very problems in the relationship that it was intended to prevent. Studies show that when men and women tend to be their authentic selves, they are better partners, which, not surprisingly, means that their spouse is happier as a result. But if they hide their true selves, their ability to function well in the relationship goes down, leaving their lover less satisfied in the relationship. Not only that, but when men are less authentic, their female partners, regardless of how open they're being, behave in ways that could destroy the relationship, such as yelling, avoiding contact, threatening to end the relationship, keeping secrets, trusting less, or ignoring their lover. So what's the take-home message here? A habit of hiding who we are and what we're genuinely experiencing usually has a way of getting us further from what we want.

It also doesn't do us any favors for our own mental health. You probably won't be surprised to learn that Fearful Frauds who have an intense fear of abandonment suffer not only when it comes to relationships, but also in their overall emotional well-being. This kind of fearfulness is associated with low levels of personal confidence and increased levels of depression as well as other symptoms of anxiety.

One more thing: Does your partner get sick a lot? People in close romantic relationships who are afraid of being abandoned have lower immunity than do those who feel more secure. Anxious folks have higher levels of cortisol (a stress hormone), as well as fewer white blood cells, which the body needs to ward off viruses.

THE SPONGE

The knot in Calista's stomach was making for an uncomfortable lunch with her best friend, Paola. She knew the only way to release her anxiety was to open up and talk about it even if it meant feeling disloyal to her boyfriend of ten months, Adrian. Once she made the decision, words poured out like a torrential rainfall. "I should be latching onto Adrian without a care. Right? He's attentive, makes me feel beautiful and special. I trust him completely; he would never cheat on me. He's really cute and supersmart. He's not some creep living in the basement of his parents' house. I mean, he has a great job. Yet . . . something feels . . . *off*."

Calista caught her breath before resuming what felt like a confession. Paola sat back, as if feeling the force of her friend's disquiet. "He seems like an empty vessel. I feel like he's always looking to me to fill up the sad void inside him. He's needy and dependent. At first it was sort of cute, like he was a lost puppy, but can I be completely honest? Now he feels like an albatross around my neck. Ugh, it's a huge turnoff. *Huge.* I mean, on paper he has it all. But in real life, he doesn't feel like a complete person and that's who I really want—someone who doesn't look to me to fill in his blanks."

If your guy is a Sponge, he's rarely satisfied or fulfilled in the relationship. He feels like he needs more from you all the time— more time, more reassurance, more everything—and the reason for his constant neediness is that deep down inside he feels an overwhelming sense of emptiness. He has an extremely unfavorable view of himself. He experiences loneliness, a lack of trust, and the absence of a guiding sense of purpose in life. Your assurances of love, acceptance, and commitment don't stick for long and they are usually inadequate no matter how sincerely they are offered. As you've probably experienced, you can't win no matter how hard you try to assure him, and yet he craves more. It's like trying to fill a bottomless container. He just doesn't feel loved or understood.

Sponge types will most likely interpret your efforts to connect and express your love in a skeptical light. He doesn't have faith that you'll stick around, and he doesn't trust your intentions for showing him love. Even when you reach out to him with loving-kindness, he'll feel this as a loss and continue to be wary, on guard, and miserable. What does this reaction look like in a day in the life of a couple? Let's imagine that you decide to make your partner a special dinner. You set the table, put out a nice bottle of red wine, give him a kiss, and tell him you love him. His reaction? "Why is she being so nice to me? Is she trying to make up for something? Did she sleep with someone else? Or maybe she's getting ready to leave me. I wouldn't be surprised. It won't be the first time that happened. I knew we were too good to be true."

Research suggests he's also feeling lonely, hopeless, and separated from most folks in his world; it's not just you. You might be wondering how he could feel lonely even if he's around other people. Remember, he carries a deep sense of emptiness inside that follows him to various social encounters. This inner emptiness is a space that only he can fill, regardless of how many people try to fill it for him. Until he recognizes that, he's probably going to feel lonely and apart no matter whether he's alone or in a stadium filled with people who really care about him. This emptiness leaves him prone to feeling quite threatened on several levels by social rejection, even if it's relatively mild. If he believes that others are rejecting him in some way, he's more likely to feel like he doesn't belong, to feel worse about himself, to feel less personal control over his environment, and to feel that his life has less meaning. Sadly, the turbulent distress within and a lack of tools to effectively understand what he is feeling and to manage his emotions make it difficult to hold on to a sense of purpose in life when he feels on the outs with others.

Since he's feeling so achingly alone, the Sponge puts pressure on you to fill that void. But it seems no matter what you do, it's never good enough. It's not that a healthy relationship doesn't add to our happiness and enhance our lives. Of course, it does. But your man expects his life to be made buoyant almost exclusively by your actions. He doesn't know how to rely on himself for a feeling of wholeness, as he should. The result, ironically, is that you grow further apart.

Have you ever seen a Chinese finger puzzle? It's a tube made of woven straw that fits snugly on your pointer fingers, one in each end. The fiercer you pull to try to extricate your fingers, the tighter and more uncomfortable it becomes. This is the same dynamic created with the Sponge's actions. The harder he tries to hang on, the more unsatisfying the relationship feels. He may, for example, try to hold on by repeatedly requesting reassurance that you love him and want you to be with only him, by giving you a hard time for enjoying time with others or pursuing your own independent goals (e.g., going to the gym, devoting time to your hobbies, spending time with friends), or—in more extreme situations—by keeping tabs on what you're doing, going through your belongings, snooping on your email or texts, or dominating conversations to keep your attention on him at all times.

Individuals with a personality style marked by inner emptiness, rocky moods, and difficult relationships are more likely to take over conversations with their partner in a bullying manner, such as controlling the discussion and directing the course it takes, or by telling the partner what to do. Desperate to hold on, he may also try to dominate you in other ways to keep you from abandoning him, such as threatening punishment if you were ever to be unfaithful to him, behaving in a threatening manner toward anyone who he believes could be a rival for your affection (whether that's actually true or not), and using sexual favors to keep you in the relationship.

• • •

Now that you've read about several different types of emotional unavailability you might have zeroed in on your man and had an "aha" moment, or you may still be unsure of where he stands. The following exercises can help you zoom in on his particular issue or issues. Even though I'm not a big believer in labels, in this case, it's worth trying to figure out where your man is on the unavailability continuum because the first step to changing a dynamic is identifying it.

Take the ID Test

This section will help you focus on your partner's type (if he is emotionally unavailable) by offering eighteen brief vignettes. After reading the vignette, rate it from 0 to 5, where 0 is the least similar to your situation and 5 is the most. After taking the test, go back and see which type received the highest scores. Keep in mind the dynamic you're dealing with may reflect more than one type of unavailability and that's often the case. Also it's possible after reading these examples that you may still be uncertain about whether he's truly unavailable; that's okay too. Be patient with yourself and try reviewing these examples again another day when you feel as though you may have a clearer perspective.

THE ICEBERG

1. From their first encounter, Aarav seemed hard to reach, kind of formal and cold, but Eden chalked it up to early-dating jitters. But now, six months down the road, Aarav is still a cool customer. Eden is wondering whether he just needs more time or if this is all he has to offer.

2. Peter isn't completely shut down. He has no problem expressing his emotions when it comes to things like enthusiasm for his professional accomplishments, laughing heartily at a comedy, or cheering on a sports team. The problem? When Miriam asks him for any feedback regarding their relationship or how he feels about her, he gets more detached. "If I ask him questions about his childhood, he shrugs that off too," she says. "You'd think Pe-

ter was in the witness protection program." They've been together for a little over a year and Miriam is wondering whether he'll ever open up.

3. "Lucas has always had a cocky, indifferent air," explains Elise, "but I overlook it because of all his positive qualities. He's brilliant, motivated, hardworking, and comes from a terrific family." And she says that he expresses interest in her work as a lawyer and is supportive of her goal to become a judge. But here's the rub: Although Elise's feelings for Lucas have grown, his have not. Or, if they have, she has no idea. "Sometimes I feel if I left him, he could just move right along and replace me in a heartbeat."

THE EMOTIONAL SILENCER

4. Talk about getting blood from a stone. That's what it feels like for Summer whenever she tries to get her boyfriend, Steve, to talk about his feelings. They've been dating for nine months and she's determined to crack his shell. "I just need the magic wand," she says with her signature determination. One evening, as they're sitting together and enjoying a glass of wine, Summer feels emboldened to give it another shot. "How are you feeling right now?" He gives her a quizzical sideways glance. "What do you mean?" Leaning over and touching his hand, she speaks softly. "I mean, what feelings are you having, right here, at this exact moment?" As his confused expression churns into a slight chuckle, he sits back. "I'm thinking that this wine is delicious!" Summer, feeling crestfallen, decides to fess up on what motivated her to ask in the first place. "Steve, I really care about you a lot, and I asked you how you felt just now because I've noticed that you don't seem to like to talk about your feelings. They're important to me

because you are, and so I didn't want to shy away from bringing this up." Steve became quiet, then softly said, "Look, Summer, I don't really know why it's so important to you to hear me talk about my feelings. I'm not *that* guy. We're having a great time together, right? Can't that just be enough?"

5. Camille will be the first person to tell you her husband, Romain, is a good man. She describes him as "calm, noncritical, nonjudgmental, trustworthy, intelligent, hardworking, and helpful." And she adds, "He engages me in debates and pushes me to reexamine my own ideas; I love that about him!" Still, all is not as rosy as it seems. Camille has had to make a major concession in their relationship. When it comes to how he's feeling or describing his emotions, Romain is a no-show. For example, after he got a big promotion, Camille asked how he *felt* about it. "I think it will be good to get started," he said flatly. Worse, whenever Camille expresses her love, her husband's standard response is "You're pretty neat yourself." "We've been married six years," she says sadly to her close friends, "and my husband has never said, 'Camille, I love you.'"

6. "All I want to do is have a heart-to-heart talk," complains Tara, "but I guess it's never going to happen with Mark." Married for three years, Tara feels the problem has only gotten worse. Not only does her husband refuse to let her in on what's going on in his emotional life, but he's not interested in how she's feeling either. Tara holds on to the little things he does to help herself get by. She reminds herself that Mark still takes the time to help her on with her coat, make her lunch, and ask what she wants to watch on television. But none of this adds up to intimacy. They're more like roommates than lovers.

THE CRITIC

7. Carolyn and Lamar have been married for eight years, and she's at a loss. She can't seem to do anything right. When she leaves clothes near the hamper after a long day at work, Lamar snaps, "Why can't you do something as simple as put your clothes away?" But when she spends time cleaning the house, Lamar (who doesn't help) asks why she has to be such a bore. "There's more to life than cleaning," he might mock. This pattern extends to just about every aspect of their married life.

8. At first Emil was the picture of politeness, but after two months of dating, Jocelyn is seeing another side of him. Emil began by making critical comments about other people—what they wear, their weight, things they say. Then he started giving professional staff, such as waiters and taxi drivers, a hard time. In fact, one day after dropping him off, a cabbie said to Jocelyn, "Lady, I don't know how you deal with that guy." In the last few weeks, Emil has been making little slights about Jocelyn: "That lipstick isn't too becoming." Although he's quick to catch himself and apologize, it still hurts.

9. "It feels like we fight all the time," Chloe complains when describing her three-year marriage to Tom. "He always has a chip on his shoulder." Tom is ready to jump at any mistake he *thinks* Chloe makes or anything that she says that he doesn't like. He seems angry a lot and Chloe isn't sure why. When she asks, "What's bothering you?" a common reply is "I'm just tired of all the crap."

THE DEFENDER

10. "Will Oliver ever admit he's wrong?" wonders Althea, his wife of four years. She loves her husband, but his refusal to take responsibility, as well as his eagerness to blame her for whatever goes awry, is eating at their relationship. When she confronts him, Oliver accuses Althea of being dramatic; he denies vehemently that he never apologizes. When she asks him to name just one time, not surprisingly Oliver can't come up with a single example.

11. Recently Julian was watching a late-night movie. His wife, Sarah, had to wake early the next morning and was trying desperately to fall asleep. She politely asked him to please turn down the volume on the TV. Even though it was blasting, Julian spat back, "I won't be able to hear it if it's any lower. Put in your earplugs!" When Sarah said her feelings were hurt (he didn't have to fly off the handle), Julian wouldn't own any part of it. "Oh, here we go again! Do you have to be sooooooo sensitive? I was just asking for one stinking favor. It's no big deal. Get off my back!"

12. Talk of problems is off-limits for Nora and Jim. Whenever they argue, he either sighs, crosses his arms and shuts down, or insists the problem is all Nora's and she probably needs to work on her attitude.

THE FEARFUL FRAUD

13. Clarence's nervousness and his eagerness to get close to Mia felt like a welcome change compared to all those guys she dated in the past who "tried to play it cool." But time hasn't calmed Clarence down. He's still anxious, fidgety, and restless around her as if he can't get comfortable. Shared silence? "That really

drives him batty," Mia says. Clarence remains a puzzle because he isn't like this with everyone. Friends, family, even his colleagues don't seem to stir up the same unease as she does. Despite her efforts to help him relax, he's still wound pretty tightly.

14. Mona and Casey have been married for two and a half years. Casey has always bent over backward to please his wife and it's touched Mona's heart. But she's growing to realize that her husband's attentiveness isn't coming from a desire to keep her happy as much as it is from a desire to keep her. Period. This makes his overtures less heartwarming and more sad for Mona. Even her assurance that she will love him forever hasn't had much effect. It's as if he doesn't trust she will stick around if he doesn't do absolutely *everything* for her. "Do you know how that makes me feel?" Mona asks her friends. "Guilty!"

15. For the past few months, Ashley has only gotten radio silence from Logan. She can tell he's upset about something, but he refuses to talk about it. Whenever she presses him, he insists it's just work related. Finally, he admitted he was hurt by something she had said months ago. After apologizing, Ashley asked him why he didn't just tell her at the time. His answer: "I didn't want to upset you." Ashley is concerned, for good reason, that Logan's willingness to bottle up his true feelings will hurt their relationship.

THE SPONGE

16. Carlos and Miranda have been dating for a few months, getting more serious about their relationship, and expressing love for each other. Privately, they've also been contemplating where the future of their relationship might go with a sense of hope and

possibility. That is, until recently. Lately, Carlos has been telling Miranda that he needs her because she is the *only* light in his world. "If you weren't here, sweetheart, my life would be meaningless," he confesses. In some ways, Miranda finds this flattering but she can't help but wonder, "Is there something a little unhealthy going on here?"

17. Married for two years, Ellen complains that her husband, Ivan, doesn't give her any breathing space. "I enjoy spending time with you, but I need some alone time too," Ellen laments. Ivan's response? "Happy couples don't need time alone." If she makes arrangements to go out without including Ivan, he won't get angry. That's not his style. But he's clearly hurt.

18. "When we first started going out, I thought Malcolm's jealousy was cute. He made me feel like I was the only woman in the world," Cynthia recalls. But after eight years of marriage, it's gotten way out of hand and she feels suffocated. When they're out, if Cynthia even gazes in a direction other than Malcolm's, he asks her in an accusatory tone, "Who are you flirting with?" He's also suspicious of her colleagues. Most recently he made comments that convey knowledge he could have only received from reading her texts and emails. Naturally, Cynthia suspects he's snooping on her.

Check Your Assumptions at the Door

Negative beliefs can cloud your ability to understand your partner's experience and see who he *really* is. This exercise will help you uncover your assumptions about his emotional availability. Complete each statement by filling in the first word or phrase that comes to mind or choosing the most fitting response from those supplied.

After completing the sentences, go back and reconsider each question. It's possible your assumption is correct, but I've also worked with plenty of clients who have strongly held beliefs they later realize are incorrect. When you go back to the list, see if you can substitute another more accurate word or phrase.

THE WORD OR PHRASE THAT BEST DESCRIBES MY PARTNER IS . . .

1. If I needed someone to help me in a crisis, he would _____.

2. He is/does _____ when I express anger over something he said or did.

3. If a stranger asked me to describe him in three words, I would say _____, _____, and _____.

4. If I share good news with him, he reacts by _____.

5. I generally feel _____ around him.

6. If I were stranded on a desert island, he would be the _____ (list a number, as if in an order, e.g., first, second, hundredth) person I would choose to be with me.

7. I anticipate my future with him to be _____.

8. When I express feelings of sadness about something he said or did, he reacts by _____.

9. He is _____ of my deepest hopes, dreams, and goals.

10. He's a _____ influence on me.

11. He is/does _____ when I express feelings of fear or anxiety.
12. My friends would describe him as _____.
13. When it comes to how good a fit we are, we are (better than, the same as, worse than) most couples.
14. When I express feelings of love/affection/joy about something he said or did, he _____.
15. When I say "I love you," he generally says _____.
16. He reminds me of (name someone important in your life) _____.
17. If I could go back in time to the day I met him and choose all over again whether to be together, I would _____.
18. We are (very similar, somewhat similar, somewhat different, very different) _____ on the importance we place on the relationship.
19. He generally treats me with _____ and _____.
20. The more I know him, the more I feel _____.
21. When I think about seeing him at the end of a long day, I feel _____.
22. The longer we're together, the more I feel _____.
23. If I could choose one word to describe us as a couple, it would be _____.
24. When we do fun things together, we _____.
25. When he faces tough times, he _____ and I _____.
26. When I face tough times, he _____ and I _____.
27. If I'm really honest with myself, I feel _____ about my relationship.

28. When I try to talk about our relationship, he

_____.

29. The best part of our relationship is _____.

30. The most difficult aspect of our relationship is

_____.

CHAPTER TWO

Assessing Your Situation

✥

If you want to fly you have to first see your wings.

—UNKNOWN

Most of us can relate to the expression "You are your own worst enemy." It probably happens more times than we realize. We shoot ourselves in the foot without even noticing we're the ones holding the gun. In fact, we're more likely to think "Wow, that hurt!" than consider we might be responsible, or at least *partially* responsible, for pulling the trigger. It's understandable since it takes courage for any of us to hold the mirror up to ourselves and look at this possibility. But self-examination is always worth the effort when dealing with any issue, including an emotionally unavailable partner. It can lead to expansiveness, connection, and just as importantly, a change in our relationships.

Let's look at Gretchen as an example of someone who is unknowingly contributing to her husband's unavailability with her constant nagging. Gretchen is a thirty-year-old professional violinist, typically soft-spoken, gentle, and caring. She's also someone who spends many hours on her own practicing, so she's a firm believer in giving others their space, though lately she's behaving differently. Her husband of three years, Darrel, has been hard to reach for the last six months, and her usual gentle, easygoing nature has turned into itchy exasperation. Now Gretchen finds herself speaking to Darrel in a way that's foreign to her.

"Hey, Darrel, do you have any interest in going to see a movie later?" Gretchen asks, offering a smile and trying to put her arms around him for a hug.

Darrel shrugs, pulling away from Gretchen's embrace while reaching down to grab a book from the table. "Nah . . . I'm just gonna stay home and read and then maybe go for a walk on the trail by myself," he says with a somber voice.

"Are you all right, Darrel? Is something wrong?"

Without taking his eyes off the book he answers tersely, "I'm fine."

"Are you sure?"

"Yup."

"Well, you seem sorta down."

"I'm not."

"Well, then why do you have that look?"

"What look?"

"The look that something is wrong."

"Nothing is wrong! I just want to read this book. Is that too much to ask?"

"Sorry . . . Okay, but can I join you later for the walk?"

"I'd rather walk by myself."

"Why can't I go with you? Did I do something to piss you off?"

"I told you I'm not angry."

"Well, something is wrong. Please, tell me what's wrong. Maybe I can help."

"I told you: NOTHING IS WRONG."

Finally, Gretchen loses it. "For Christ's sake, Darrel, say *something*. Anything! How am I supposed to know what's going on if you won't talk to me?"

When confronted like this, Darrel snaps back: "Well, Gretch, ending all this damn nagging would be a good start."

Gretchen insists, "All I want is a crumb of human contact. I didn't know I was marrying a stone wall!"

Her heated retort triggers a flood of emotions, which overloads Darrel. "Nice going, Gretchen. Bring up our marriage and how I'm always failing you. I'm going out. Don't wait up for me."

It's pretty common to end up continuously urging (or let's be real—*nagging*) our guy out of frustration. For goodness' sake, we just want him to communicate! But this tactic is almost a guaranteed no-win strategy; the receiver of these relentless pleas usually ends up withdrawing and moving further away emotionally. Just look at the way Darrel is checking out. No one wants to hear they're not meeting expectations.

It Takes Two

Despite your very best efforts to do otherwise, there is a chance you may be priming the pump of unavailability. It doesn't necessarily mean you caused your partner's unavailability; it does mean, however, that you play a role in maintaining its presence. There's no need to judge yourself. Acknowledging that you have a part in whatever is going on in your relationship just means you're being realistic. You're human.

Try this: Think about your relationship as a system, similar to the way chains and gears work interdependently on a bike. You can't change gears without changing the alignment of the chains, and you can't change the alignment of the chains without switching gears. Similarly, you and your partner, or for that matter you and any other person with whom you have a relationship (friends, family, colleagues), form a system, and the parts of the system rely on one another. The way you behave toward someone else sets the conditions for how they'll react to you, whether it increases the chances for distance or enhances a closer connection. Or to put it another way: Your behavior affects the thoughts, emotions, and behavior of your guy, and vice versa. So you're in it together.

Is This *You*?

In the following section, I'm going to list and describe several behaviors that can create distance between couples and how you can work to avoid them. It's a tricky business because, ironically, we often create strategies for the sole purpose of avoiding problems, but in reality they can make the situation even worse. You might think the tactics you've been using can:

- Protect you from being hurt
- Bring the relationship closer
- Encourage your guy to change

You act a certain way because you believe it can help. Right? But more often than not, the following strategies can further damage your relationship. Please be assured my goal isn't to blame you in any way. My purpose is to bring these self-sabotaging acts to your attention so you can work toward changing them and opening your relationship to greater emotional availability.

While going through the following possibilities, ask yourself these simple yet crucial questions:

- Do I do this?
- Does it help or hurt my relationship?
- What can I do to change my behavior?

Withholding Sex

It may seem tempting to shut down physical intimacy or to leverage sex as a way of letting your guy know how serious you are about needing him to change. And don't get me wrong: I'm not suggesting that people always have sex even if they're upset and not in the mood. Distressing feelings can sometimes really dampen sexual desire—and that's not surprising. But I am saying that you don't want to shut the door to sexual connection and lock it out habitually.

Sex is a huge part of our relationships. According to results from the National Survey of Sexual Health and Behavior (NSSHB), roughly 47 percent of married men and women between twenty-five and twenty-nine years of age report having sex once a week, and approximately 36 percent have intercourse two or three times a week. Just about 49 percent of married couples between thirty and thirty-nine have sex weekly, and 24 percent have sex two to three times per week. About 49 percent of married men and women between forty and forty-nine years of age say they get it on once per week, and 20 percent do it two to three times per week. For married couples between the ages of fifty and fifty-nine, the frequency for 37 percent is about once per week—and two to three times a week for 16 percent. Among married men and women between the ages of sixty and sixty-nine, about

35 percent are having sex once a week—and 8 percent are canoo-
dling two to three times weekly. Approximately 17 percent of
couples seventy and older continue to have sex once a week—
and 4 percent go for it two to three times a week. The take-home
message? Many couples really don't stop being sexual. And that's
good news because making love is a healthy and super-enjoyable
expression of intimacy.

Ideally, when you're having sex with the man you love, all of
your attention is focused on each other and you're engaged in an
act that is a powerful physical and symbolic expression of your
desire and love. Oh, and as if I have to tell you: Sex can also be
wonderfully fun! But that's not all. Sex also offers heaps of health
benefits. Regular sex is connected to:

- Higher overall emotional well-being
- Greater happiness in a romantic relationship
- Improved physical and emotional awareness
- Enhanced mood
- Less physical pain
- Better vaginal circulation
- Stronger pelvic floor muscles
- A dip in blood pressure
- Elevated testosterone
- A surge of dopamine (a neurotransmitter linked to rewards)
- Better prostate health and lower risk of prostate cancer
- A lower risk of breast cancer

Not having sex? Well, that has consequences too. A population-
based survey conducted in 2011 revealed that men and women
who are dissatisfied with how frequently they have sex are more

likely to say they're generally unhappy not only in their sex lives but also in their relationship as a whole. This is in line with another study showing that for men, the most annoying problem they're dealing with right now is their partner withholding sex.

If you go through a sexless phase for a short period of time, that's okay. Sometimes we really are just not in the mood, or we're too beat, overstretched, or frazzled. But if it's ongoing, well, couples have a whole new reason to feel dissatisfied, disconnected, angry, and hurt.

To sum it all up: It's fine if you're too ticked off to cuddle, but it's important for your relationship to get past the anger. There's something called "physiological down regulation," which means that when couples are in a positive emotional state, their physiological arousal decreases and they're in a better place to handle situations constructively. If you're willing to reach out and use sex as a way to connect and have pleasure, this may help your relationship distress. Did I hear win-win? *Yes!*

Shutting Down

Lila wholly adores her husband, Finn, which gives his aloofness the power to hurt her even more. She yearns for a little indifference of her own, but realizes she's kidding herself: She is as devoted as he is distant. One day she finally decides to open up about it to a friend over lunch, unable to hold the secret of her dwindling marriage any longer.

"Things aren't really going too well between us. They haven't been for six months actually," Lila confesses as she fidgets with her straw. "And the hardest part is that I have no idea why, so I

NOT IN THE MOOD?

⟡

What if your partner is the one who is less interested in sex? In that case, you have a few options:

- You could decide to let it go for the time being and focus on other ways to connect that you both enjoy, such as hiking, concert-going, trying out different restaurants, spending time with friends, or playing board games. This is an especially effective way to go if you believe there are other reasons beyond your control for why he's not interested in sex (e.g., insomnia, work stress, low testosterone, a chronic condition, or medication side effects).

- A second option (which does not necessarily contradict the first option) would be to only engage in whatever degree of physical intimacy he feels comfortable with. Maybe intercourse isn't an option right now, but making out or a massage is a possibility. Go for it! What you want is physical connection, and if you can maintain a level of intimacy and continue working to close the emotional wedge in your relationship until he's ready, this approach could work very well.

- Third, the next time you initiate sex and he turns you down, gently broach the topic with an attitude of nonjudgment, acceptance, calmness, and understanding. You want to discuss the issue in a nonthreatening manner. Ask him if there are ways that you can enhance his sexual experience, or if there are any steps that you can take to make it easier for him to talk about. If he doesn't want to talk about it, don't push the issue. You don't want to drive him further away.

don't know what to do or not do to stop it from getting worse. He just feels so standoffish and uninterested in me. It's been confusing the hell out of me, so I've just been going along with it all. It feels awful and I'm so scared to push him away that I feel like I've stopped being *me* around him. Normally, I tell him I love him practically every day, but I don't say it anymore in case he feels smothered. He always forgets to take out the trash, and I used to tease him about it, but I don't do that anymore either. I just take it out myself. In fact, I don't really say anything to him other than maybe asking him what he wants for dinner or letting him know when I'll be home from work. This will probably sound silly, but I feel like a ballerina in the house, standing on my tippy-toes trying not to disturb anything or get in the way. I feel so trapped and I don't know how to get out. What should I do?"

We all want to avoid what makes us uncomfortable. That may be the crux of why you're choosing not to share important information about you or your life with the man you love. You may be shutting down open communication because you're:

- Afraid of rejection
- Avoiding possible conflict
- Unsure how to communicate what you're thinking and feeling

But the backlash for shutting down is high. When you push a thought or feeling away, it's likely to come back, and when it does, the impact can be even stronger. Plus, when you try to suppress the expression of emotions or thoughts to your loved one, you end up having to monitor yourself. You might become quiet and distant because you're afraid if you speak, the truth will slip out. Trying to self-monitor like this requires a lot of effort. Indeed, it requires so much effort it takes attention away from the present and interferes with your ability to understand what your partner is telling you or even to remember what he said.

When you hide information about yourself from your other half, everyone loses. So, if you conceal something from your partner, it's likely you'll not only feel less satisfied with the relationship, but he will too. Also findings show you'll both end up being less committed to each other.

What's more, daily concealment brings even more conflict between couples. If you're hiding your emotions and thoughts from your guy because you want to avoid conflict or keep the relationship intact, paradoxically you'll increase the odds of those very things happening. That self-protective layer of silence actually creates a wedge. When you notice you are holding back from sharing your thoughts and feelings:

1. Ask yourself, "What do I think will happen if I tell him what is really going on?" This doesn't mean you actually have to open up and tell all, but just asking the question will help you investigate the reason(s) behind your reticence.

2. Write down as many details as you can of an upsetting situation you encountered together. Describe your deepest emotions and thoughts, as well as the facts as you see them. Writing down our most deeply held thoughts, feelings, and emotions can be cathartic and help release all kinds of distress around the situation.

Fundamentally, when you shut down and pull away from the relationship, this is a form of emotional unavailability, and it probably looks a whole lot like what you've been observing in your partner. The goal in pointing this out is not to blame you (and I truly hope that you don't blame yourself either!) for putting a wall up and trying to protect yourself. It's an all-too-understandable instinct. Instead, my intent is to shed light on how anyone could be unavailable, and to give you a clearer window into how your partner may be feeling when he shuts down from you.

So try sharing something about yourself that you've kept guarded from your partner. It doesn't have to be a huge revelation. No risk is too small; it could just be the mood you left work in. This gives you practice in opening back up. In the process, you may make the happy discovery your mate will open to you in return.

Buying Into Your Story

For virtually any situation you're experiencing in your relationship, there are two layers of experience:

- **The objective layer:** This is what actually occurs, like the facts you read in a police report.
- **The subjective layer:** This is how you interpret a situation through your own personal viewpoint.

Imagine you're walking down the street, you see a friend, and you call out to her. Rather than respond with a smile, a wave, or a few kind words, she doesn't acknowledge you and walks right by. You could interpret this situation in different ways:

- You could think she was angry at you for some slight and chose to ignore you.
- You could think she was preoccupied with something else and didn't hear you.
- You could think she wasn't wearing her contacts and didn't recognize you.

You get the idea. The point is, whatever story you tell yourself dictates how you're going to feel and what you're probably going to do next. It's no different when it comes to explaining your guy's behavior. You come up with an explanation for how and why he did something, how he feels about you, and even what he's likely to do next. Your interpretation will affect how you react to him. Right?

There's nothing wrong with seeking understanding and trying to explain behavior, but the challenge comes when you buy into your personal explanation too readily without checking your assumptions. To look at it another way, let's say you notice your husband is being unusually quiet and withdrawn. You could think to yourself:

- Ugh. He's not even giving me the time of day. He chats up a storm with his friends, but when it comes to me, nothing. He's being so selfish!
- Uh-oh. He's super quiet. He never used to be so preoccupied when we were together. He must be bored.
- Hmmm. Silence from such an outgoing and chatty guy? He gets this way whenever he's mad at me. Now what did I do to annoy him?
- Gee. It could be all the stress from work that's exhausting him. I wonder what I could do to help him relax.

Each of these different stories influences how you would treat your guy when he shuts down. Think about it: By accepting the story you create in your mind, you can end up making it a reality. Your interpretation can become a self-fulfilling prophecy.

The stories we weave about our relationship can either support a stronger fabric of togetherness or create holes in intimacy. Don't be discouraged since there are effective methods to help you work on this dynamic. Next time you find yourself jumping to conclusions:

1. Imagine a stop sign or some other cue to help you put a pause on your conclusion.

2. Visualize your assumption as if it's a cloud floating by to help you treat it as a passing idea.

3. Remember even if your story is upsetting, it may be so compelling in the moment that it may be tough to let go of. If that's the case, take a few deep breaths and do something to change your focus: Go for a walk, watch a comedy, read a novel.

4. After you get that needed distance, ask yourself: "What if there's another way to see this?" Then try to entertain different perspectives. Put yourself in his shoes. Or think about the way a favorite literary or television character might see the issue.

Of course, in the end, there's no substitute for just asking your partner what the heck is going on. The only way you can be sure of any assumption is to check it.

Not Trusting He Really, Truly Loves You

Let's take a look at Jack and Josephine, who have been dating for three years. Jack tells Josephine that he loves her and it's true that he's a pretty affectionate guy. However, he's also an extremely hard worker, putting in long hours at the law firm in an aggressive attempt to make partner. He insists that he can't wait for this phase of his life to be over so he can spend more time with her, but Josephine can't seem to shake the notion that if he loved her, he would make their relationship more of a priority.

Josephine's inability to believe in Jack's genuine feelings might sink the relationship. It turns out our perceptions ultimately predict how dependent we're willing to be in a marriage. Our perceptions can also predict the course of a marriage's success over the long haul. That's why when your partner shows you who he is or tells you his feelings for you, believe him. Easy to say, but if you have low self-esteem, you might find it's really tough to believe you're lovable.

Struggling with insecurity? Here are some strategies that can help:

- Keep an eye out for all the ways he shows he's into you. Rather than focusing on behavior pointing in the other direction, shift your perspective and you're likely to notice a big difference.
- Consider your past. Have you encountered this kind of insecurity before? Or is it just with him?
- Recall other forms of feedback you've gotten over your life. Make two lists: one containing the negative feedback you've received, and the other containing positive feedback. Notice which types of feedback you accept and those you reject. If you're more likely to reject positive feedback and accept the negative stuff, consider what this means in your relationship.

Avoiding Rejection

Moyra lit candles and put the champagne on ice in a bucket in the bedroom, then slid into a vampy faux-leather number that she just bought. As she lay on the bed, waiting for her husband,

Angus, to get home from work, her thoughts were anything but sexy and confident. "Okay, honestly, what am I doing?" she thought. "It's either a T-shirt and sweats or being bare-ass naked for me. This isn't me! Ugh! But that assistant of his is just so exotic and sexy, and I have to do something. I have to stop him from getting blasé about me; otherwise Miss Gina's gonna put some zip into him. Hopefully he'll hate this and want me to take it off. And, if he likes it, well, it's just for a little while . . ."

Is rejection your big bugaboo? And do you spend lots of energy trying to avoid it? Well, all that effort may be sabotaging your connection. A recent study shows that when you focus on avoiding rejection and displeasure with your partner, instead of just enjoying each other's company, the relationship suffers over time for both of you. This makes sense when you consider what avoidance does, or rather what it *doesn't* do. It won't create a positive, trusting, connection-building mind-set. Instead it feeds a cautious, fearful, distancing dynamic. If all you're trying to do is prevent your guy from getting upset, you're putting a Band-Aid over the real issues. Nothing is being worked on.

In other words, avoidance is really a more negatively tinged attitude and mind-set that we can take on with our partner. The name of the game is to make choices in the relationship to steer clear of a partner's disquiet or displeasure. If you think this resembles what we covered earlier about shutting down and putting a lid on yourself to prevent rejection, you're absolutely right. But avoidance is actually a larger, more general style of communication. When we shut ourselves down, or clam up to prevent rejection, these two tactics reflect avoidance, but there are others. As Moyra's story illustrates, we can seduce our partner with the intention of preventing them from straying. We may use humorous overtures to assuage our fear that our spouse will get bored unless we step it up. A swiftly made meal might be a means of trying to forestall a partner's annoyance when he returns home hungry after a long day. Avoidance is at odds with a more upbeat, affection-building mentality. When we aspire to foster closeness and bliss rather than merely to halt our partner's displeasure, then we seduce because we want to sexually enchant our spouse and revel in carnal gratification. We crack jokes to amuse our partner and savor watching him laugh. Busy kitchen bustling over a new meal for our partner feels more energizing than anxiety provoking because our aim is to surprise, to create enjoyment, and to express love. See the difference? Oh, and if you're recalling times when you've been in an avoidant mind-set, that's okay. We all have the capacity to switch into an avoidance mind-set, and we do from time to time. The key is to be mindful of it and bring down how often it happens.

To help you take on a connection-building mind-set, try the following:

- **Catch your avoidance.** Ask yourself, "Why am I doing this [fill in the blank with your behavior] right now?" If you're saying or doing something to avoid your partner's anger, displeasure, or possible rejection, then allow yourself room to pause and stop. Then hit the reset button and change your mind-set.

- **Move toward, not away from.** What does this mean? It means that instead of acting to prevent the rejection you fear, act to maximize the happiness that you want. A great way to do this is to ask yourself, "What can I do today to be good to my partner?"

- **Make a list of relationship goals.** Be sure that these are all goals you can move toward, not results you are trying to avoid (e.g., communicating more effectively, having more sex, being more humorous with your partner, enjoying fun activities).

Not Hearing Your Own Voice

Never mind those singing competitions on television; did you know the pitch of your voice can make a big difference in maintaining intimacy in your relationship? The pitch of your voice is basically how high or low it sounds. The pitch of your voice is different from the volume. You can get a gut sense of the contrast if you try shouting, and then adjust it from a low, booming roar to a high shriek. You'll see that even though the volume of your voice doesn't change, the pitch does. (Oh, and just as a friendly FYI, I highly recommend trying this yelling experiment either when you're alone or around an open-minded buddy who's game to play along with you!) Psychology researchers conducted a study in 2013 on the impact of vocal pitch in which they examined what partners really communicate to each other with the pitch of their voices. The scientists found that the range of pitch level conveys your emotional distress to your partner. It's also related to everything from our body's arousal—including heart rate, blood pressure, and levels of cortisol (a hormone that's released when we're stressed)—to how couples communicate with each other during a conflict. The researchers concluded that raising the pitch of your voice is also associated with nonproductive behaviors during a conflict, such as criticizing, making angry expressions, knowingly suggesting a detrimental solution to a problem ("Well! I'll just go out by myself and leave you here!"), and pointing at, quarreling with, or ignoring your partner. In a similar vein, there's a connection between a higher pitch and:

- Long-term risk of divorce
- Poorer communication
- Less benefit from couples therapy

Also if you vent with tactics such as yelling or name calling, your own mental and physical health suffers too. This type of angry exchange heightens the stress felt by both partners, and we know the negative health consequences of stress (high blood pressure; turning to food, alcohol, drugs, or tobacco to relieve stress; sleep problems; and all the diseases associated with these issues). In fact it takes us longer to get to sleep at night following angry exchanges. Unfortunately, this creates a self-perpetuating cycle, as couples are likely to fight more on the days after a poor night's sleep, regardless of their emotional well-being or their satisfaction in the relationship. Then the day of conflict makes it harder to go to sleep that night—and a sleep-deprived fight cycle can be set into motion.

Put all this together and you'll find a vicious circle. Whether it's out of frustration, hurt, desperation, rage, or a last-ditch attempt to reach your guy, screaming or threatening to leave doesn't help. The hole you're trying to dig yourself out of only gets deeper when you yell. Your partner feels bad, you feel bad, you both sleep poorly, and then you each feel worse and less able to tackle challenges.

To train yourself out of this habit, try to pay attention to the difference between how you sound when you're upset and how you sound when you're calmer. Does your voice get louder? Do you use sarcasm? Does the rate (speed) or pitch of your voice change? The next time you get annoyed or upset, make a conscious effort to speak more slowly and quietly, with a lower voice. And when you're tempted to use sarcasm, don't. Instead, strive to be less witty and just be honest about how you feel.

All of that is easier said than done, isn't it? When you're feeling more keyed up, stop and take a nice, slow breath. Then picture something cheerful and happy. It could be about your partner (e.g., what you love about your partner, a shared ridiculous moment you both had, something really sweet he did for you, or what you value most about your relationship with him), or about life in general (e.g., a favorite childhood memory, a favorite joke or movie scene that cracks you up, or mental pictures of adorable puppies if that's what works. And why wouldn't it?).

Speaking Without Words

There are plenty of other ways nonverbal cues can create distance in our relationships. For instance, in one study, researchers observed couples talking with each another as they described a time in their relationship when they felt hurt or insulted, or loved. Surprisingly, those couples who were talking about their hurt feelings looked at each other more, not less. The researchers concluded that intense staring conveys an inflexible mind-set that could fuel a desire for the partner to withdraw from the discussion. What relevance does this have? Well, if you're airing a complaint, you might want to keep your gaze on your partner at a more moderate level, taking time to look down from time to time so you don't inadvertently spark your partner's desire to run from the conversation.

The general emotional tone exchanged between you and your

partner over a period of time (e.g., several days) plays a role in how you'll express and, in some cases, read emotions in each other during a conversation as well. A study on how married couples communicate and express difficult emotions, such as so-called hard anger or soft sadness, found that an emotional backdrop of anger in a relationship can influence what emotions partners display to each other, as well as what emotions they see. If partners are angry, they're prone to showing it and holding back from revealing sadness, a softer, more vulnerable feeling. Not only that, but couples in an angry place tend not to notice each other's sadness. In other words, when couples are mad, they share less sadness and miss seeing it in each other, like two emotional ships passing in the night. As you might imagine, this mis-signaling can convey more anger than is actually present, as well as increase the gap in communication and emotional connection.

When it comes to figuring out whether your partner's smile is real and a true expression of his pleasure and happiness, pay attention to the signs of authenticity, which include crinkled eyes and lifted cheeks. This is in contrast to a weaker, perhaps less authentic smile, which will be more static and won't exhibit eye and cheek movement. If you're seeing a halfhearted smile, it could not only mean he's feigning happiness, but also signify a negative emotion, including anger or disappointment. But be careful. It's best not to assume he's faking happiness. All we can say about halfhearted smiles is that they could mean mild (rather than ebullient) happiness, or a host of other possible emotions.

A 2011 study showed another way in which we share nonverbal clues is by how much we touch our partner, or how much they touch us, while sharing a grievance and/or asking for some kind of change. When wives talk to their spouses about changing something, researchers observed they touch their husbands more often. The scientists also pointed out that touch can also be used to influence others to meet our requests. This could end up being problematic if your man winds up repeatedly agreeing to changes that don't reflect his true desires.

So what is the take-home message here? I'm definitely *not* telling you to mask your expressions of emotion or to monitor your every gesture when you're upset. Emotional expression and addressing important issues in the relationship, rather than burying them, are healthy. What I am saying is that any message we deliver to our partner can also be colored not only by what we say, but also by what our face, body, and tone of voice are delivering. These unspoken cues can promote connection or distance.

The goal for us all in any relationship—marriage, friends, parents, children, coworkers—is to take personal ownership of our emotions and of our choices for how to express them. Intense feelings are compelling, but we're not their prisoner, and we can choose to find ways to soothe ourselves and others, and to choose our words and nonverbal actions in ways that will make others more likely to hear us.

Trying to Change Him

Wilma and her best friend, Jane, are reading the paper together and sipping coffee in a nearby café on a crisp fall Sunday. Suddenly Wilma thrusts the paper down onto the table.

"Okay, that's it. I can't take it anymore. How's it going with Ken?"

Jane peers around her paper. "What do you mean?"

"Oh, stop!" Wilma guffaws. "You know exactly what I mean.

You told me you told Ken what's up in your marriage, and I've been waiting to hear how it's been since then! Has he changed?"

Jane's head fell back as her paper fell to her lap. "Ha! No!" She sat up and continued. "And it's so frustrating because I don't think that what I'm asking him to do is at all unreasonable. I'd like him to help around the house more with five—count 'em—just five extra chores. I'd appreciate a little more conversation and detail when I ask about his day. The man won't talk! A boost in the romance department would be nice. Maybe some flowers, a date night here and there, and upping his game a tad to make me feel wanted—is that so tough? If he could bring in some extra money, that would be ideal too. I've mentioned that one, but I'm not really pushing it."

Wilma shrugged and nodded. "Yeah, that seems fair. So what did he do?"

"Effective last week, he decided to add sarcastic comments to his repertoire, which is not an improvement on the fact that he's spending more time with his buddies after work. He used to come home at five thirty. Now, it's seven p.m. He's just digging his heels in like a petulant child and it's insane. It's not like I'm asking him to change who he is as a person, right? If only he would change those few things, then the relationship would be perfect, I would be happy, and I wouldn't have to bug him about anything."

"Happy wife, happy life, isn't that what they say?" Wilma smiled wryly.

"Yes!" Jane cheered as she leaned forward, grateful for the validation. "Why can't *he* get that?"

Situations like this are so common, aren't they? People tell themselves that if only their partner could change X, Y, and Z, then everything would be golden and secure. In their eyes, their partner reflects the problem and they try to change him in an earnest, usually well-intentioned attempt to uplift or save the relationship. Of course, it's certainly sensible for people to expect change in some circumstances if a relationship is going to continue. For example, it's self-preserving for people to demand that their partner never slap them across the face again, never sleep with someone else outside a monogamous relationship again, or never call them vile names again. These are examples of appropriate boundary setting in a committed relationship, not to mention basic self-care. But the vast majority of situations don't fall under this umbrella. As a general rule, when we put the onus on our partner to make corrections and adjustments for our happiness in the relationship, it's actually unhealthy. In fact, if I could say this next statement through a megaphone to, well, everyone, I would:

IF YOU FOCUS ON WHAT YOUR MAN NEEDS TO DO TO CHANGE INSTEAD OF WHAT YOU CAN DO ABOUT *YOU*—YOU'RE IN FOR TROUBLE!

In fact, attempts to change your mate generally make the relationship worse. Unfortunately, just working on yourself won't guarantee your relationship problems will be solved either. But research points to the fact that if you focus on changing and improving what's going on within you and your guy sees and recognizes these efforts, then your relationship will get closer.

When you find yourself ready to explode in anger or react rashly, try one of the following:

- Envision yourself sitting on a cloud in the sky and look down on what's going on as an objective observer. How can you change your reaction?

- Imagine tomorrow is the last day of your life. Ask yourself, "Would I be investing all this distressing emotional energy into this problem during my final hours on earth?" Asking this question will certainly help put your reaction into perspective.

- Envision *your* best possible self as a partner. What qualities does she possess? For example, is she nonjudgmental? Open? Patient? Calm? Exuberant? Energetic? Decisive? Contemplative? Affable? Conscientious? Now take a look at your current situation and notice some of the ways in which you're thinking or handling a problem you're facing. Let your best possible self take over.

- Finally, when you're feeling overwhelmed and really upset, the best strategy is to keep it simple. You probably won't be able to figure out strategies in the heat of the moment. That's why I suggest taking time to create a plan in advance with simple strategies you can put into play when you're feeling like yelling or hurling insults. One of the simplest is to stop and take deep, slow breaths. Another is to remind yourself that you needn't respond right away. A soothing word or phrase that you can repeat slowly and silently, such as "calm," "easy," or "I'm okay," can also help soothe and smooth a heated situation.

Setting Unreasonable Expectations

Viv believes a truly caring, loving, good man will always be willing to try whatever their partner enjoys. For example, Viv loves sewing and wants Tyler to join her weekly class. "Now don't get me wrong—I think it's a cool hobby," Tyler says. "But sewing isn't for me. Can't we just meet after and go out for dinner? You choose the place." With hurt and a touch of sarcasm, Viv counters, "I thought you'd jump at the chance. If you invited me to your Dungeons and Dragons meet-ups, I'd be all over it."

If you have a strong desire for your guy to meet impossible expectations, you may find that you are disappointed again and again. Even if your partner tries to meet these expectations, it will probably never be exactly what you want.

In all reality, if things always happened the way we hoped or expected, life would be utterly predictable and completely unexciting. The possibilities are endless, but if we are resistant to letting life unfold as it is meant to, we tend to paint unexpected occurrences in a negative light. So, let it go. Holding on to expectations can make your reality unbearable when it doesn't need to be.

That may be easier said than done. We all have expectations, and we have them for just about everything. The first step is to distinguish between realistic and unrealistic expectations about your partner and your relationship. It's pretty easy for us to notice what our partners are doing "wrong." Yet we are frequently blind to the yardstick we inwardly carry around. You know, the ruler that judges and measures. It forms the basis of our expectations. If your partner meets the marks on the yardstick, then you're likely to feel happy in the relationship. If he exceeds them, then you're probably drifting on cloud nine. On the other hand, if he doesn't meet the self-imposed mark, you're likely to feel dissatisfied—and maybe even miserable.

As you can imagine, expectations matter. A lot. They shape what we label as acceptable versus unacceptable behavior. They allow us to categorize his actions into kind versus rude, selfish versus healthily assertive, obstructive versus helpful. And yet we often aren't clear on what our expectations are, making it hard to know whether they are realistic or not, or how to convey them to our partner.

Here are a few questions to ask yourself in order to help sort through your expectations:

- Where are my expectations coming from? Are they based on my own experience? What my friends think? What the media is presenting?
- Do I have a double standard? Am I expecting my partner to react in ways that I would find difficult? Or to do things I don't do?
- Am I allowing my partner to be a complete, separate individual with his own ideas, gifts, strengths, struggles, idiosyncrasies, likes, dislikes, and abilities—rather than a vision of someone who I think my partner should be?

For a specific example, let's say you believe that part of what makes an emotionally satisfying relationship is when couples are always willing to try everything their partner enjoys. As long as your partner agrees, all is golden. But what happens when inevitably he has no interest in something you want to do? If your expectation isn't met, there's the potential for conflict. You might take his unwillingness to join in as a signal that he doesn't care to share his life with you. But of course, no one has exactly the same interests and that's why this unrealistic expectation sets you up for disappointment. Now let's change the expectation. Instead, tell yourself that it's perfectly appropriate and healthy for partners to have both overlapping and separate interests. Then the next time he declines an offer to see a romantic comedy or go scuba diving, you can still move along quite smoothly as a couple.

Being Unresponsive

If you have a mate who is willing to share personal information about himself, whether it's positive or negative, he's letting you in on his world. It doesn't have to be a big reveal to create intimacy. He might just tell you he ran into an acquaintance unexpectedly. Or it could be heavier, such as the loss of a very close relative or friend, or a different kind of life-changing event, such as a new career opportunity. It's not the information that makes the difference, but how you react to it. Your response gives him clues on how much support, love, caring, and affection he can expect from you; it also predicts the success of a relationship.

Responding or not responding doesn't mean saying something or saying nothing. There are subtle cues of communication.

Let's look at some examples:

He says: "I ran into Jane on the street."
RESPONSIVE: "Wow. It's been a long time. What's she up to?"
UNRESPONSIVE: "Oh, that's nice."

He says: "The cabdriver I had today was so rude. He was honking at other cars and yelling out curses!"
RESPONSIVE: "That behavior is completely uncalled for!"
UNRESPONSIVE: "Well, you should have just gotten out and walked the rest of the way."

He says: "I'm so angry at the way I was treated by my boss."
RESPONSIVE: "It's entirely understandable why you feel that way. Anyone would be upset if they were treated that way."

UNRESPONSIVE: "Don't get angry about it—it's just a waste of energy. I would just let it roll off my back."

Remember, you also express support through your body language. For example:

RESPONSIVE
- Maintains eye contact
- Smiles
- Reaches out to touch

UNRESPONSIVE
- Eye roll
- Looking away or at something else
- Standing away or sitting back with arms crossed

I'll wager that less-than-responsive moments are probably flitting through your mind right now. Why would I assume that? Because everyone—and I mean everyone—has junctures when they are not shining beacons of responsiveness. So if you're cringing and mentally drubbing yourself for being unresponsive and missing windows of connection, lighten up. It's just not possible to be completely responsive and receptive 100 percent of the time. You're human, right? Well, humans don't always smile; sometimes they forget themselves and roll their eyes; occasionally they sit back rather than lean in; and they blunder from time to time when it's their moment to be a reassuring, engaged partner or friend.

And that's okay. We are all going to miss the responsiveness boat sometimes. There may even be periods of time in life when we've been really unresponsive; those missed boats resembled megafleets. The gist is that no matter whether you've been just a little unresponsive or a whole lot, every moment presents you with a new opening to do something different and make a new choice.

So when you think about moments of responsiveness, try looking toward your present rather than your past. Remind yourself that you are in today, in your own right now, and that this is the only place where you have the power to do *anything*. If you miss a boat of opportunity to be responsive to your partner in one moment (and you inevitably will), rest assured that another one will almost always come before long to give you another shot.

How can you start being more responsive in your relationship today? The good news is that you have a cornucopia of avenues to choose from. Below are a few examples to think about. You may choose to put all of these to use, or just a couple of them. Depending on the situation, some ways may feel more appropriate or useful than others. But no matter which of these approaches catches your eye, I hope that you'll give yourself the freedom (and the patience—it's all about practice) to play with responsiveness and find what resonates with you!

• Apologize when you catch yourself being unresponsive: "Todd, I'm so sorry. You were telling me about your day and I had my face buried in this damn smartphone. I got distracted by an email, and I didn't mean to do that. It's getting banished to my purse right now."
• When you're having a conversation with your partner, try to keep the focus on him rather than letting your eyes drift over to the television, your computer, your smartphone, your tablet, etc.
• Smile at him when you see him.

- Express empathy and attention when he shares difficult moments, stresses, or inconveniences: "Argh! You're so right. Rush-hour traffic is such a drain! Is it always that bad, or are some days worse than others?"
- When he shares good news, no matter how big or small, show him with your words and gestures that it matters to you: "You got a hole in one today? That's so awesome! Let's have a glass of wine to celebrate!"
- When he shares something that irks you, resist the urge to lay out blatant displays of annoyance, such as rolling your eyes, sighing with exasperation, or mumbling an expression of frustration under your breath.

As this chapter comes to a close, let's look back at the ground we traversed: The core message is that when we look within ourselves and honestly consider our role in the relationship's system, we're empowered and it's clear we have a measure of control over the dynamic of emotional unavailability that exists in the relationship. Your 50 percent role in the relationship means that there may be unseen ways in which you're unwittingly stoking the embers of unavailability. Even more importantly, it means that you have what it takes to stop adding the fuel by working on the only aspect of the relationship you can—you!

So what tools do we have to counteract our partner's unavailability? We can continue enjoying sex rather than leveraging it to withdraw, punish, send a message, or push our partner to change. We are able to openly communicate and center our focus on how we can strive to build closeness with our partner and make him happy rather than on how we can prevent displeasing or losing him. We are capable of challenging our own beliefs and assuring ourselves of our partner's love, particularly when he's given us good reason to trust in it. Even if it's difficult to do when we're upset, it is nonetheless within our power to use a softer, lower pitch when we speak and to be mindful of the messages we're sending with our body as well as our words. We've learned that we actually gain more when we focus on changing ourselves rather than our partner, and when we set expectations for him that are reasonable. Another essential tool is to be responsive with our body language and words when our partner opens up and shares with us. Let's move on to the exercises and start putting some of these tools into practice!

If I Had a Magic Wand

PART I

Imagine you have a magic wand that allows you to change five things about your man that you believe will improve your relationship. What would they be? Take your time and write them on the lines below.

This exercise works best if you do it at a time when you're feeling calm and reflective rather than angry. If you're mad at him, your responses could be more sarcastic than sincere.

1. _____.
2. _____.
3. _____.
4. _____.
5. _____.

PART 2

This time, imagine you receive a brand-new magic wand. But the latest wand only allows you to change five things about yourself. What would you improve? Try to reflect on deep changes that might help boost your relationship rather than less substantial or shallower ones (such as getting rid of cellulite). This exercise gives you a chance to relinquish the notion of changing your partner (which is really not possible to control) and focus instead on the changes within you (that you can control).

Just as with the first part, I recommend doing this at a time when you're feeling calm, reflective, and nondefensive.

1. _____.
2. _____.
3. _____.
4. _____.
5. _____.

Discover Your Attachment Style

Attachment style totally influences how we connect in our relationships.

For this exercise, read these three statements, based on research on attachment, and think about which one most closely reflects your personal attachment style:

1. "It feels rather strenuous to be emotionally intimate with people or to let go and rely on others. I have a boundary line for how close I'll let partners get, and I set it farther out than most of them would like. If someone crosses that line, it really sets me on edge."

2. "Oftentimes, I crave far more emotional intimacy than my partners want, to the point that I feel like I just want to meld with them. My intense longing for such a connection winds up creating more distance, as partners back away, startled at times. When I'm in a relationship, I tend to agonize over the possibility that my lover's feelings aren't genuine or that he'll go away."

3. "I'm reasonably unperturbed allowing myself to be emotionally intimate with people. The experience of placing confidence in others or of being a sturdy presence for them is a pretty contented one for me. Thoughts that a partner will break away or that

we might have too much emotional connection are not ones that I ordinarily fret about."

Now ask yourself: "Which statement resonates most?"

This is likely your attachment style. The first one on the list is an avoidant attachment style, the second is an anxious-ambivalent attachment style, and the third one is a secure attachment style. Recognizing it can help you gain a greater understanding into your possible unavailability dynamic. Please keep in mind, there's no right or wrong. There's only understanding. Gaining awareness without judgment is one of the best tools to help your relationship stay real and heal.

CHAPTER THREE

Deciding Your Next Move

❖

We need to accept that we won't always make the right decisions, that we'll screw up royally sometimes—understanding that failure is not the opposite of success; it's part of success.

—ARIANNA HUFFINGTON

Sharice was at a bumpy crossroads in her two-year relationship. Her anguish was obvious as she knotted a tissue in her fist and tapped her slim foot against the chair. Barely speaking above a whisper, the thirty-five-year-old explained her dilemma: "Lamar's a good man. Loyal, kind, responsible, and hot in bed . . ." She let out a sigh. "But I can never talk to him about how I'm *really* feeling. He shuts down like a bar after hours. He can be sitting right next to me and I swear it feels as if I'm absolutely alone."

Sharice was quick to admit she "loves Lamar like crazy," but wants a man who is a genuine confidant, not, as she puts it, "a stone fortress." Her overriding issue? "I don't know whether to stick it out and hope he'll *eventually* turn into someone else—or admit to myself that it's hopeless and just cut my losses now."

You might be considering your options too. Lots of couples go through rocky patches and it doesn't mean it's the end of the road. If you've invested time and energy in your relationship, it's likely you will want to try to work it out regardless of how consistently shortchanged you may feel or how bad things have become. Sometimes this means it can be hard for you to recognize when your relationship is failing and when it's best to let go, or on the flip side, when it has the real possibility of turning around.

Even if you have an understanding of what's making you unhappy—including taking into account your guy's unavailability and your own potential role in the dynamic as discussed earlier— deciding whether to hang in there or cut your losses can be a hard-edged diamond to cut. You may know exactly what's going on in your relationship and yet still be left wondering: *Do I want to move forward and fight for my relationship or do I choose to walk away?*

Maybe you have the answer to this question and there's no inner debate going on. But if you're not sure, this chapter is for you.

Getting Off the Fence:
Ending Ambivalence and Moving Forward

Deciding whether you want to let go is rarely an easy choice. Regardless of the specifics, you're probably feeling uncertainty and ambivalence. It's tough to trust yourself when you feel pulled in different directions. You might be wondering whether you should focus on:

- What your gut tells you
- What your mind is saying
- What your emotions are relaying

Your emotions are probably the strongest influence, but they aren't necessarily the only, or best, guidepost. When you're making a choice between two possibilities, emotions tend to kick in first and motivate your decision. Mindful reflection comes into the picture later on—*if ever*. But deciding whether to break up can be so emotionally wrought, I've had clients ask *me* to make the decision for them. As much as I wish I could pull out a crystal ball and show them what will happen if they stay or if they leave, I can't do that! And of course, I can't tell you what to do, because you're the one who's going to be living with your decision either way.

This is what I *can* do: I can ask you crucial questions to help you decide, and I will ask these questions later in the chapter. I can guide you to focus on the biggest issues so you'll be able to make a decision and move forward. Ideally, with no regrets.

> **TIP:** Resolve to make a commitment to yourself to step away from ambivalence at some point. Keep in mind that you aren't committing to knowing right now whether you'll stay in the relationship or leave it. If you make this commitment to yourself, it will only mean that you are choosing to spare yourself a life of sitting on the fence.

The sections that follow detail the different emotions, signs, intuitions, and practical considerations that you will need to take into account as you make your decision about where to go from here.

Cold Feet

If you have doubts *now* about whether to continue together, think back to how you felt when you were just starting to get serious. Did your inner voice whisper warnings that he might not be for you? If you're married, did you have "cold feet" before your wedding or were you racing down the aisle with the wind at your back?

You may be surprised how many women say they had huge doubts before getting married but shrugged them off, thinking everyone is uneasy before their big day. However, research shows if you're feeling wary, attention needs to be paid. According to a 2012 study, if you feel uncertain before you say "I do," you're more likely to be divorced by your four-year anniversary compared to women who have never had misgivings.

If you did happen to have doubts at the start of your relationship or just before marrying your spouse, don't fret. Doubts aren't infallible fortune-tellers. They don't necessarily mean your partner isn't the one for you or that your relationship is doomed to fail. Not everyone who was uncertain before walking down the aisle ends up in divorce court. Nor does everyone who was assured and confident remain married. Doubts, indecision, and hesitations are information: They are signals of a concern. They should not be treated as an absolute verdict of whether your partner is right for you, nor should they be dismissed. They could reflect an issue in your relationship that needs attention, such as a fear of commitment or nervousness about crossing a milestone in life. Maybe you had a feeling of uncertainty in the past and are trying to make sense of it now, or perhaps you have a lack of conviction now and are trying to sort it out. Either way, exploring your questions is a way of gaining greater clarity.

TIP: Is your mind flooded with memories and contemplation of your feelings in the relationship? If so, that's understandable. It's not always easy to look honestly at ourselves. So this may be a good time in the book to step back and take a break. Devote some time to relax and unwind. You might try some soothing music and a hot cup of tea; a walk on a warm, starry evening; or another pathway to tranquillity that you know works for you. When you return, give your doubts a second look with fresh eyes. Consider what they may be telling you, but you needn't come to any conclusions yet.

Disharmony

Your daily feelings really take a toll. If you're living in an unhappy situation, studies show it can be detrimental to your overall well-being. When you are unhappy in your relationship, it can have a negative effect on several other areas of your life, from problems fulfilling one's role as a friend and family member and difficulty performing one's job to general emotional upset and poor health. Studies show that, for men who derive self-esteem from their romantic relationship, when the relationship is on poor, unsettled ground, they are more likely to take up alcohol as a coping strategy.

Trying to lose weight? It'll be harder if your relationship isn't going well. Relationship conflict increases the odds of a higher body mass index (BMI) and an increased waist size (even when taking into account a host of other explanations related to lifestyle, including general health, personal background, and mental health).

The good news is that research also reveals the tide can be turned. When folks get couples-based treatment, their emotional issues improve. So if you're in a relationship fraught with conflict, you might want to think twice before allowing the situation to remain as it is. This doesn't necessarily tell you whether you'll stay in the relationship or leave it (hopefully, you'll figure that out), but it does prove that you are making a positive change by attempting to work through these issues.

How You Think He Sees You

Does it matter whether your guy is happy with you, respects you, and looks at you with fondness? I'm guessing your answer is yes. Just think back over those times when he gazed into your eyes with love, or told you how overjoyed he was to be with you. I bet your heart soared. How about the opposite? What if he's indifferent, dismissive, or downright mean? Does your heart feel weighed down like a stone?

You're not being hypersensitive. It's normal to care about how he sees you. After all, this man is probably one of the most important people in your life, if not *the* most important person. I've had clients insist they're indifferent to the opinions of others, but I'm skeptical. Virtually all of us care about how *someone* thinks or feels about us, and the person with the most influence is usually our partner.

How he regards you and your perception of that regard also has consequences. In fact, positive perception is the glue in your relationship. If you believe you're seen in a positive light, you'll be more likely to experience intimacy, value your partner, and be more satisfied with the relationship over the long haul. But the opposite is also true. If you believe your spouse sees you in a bad light, a division is likely to develop. Your feelings of security and intimacy are compromised and ultimately there's a greater chance of divorce.

> **TIP:** Put yourself in the driver's seat and take fifteen minutes to write down how you believe your partner actually sees you. I don't mean how you *want* your partner to see you. I mean how you really believe he does! Then write down the evidence you have for your perception.

If you discover there's more projection than hard evidence, ask yourself: "Is there really just one way to understand what I'm feeling?" To test it out, notice how many of your observations are favorable versus how many are negative. If you have a lot of unflattering perceptions on your list, you could be zeroing in on the negative because your relationship is in a painful place right now. If you can, try to even out the list a bit more; consider other signals that reflect the valuable qualities he sees in you.

You may feel a desire to talk with him about the list to see whether it's accurate, and that's understandable. But hold off for now—at least until your relationship is in a stronger place and you've gained the tools to relate more effectively.

How You *See Him*

Let's turn it around now and check in on how *you* see your partner. Has your view of him changed over time? You're reading this book, so I'm guessing your regard has probably moved in a more negative direction, but I could be wrong. You might be trying to reach out to a person you still hold in high esteem, but for some reason, he's not reaching back. What's most important is to be honest with yourself. If you don't see your lover as positively as you once did, that's okay. The main point is to recognize it, and then decide whether it's something you want or are able to change.

Ironically, you may conclude that *he* hasn't changed, but your feelings have. Dr. Diane Felmlee, a psychology researcher at the University of California at Davis, found that 44 percent of the people in her study reported what she calls a "fatal attraction." In this case a fatal attraction is the quality that first attracted you to him but eventually becomes the very thing that repels you. In other words, what you thought was so charming about him is now a huge turnoff.

Let's say you used to admire your husband's careful weighing of pros and cons over every decision because you thought it reflected his considerate nature. But now you think he's just a wishy-washy wimp and his indecision drives you up the wall. That's an example of a fatal attraction. Felmlee notes a person can go from being "nice" to being "passive," from being "strong-willed" to "stubborn," or from being "laid-back" to "careless and late." In cases such as these, it isn't your partner who has changed, but *your* perception of him.

> **TIP:** Take a sheet of paper and draw a line down the middle. On one side, make a list of the qualities you noticed about your guy when you first met. Then in the second column, write down qualities you perceive in him now. After you're done, compare the two lists. Do the qualities on either side of the line reflect the same general trait or ability? If so, ask yourself, "Is it my partner who has changed? Or has the way I see him changed?"

Honesty

Some folks feel like they can share almost anything with their partner, whereas others feel more reined in from saying what's truly going on. If you're dealing with unavailability issues, you may feel like you have to walk on eggshells. Are you reining in what you talk about? Not surprisingly, research shows if you can't share what's going on in your life, you'll experience less intimacy and less overall happiness together.

TIP: For one week, write down what you're thinking but not saying to your partner. At the end of the week, read over what you've recorded. Ask yourself, "Why didn't I share this?" The goal is not to encourage you to share or to imply that you should have shared. The purpose of this activity is to increase your awareness of what you hold inside and to discover why. Look for themes that emerge in your reasons for holding back. For example, because of fear of rejection, do you hold back from sharing loving feelings toward him? Asking him to spend time with you? Or revealing your hopes and dreams? Are you holding back because of anger, irritation, or anxiety about the state of your relationship? Are you concerned that speaking up will be counterproductive and he'll just move further away? Do you resist telling him about your day or other aspects of your life in an effort to avoid signs of a lack of interest?

You don't have to do anything concrete with your insights right now. The main point is to start noticing what makes you feel like sharing—and what holds you back from opening up. You don't have to bring all of this up quite yet. The point is, you're aware of why you are, or are not, feeling free to express yourself.

Early Signs

Research shows the biggest predictor of a couple's happiness over time is the level of satisfaction at the beginning of their marriage. So if you want to know where your relationship is heading, a good indicator is where you were at the start. Spouses with low satisfaction early in their marriage have divorce rates three to four times higher than husbands and wives who report higher levels of happiness from the get-go.

I bet you're thinking: "Well, I know plenty of couples who seemed completely in love and totally satisfied at the start of their marriage, but they went on to divorce. *What about them?*" All I can say is this: They may have appeared completely content, but as the old adage goes, *who knows what happens behind closed doors?* Negativity, even when couples say they're happy, can create a subtle emotional division in a relationship—and it's likely to widen over time.

> **TIP:** Want to get a clearer picture of the negativity and positivity in your marriage? Devote one week to noticing how you're talking to your partner and give yourself a rating from 0 to 10 for how much positivity you communicated and how much negativity you conveyed. A rating of 0 means no positive (or negative) communication, and a rating of 10 reflects a ton of positive communication (or negative communication). The next week, notice how he's speaking to you and use the same rating system on him. Be careful not to base the rating on how much you like (or didn't like) what he said or what you said, but whether it's positive or disrespectful, damaging, and hurtful.

Children

If you share children with your emotionally unavailable partner, your child's fate adds a thick layer of complexity to your decision of whether to remain together or head for the exit door. You may be anxious about visitation and custody decisions or dread the thought of your child feeling resentful because of the breakup. You may worry about missing pivotal moments in your kid's life if you split up or about angst over harming your child's develop-

set time frame. However, when you're out of ambivalence, you'll know it. Where you felt confusion, there will be clarity, and where you felt anxious about making "the wrong choice," you'll know in your heart that you can move forward with no regret even if there is a difficult road ahead.

When people have fully made their choice, it's clear. They transform from a state of turmoil and upset to one of calm relief. I help people get to this place with a number of guiding questions, and we'll get to explore these questions together at the end of this chapter.

Let's be frank: standing stuck in the muddle of indecision about a relationship is excruciating. We can dwell in ambivalence for a while, but we undeniably don't want to be there forever. The considerations and questions asked in this chapter will help you in reaching a resolution about whether to sit snugly in your relationship or to stand up and walk away.

How sure were you when you married your spouse? Did you have wind at your back, or did doubts hound you? What about the early signs in your relationship? Was it happy and filled with constructive, caring communication, or was it marred by conflict, uncertainty, hurt, or just a "meh" quality? What impact is this relationship having on your health, and what kind of example is this relationship setting for your children? How do you see your partner and how do you think he sees you? Are you and your spouse honest and open with each other, or do you keep mum about your life? Is the relationship abusive? Are you still on the fence about the relationship? Do you have both feet on one side or the other, or are you straddling the fence? Try to remind yourself that ambivalence is not a place where you can remain forever, even though it's okay to be in it right now. We can sacrifice our would-like-to-haves, but not our must-haves, and this kind of bald, concrete contrast can help us choose.

ment. Like most parents, I suspect you share many, if not all, of these big concerns. You might also harbor worries about the harmful effects on your child's development if you remain in an unloving relationship. If your husband is unstable, has alcohol or substance dependence, or is an abusive parent, this adds another serious dynamic as well as urgency to your decision.

Whatever you decide, consider what kind of example you're setting. Successful marriages tend to get passed down from generation to generation. Studies show couples who are happy and secure are likely to raise children who enjoy happy, securely connected relationships. Unfortunately, the opposite is also true: Unfulfilled couples are more likely to have children who feel dissatisfied in their own relationships.

What is the gist of all this? Thankfully, it means that you are capable of modeling a blooming, connected relationship for your children and the key to doing this is to forge a relationship that is worthwhile and emotionally fulfilling for *you*. If you can build that type of relationship with your partner—fabulous. However, not all relationships can heal and become healthy ones, and if you ultimately decide that yours cannot, it's okay. Don't mentally thrash yourself. Instead, focus on where you are now and where you want to go from here in order to model a gratifying relationship. Perhaps you'll decide to search for a more enjoyable, affectionate bond with another partner to attain this goal. I'm not sure what you'll choose, and right now you may not be either. That's understandable. Choices can take time, and it is not my aim to pressure you into deciding whether to leave the relationship or not. This is only a decision that you can make on your terms. However, I am bringing up your children to guide you in your decision if you're spinning in uncertainty, unsure of what to do. Sometimes, when we think over a few critical aspects of life that really matter to us, it can aid us in getting off the fence. So if the model your children witness is profoundly important to you and you're unsure whether to stay in your current relationship, then you might want to use that knowledge to show you the way.

> **TIP:** Ask yourself, "Do I want my children to have the same kind of relationship I have now?" If your answer is yes, great! If not, ask yourself, "How would I want it to be different for them?"

Abuse

If your relationship has become abusive, don't wait to create an escape plan, hoping the situation will get better. Do it now. If your partner sexually, physically, or emotionally abuses you, or if you feel unsafe with your partner in *any* way, think of a plan now for how you can reach out for help and support as well as receive guidance on how to leave the relationship as safely as possible should you choose to do so. Consider having the phone numbers on speed dial of people you can stay with at a moment's notice. Make sure you can do this safely without your partner suspecting anything. Memorize the number for the National Domestic Violence Hotline, which is 1-800-799-7233 (SAFE), as well as that of your local police department. In an emergency, don't hesitate to call 911. Also think of a public place (ideally, one that's open late) where you can go if you need to get out of your home quickly.

No one can tell you when to leave the relationship. Only you can do that. But know that if you're being abused in your inti-

mate relationship, you're not alone, and you don't have to handle your safety or the decision of whether to leave in isolation. Reach out to the National Domestic Violence Hotline, friends, family, police, and your local emergency room for help.

Ambivalence

One thing I urge against is straddling the fence for too long. Of course, it's crucial to gather your feelings, reflect on them, and then weigh your options. But it's not good for anyone to keep one foot in and one foot out the door forever. As long as you feel confused or trapped, you'll also feel stressed-out and unhappy.

I'm not trying to say that ambivalence is unacceptable. It's perfectly okay to feel stuck right now, even though it may feel awful. When you're ambivalent about staying in a relationship, it means that you have reasons for wanting to stay and reasons for wanting to leave. No matter how uncomfortable it may feel, both sets of reasons need to be acknowledged, understood, and evaluated. That's why I never tell couples whether they should get divorced or not—even when they ask me straight out. I can't see into a person's heart. I can't know whether they are truly at peace with a decision, one way or the other. In fact, usually when people ask me that question, I know they're not ready to decide because they're asking me to do it for them.

But there is an important step you can take *right now*. Acknowledge that no matter whether you choose to stay in the relationship or whether you ultimately decide to leave it, permanently staying exactly where you are now emotionally is not an option. How much of a grace period should you give yourself to stay in ambivalence then? This is different for each person—there is no

WHAT IS ESSENTIAL VERSUS WHAT WOULD BE NICE

When making a life-changing decision, like whether you should end or work on your relationship, how can you distinguish between issues with room for give-and-take and those set in stone? One way is to make a list of "must-haves" versus "would-like-to-haves." You can identify the must-haves by considering the following statement and filling in the blank: "If my partner _____, then I absolutely cannot remain in this relationship." Do not compromise on anything in the must-have list. If it's essential to you that your partner wants to have children, wants to spend vacations traveling the world, and shares your religious beliefs, don't negotiate.

On the other hand, your would-like-to-haves are preferences, but not deal-breakers. Perhaps you prefer living in the country but would be willing to live in the city, or you would prefer a partner who goes out a lot to bars and restaurants with friends, but would settle in just fine with someone who enjoys staying at home. Don't put pressure on yourself to complete the list in one sitting. It will work best if you allow different qualities, lifestyles, and life goals to come to mind as you move through your day. If you get stuck, try thinking about past relationships that didn't work out. What must-haves were missing?

A Helping Hand: Could Therapy Be the Answer?

Individual Therapy for You: Someone to Talk To

The only thing that hurts more acutely than straddling a fence is straddling it all alone. Not fun. Thankfully, you don't have to navigate the waters of uncertainty solo. A therapist can be a wonderful resource in helping you unhinge from doubt, find clarity, and get off that fence for good. In spite of the immense benefits of therapy, stigma about seeing a therapist lingers, much to my irritation. I've heard people say that they think they've got to be crazy, weird, "messed up," or weak to see a "shrink," but this is utterly off the mark, in my opinion. Truly, it takes an exceptional amount of boldness and grit to come nearer to what we would much rather avoid and then to share profound thoughts and feelings with another person. For those who are willing to brave their fears and see a therapist, they reap the hefty advantage of wholehearted encouragement and backing as they explore which side of the fence they want to be on. Just imagine—you're in a room with someone who is not part of your daily life, and who is sworn to secrecy when it comes to almost everything you tell them, unlike your sister, your dad, your mom, your opinionated best friend Carla, or your buddy Saul at work. Not only that, this person can focus, right alongside you, to help you understand yourself and what you really want in a more transparent, lucid light. Sounds good to me!

Couples Therapy:
Getting Out of the House and into the Office

I've heard people say they don't think it works, and I've even had couples walk into my office and tell me they don't think couples therapy will help them. They could have plenty of reasons to be skeptical. Maybe they are just willing to try anything at this point and they are going in for that last-ditch effort, or they've already tried to fix what's broken by seeing several couples therapists without any results. Yet I also understand that they wouldn't be sitting with me if they didn't have some speck of hope. So when they tell me that they don't really think it will help them, I respect their honesty. But is it true? On the contrary! Studies show roughly 70 percent of couples who have therapy report an improvement in their relationship. Just keep one thing in mind if you do seek couples therapy: You need your therapist to feel like a good match and this may take some "shopping" around to find a therapist with the personal style and treatment approach that works best for you and your partner.

Couples therapy is an excellent resource for a broad range of couples. It's a sage investment for close, happy couples who want to maintain their bond and elevate the caliber of their connection and for those who are struggling but committed to overcome a relationship impasse, as well as for those who want guidance severing their union. Even as couples therapy is hugely beneficial, it's imperative to go into it with reasonable expectations about what you can and cannot accomplish in couples therapy.

Have you ever gone to your physician when you're sick? If you're like me, you sit with optimistic anticipation in the waiting room, believing that the doctor will take a good look at you, figure out why you feel so crummy right away, and give you a remedy to make it disappear. Thankfully, your physician's office really can be a place where your fantasy visit comes true. In several instances, there are simple cures to what ails you just a trip to the pharmacy away. So it's wholly understandable that when people go to a couples therapist, it's awfully tempting to envision the therapist as a couples physician who has the ability to "fix" them. I hate to disappoint, but couples therapists don't have this power, and believe it or not, I'm actually glad—really glad, because then couples have the chance to learn, take chances, evolve, and grow, as opposed to being "fixed," which seems sort of mindless, doesn't it? Couples therapists can offer you unique third-party perspectives on your relationship and they can ask you questions you may not have thought about. Therapists can also teach you new ways of relating to each other and to yourselves. However, a therapist (a) cannot change either of you (that's up to the person who wants to change), (b) cannot make either of you share what you are honestly thinking and feeling, or control how reflective you are willing to be in therapy, and (c) cannot alter your or your partner's feelings. In essence, a great couples therapist can hand you the tools, but you're putting in the effort, and it's crucial to continue doing so. And what if couples find themselves hitting rough ground later on? They can always return to couples therapy for additional work to repair and tighten their bond.

Individual Therapy for Him:
Mentioning Therapy to Your Partner

I'm a huge believer in individual therapy. I'd better be; otherwise I'd need to get another job, right? Although I think everyone can benefit from engaging in therapy, there is a right place and time for it. If we boil it down, therapy is actually a commitment—of time, money, vulnerability, and effort. So I highly recommend waiting until you're feeling motivated and game to jump in. If you're interested in therapy and feel ready, I sincerely invite you to give it a try. Not only can a therapist help you make effective decisions in your relationship (including whether to stay in or leave the relationship), but you also have a space to explore and address other concerns for you personally. Perhaps you have some unfinished business from your past that rears its head, or maybe your self-regard isn't where you'd like it to be, or possibly you find life somewhat unfulfilling and you're unsure how to transform it. Individual therapy is excellent for all of these issues, and plenty of others.

But what if you've seen your partner wrestle with distressing or disquieting concerns (e.g., emotional unavailability) and you believe therapy could help him? If you choose to approach him about therapy, how do you do it? Just as in comedy, delivery and timing are everything, so they're paramount to consider.

In the ideal situation, your partner brings up the problem in some way on his own. When that happens, he's just opened the golden door of opportunity where you can raise the idea of therapy as a possible solution for him. The simplest scenario is if he refers to the problem directly: "Life is just shitty. I'm so done with feeling 'blah' all the time." But this approach still works if he says something vague that you believe could pertain to the problem you're seeing. Here's an example of this: "I dunno—I guess I haven't really felt like myself around you or other people for the last two years." And what is your response? After you listen and offer an empathetic ear, you can plant the seed: "I'm so sorry you've been having such a tough time for so long. That must feel pretty awful. Have you ever thought about therapy? I've heard great things about it, and maybe it could help. What do you think?"

As much as you may understandably yearn for your partner to try therapy, the key is to plant the idea like a seed, not force it down his throat. A well-timed question about whether he'd consider therapy lays the groundwork, but trying too hard to sell it can work against you, putting him off and building a blockade between you and his ears. Definitely not what you want. Here's an illustration of overselling so you get the idea: "I'm so sorry you've been having such a rough time for so long. That must feel pretty awful! Have you ever thought about therapy? I've heard great things about it and I really think you should try it. I mean, why not, right? You've got nothing to lose. In fact, I can even find a therapist for you. Can I get you to agree to go one time?" Instead, keep it nice and mellow, like a solution that you pop out there, leaving him to choose.

It's all well and good if he brings up his own troubles, but what's your game plan if he doesn't? Now you're muddling through murky territory. You don't know whether he's on the same page and realizes the foe he's internally grappling with, or whether he's on a different page, in a completely separate book. This puts you in a pickle, because now you have to find a time to bring up a solution that he may not want to a problem that he may not even believe he has. This isn't easy, but it's not impossible either, so let's consider how you can broach therapy with your partner across the six emotionally unavailable subtypes. Although I'm going to lay out approaches that I believe are most likely to work, I'm also keenly aware that people can surprise you. Your partner can surprise you too by being more or less receptive than you expect, so try to keep an open mind. Depending on the type of emotional unavailability that he exhibits, his reaction could vary widely. Here is some advice on how to broach this topic with each different type from Chapter 1.

THE ICEBERG

He's cold, removed, and distant, and he has a tendency to veer from the personal and emotional. This also means that you're probably not going to find him at the front of the line, itching to talk with you or anyone else about intimate issues. Here you'll want to mention therapy in a roundabout way. You could mention something you read on how helpful therapy is for people. You could bring up an article, opinion piece, or news story related to therapy. Or you could make a general statement about how it seems like a lot of people are in therapy and really seem to get a lot out of it. Then you could casually bring it up. "What do you think? Do you think you'd ever want to give it a try?"

THE EMOTIONAL SILENCER

He is distant from his feelings, and possibly his body too. However, unlike the Iceberg, he probably isn't going to project coldness toward you. It feels more like he's running from his own emotions than from you. So here, if you find that he could benefit from therapy for reasons that involve a little less soul-searching, bring that up instead. For example, let's say that you know he hates his job or that he's upset he didn't break a personal record in his weekend 10K road race. You could wait for him to mention how mind-numbing his job is, or how he missed that coveted record by just minutes, and then say something like "You know, I'm hearing about how lots of people are working with psychologists and getting great results toward making a career switch or reaching their goals. Maybe it could help. What do you think?" If he tries it, at the very least, you planted that seed and helped make therapy more approachable. And once he is there, if the therapist can spot his more inward struggles and help him in the process, even better.

THE CRITIC

It's as though you can do nothing right. The Critic scans for what's wrong, easily flitting from one fault to the next, peppered over the days, weeks, months, and years. Most likely you'll need to be careful when you mention therapy to a Critic. Depending on just how critical he is, your suggestion that therapy might be the ticket for *him* could also be his ticket to shoot *you* down again, scoffing at the absurdity of your idea or your gall to imply that he needs help. Obviously, you're the problem, as far as he's concerned. So introduce a legitimate suggestion that he's likely to hear: Therapy is a way for him to address and get some support around his displeasure with you. I want to be clear that I'm not recommending that you throw yourself under the proverbial bus. Even if you're not at fault, and this is more about him than you, his distress is still real. And if he's irked with you all the time, he could probably benefit from someone to talk to. Even if the "real" problem is something other than his criticism, like depression, the underlying problem may be fueling the criticism.

Again, timing and delivery are crucial. If you can, wait until a lighter, less critical moment; his body will be calmer, rendering him more able to hear your idea. If this isn't an option, that's fine too. In that case, wait until the next time he seems rankled by you and proceeds to criticize, and then bring up the idea. In either scenario, you could utter something like, "I feel like it's been a rough go for you to be with me. You've seemed pretty unhappy and stressed in our relationship, and it seems like you're dealing with it by yourself. Have you ever thought of talking to someone else about what's bothering you about me/us, like a therapist?" Perhaps he'll bark back that you should go to a therapist. In that case, you could support that notion, and then put out the idea again of both of you having therapy. Once he's in therapy, his clinician might figure out that there's more to the story.

THE DEFENDER

He's watchful for threats and puts up his guard at the smallest sign of discord. A tip for him to seek therapy is apt to skyrocket his defensive shields, as he potentially perceives it as a critical or intrusive overture on your part. With the Defender, a playing field that feels level has the best chance for success. So you might want to start by gently plugging individual therapy for both of you. What about timing? You might choose a calmer moment to share your own concerns that you want to address in therapy, or a personal goal you want to aim for, noting that you've heard therapy is exceedingly useful and that you'd like to give it a try. Then you could ask him if he'd like to give it a whirl too to improve how he feels in some way. Who can't benefit from therapy in some way, truly? (Hint: The answer is "no one!") This will allow you to suggest therapy without triggering his defenses as much. Here's an example of what this can look like: "You know, I've always struggled with public speaking. Sometimes I get so nervous, it's like I can't get out of my own way. So I've decided to do something about it and give therapy a try. I figure it can't hurt. It'll give me a chance to deal with something that's been bugging me, and I hope I'll grow and be a wiser, happier person while I'm at it, right? Hey, would you want to try it at the same time? Maybe we could both see what it's like and do something positive for ourselves!"

THE FEARFUL FRAUD

The Fearful Fraud is exceedingly fearful of your rejection, so arguably, any suggestion of therapy pairs best with remarks (assuming they're sincere) extolling therapy's worthiness, and pointing to the impressive courage of people who seek it. You can take a similar tack as with the Defender, sharing your wish to also engage in therapy and inviting him to try it too. Let's start in the same way: "You know, I've always struggled with public speaking, so I've decided to do something about it and give therapy a try. I really respect people who reflect on themselves and take the risk of being honest with themselves, even if it's hard to do.

Besides, I figure it can't hurt. It'll give me a chance to deal with something that's been bugging me, and I hope I'll grow and be a wiser, happier person while I'm at it, right? Hey, would you want to try it at the same time? Maybe we could both see what it's like and do something positive for ourselves!"

THE SPONGE

He feels empty inside, so he relies on you for his happiness, self-worth, and sense of meaning. He looks to you to reassure him that you're not going anywhere, yet he can't take it in, second-guessing you and concocting stories of impending rejection. He's unlikely to veer from a conversation about emotions like some of the other subtypes, but he may see your advice to seek therapy as a confirming signal that he's coming up short in your eyes. A solid approach is to share your intuition that something has been troubling him, and let him know that you want the very best for him because you love him or care about him. You could mention hearing how beneficial therapy is for helping people to relieve themselves of the burdens they carry, and then ask what he thinks about the idea. Time this with a peaceful, quiet moment if you can. For instance, you might say something like this: "Can I talk with you about something? I care about you very much, and I've been feeling as though you've been more stressed and have been carrying a heavy burden. This saddens me, because I know that you deserve better. I've heard that therapy is a powerful way for people to gain a deeper sense of inner peace, and I wonder what you think of it. Do you think you'd want to give it a try?"

Remember, you may see a close match between your partner and one of these subtypes, or you may find that your partner is emotionally unavailable, yet does not look anything like these types. Either way, please keep in mind that these subtypes are intended as useful categories only to help us pinpoint examples of what emotional unavailability can look like. Emotional unavailability really lies on a spectrum rather than actually being a specific type. If your partner does not match any of these types, look through each of the approaches and try the one that you expect your partner will most likely be able to hear.

No matter which subtype your partner resembles, wouldn't it be grand if it worked and he opened up to therapy? Absolutely! Unfortunately, there's no guarantee he'll be willing to try it, or even that he'll hear your suggestion. This is an illuminating example of the contrast between what we can control and what we cannot. Given that his journey into individual therapy strictly depends on his willingness and decision, the choice is his alone to make. Remember, therapy is a commitment of time, money, vulnerability, and effort, and the only one who can choose to do it is him. So if he says no, then the answer is no. He's like the horse that you can take to water but can't strong-arm to drink. At that point, all you can really do is focus on the only thing you can control: Accept his decision and figure out what *you* want for yourself.

Some of us have our feet firmly planted in our relationship, some of us swing both feet out, and others of us straddle both sides, with feet achingly unsure what to do. In Chapter 3, we paid attention to an indispensable simple truth: A relationship is a choice. Based on the fact that you're reading this book, I'm guessing that, as you read this sentence, either you want to make the relationship work, or you're on the fence. The goal of this chapter was to give you the tools to get off that fence. Thankfully, you don't have to face the indecision alone with individual and couples therapy there to help you navigate this hazy landscape. Individual therapy for one or both of you can also help you and your partner handle personal issues that may be pulling down the caliber of your life and your relationship. The added plus is that you're liable to gain additional insight and information to help you make a decision about your union's future. The exercise in the next section contains questions designed to help you move toward a decision about your partner if you're feeling stuck, but I recommend the exercise even if you're not stuck. It's worthwhile to reflect on your bond.

21 Important Questions to Ask Yourself

Whether you decide to remain together or leave is up to you. The goal isn't to impose what I personally think might be best, but to ask the kinds of questions to give you the ability to trust yourself. Keep in mind you may not have an answer to all these questions now, but as you complete the steps in the coming chapters, the picture before you will likely get clearer. Also ask yourself these questions more than once. Over time, your answers may change.

1. Is your decision based *only* on whether he changes, or are there other factors influencing you, such as concern for children, financial barriers, fear of being alone/dating again/not finding anyone better, etc.?

2. If your guy would change even a little bit, would you be willing to stay in the relationship? What is the minimum your guy would need to do in order for you to stay? Give specific changes here to make it useful. Examples could be: talk about his emotions with me; hold me/cuddle; praise me more/criticize me less.

3. If your answer to 2 is yes, what is it about your partner that makes you want to stay? On the other hand, if your answer to 2 is no, what personal qualities and/or behaviors do you find intolerable?

4. What was the beginning of your relationship like? Did you both connect easily and get along really well? Or did you feel more like two people who loved each other but struggled a lot?

5. If you were to walk away from the relationship today, would you feel any regrets for the decision, or would you be sad but know it was the right thing to do?

6. When you listen to your gut—that silent, calm, knowing part of you—does it tell you to leave or to stay?

7. When you were getting serious about your partner, or when you were about to be married, did you have doubts about whether you were doing the right thing?

8. Think about your happiness over the course of your relationship. Has the relationship made you a better person (e.g., brings out the best in you)? Has it improved your quality of life? Have friends commented on how you've changed? Has the change been for the better or for the worse?

9. Let's imagine your relationship is in the form of a line (like string that can be bent or straightened). If you could describe the shape of your relationship, what would it look like?

10. If you could get in a time machine and go back to just before the moment you met, would you stop yourself from meeting your partner, or would you encourage yourself to meet him?

11. Are your parents happy in their marriage? Are your guy's parents also happy in their marriage?

12. What is his attachment style? What's yours? Has it always been this way or did it change for either of you? If there was a change, what do you think caused it?

13. Let's say your partner wants you to make changes in order for him to (a) stay with you or (b) be happy with you—would you try to make those changes?

14. Are you willing to do anything differently in the relationship to make it feel more connected? If yes, what are you willing to do differently? If no, what gets in the way of your willingness to do something different?

15. What are your deal-breakers—those qualities and behaviors that you simply are not willing to live without?

16. What are your must-haves—those qualities and behaviors that are essential for your partner to possess?

17. When you think about spending the rest of your life together, how do you feel about it?

18. When you think about leaving him, how do you feel about it?

19. What do your friends think of him? Do they like him and say you're a great couple? Or are evenings out awkward because your friends really don't approve?

20. Do you hold on to lingering resentments? If you do, can you truly forgive him, renew a sense of trust, and move forward without bringing up the past?

21. And finally: Do you like him? If you had never met him in a romantic context, would you have felt drawn to him as a friend?

CHAPTER FOUR

Understanding Why

❖

Each has his past shut in him like the leaves of a book
known to him by his heart, and his friends can only read
the title.

—FROM *MRS. DALLOWAY*
BY VIRGINIA WOOLF

How are you doing? Have you gotten off the fence? At this juncture, perhaps you know with steadfast certainty that this relationship is worth saving. You can just feel it in your gut. On the other hand, maybe you're not 100 percent sold on staying the course with him, sensing that you need to know that the relationship has what it takes to triumph over emotional unavailability before you can steadfastly commit. That's okay too. Sometimes we need more information to make a choice that suits us well, and it takes more time. Regardless of where your footing lies, the standout truth is that you are choosing to take steps toward leaving emotional unavailability and the chasm that separates you in the dust.

The cardinal purpose of the rest of this book is to open doors for you to do just that—to get the better of emotional unavailability in any way that you can. From this point, we'll move onward in a systematic, step-by-step fashion, each chapter building on the preceding one to help you head toward connection and healthy intimacy. As tough as it is to be patient when you want attachment *now* (Who can blame you? Certainly not me!), try to bear in mind that the gorge between you will likely close in steps, not leaps. I'm guessing that you can't hop a massive meadow in one go, right? It's essentially the same dynamic here. However, if you keep going forward and your partner is willing to do the same, then you can find yourselves next to each other, united. And if you are still on the fence, my earnest wish is that this book and the journey you are about to take will help you make a surefooted dismount. To those of you who know you want to salvage your relationship, I hope you make it.

So let's get going! How will the remainder of the book help you start traversing the distance between you? In this chapter, we'll explore various reasons why emotional unavailability creeps into our lives and relationships. The goal is for you to come away with a more thorough understanding of what your partner is dealing with. If we can wrap our minds around a problem and why it's occurring, it's a little easier to muster our inner reserves to cope with and navigate it effectively. Chapter 5 equips you with tools to lay the foundation for greater connection by creating boundaries and guidelines in your relationship, and fostering trust and goodwill. Once the groundwork is set, in Chapter 6, you'll start breaking barriers that divide you and your partner. Once the barriers are down, with Chapter 7, you'll move on to cultivate and safeguard your emotional connection. In Chapter 8, you make peace with the past and work toward forgiveness, setting a path for your future unburdened with resentments of yesterday. Chapter 9 invites you to pay attention to restoring your emotional and physical wellness after what is probably a lengthy and formidable trek, whether you emerge bonded with your partner or single again. You'll find tools to heal together as a couple as well as tools you can employ independently. All that said, ideally you're taking good care of yourself throughout this journey. After all, you're the only tool you've got, not to mention the best one!

The Whys of Unavailability

After a jaw-clenching day at work, you're greeted at the door by your adoring husband. "Sweetheart, you look beat," he says. "Tell me everything." Wrapping his arms around you, he leads you to the couch, where you cuddle, relax, and share all. He hangs on to your every word, listening carefully and offering comfort. Then he tells you about his day. You're also totally tuned in. Eye to eye, heart to heart, you feel boundless intimacy and endless connection. And it's like this *every single day*.

Okay, now you can stop dreaming. Of course, you know that no one is available 100 percent of the time and you wouldn't expect your mate to be on call 24/7, especially after a long, hard day's work. You get this, but you also know your situation is different. Your guy is unable to connect on a deep level most of the time—if at all. With this kind of profound distance in your relationship, it makes sense to wonder, *WHY?*

Unavailability can happen for an assortment of reasons, and you've probably thought about many of them over time. But narrowing in on the "why" can be really helpful in understanding your partner and increasing communication.

As humans, most of us have an innate sense of wonder and a longing to understand why. When it comes to relationships we want to know *why* our loved one is reacting (or not reacting) in a particular way. We look to him, we look within ourselves, and we look to the outside world for answers. This yearning to understand is inherited from our ancestors. Back then it was a matter of survival; unexplainable behaviors looked and felt unsafe. Today we tend to be uncomfortable with confusing reactions because they leave us floundering—clueless about how to respond.

If your partner comes home and silently walks into the bedroom, shutting the door behind him, awareness about *why* he's behaving this way would give you valuable information and help you choose a supportive, heartfelt response. Is he angry with you? Did he get terrible news about a family member? Did he get a speeding ticket on the way home from work? Is he trying to push you away? Or did he just have a crazy hard day at work and now he needs to crash?

Whatever the reason or why behind his actions, there are probably similarities in the way you could react. You might check in, offer an ear, ask him if he wants some space—or all of the above. But beyond those responses you would be at a loss for what to do next. If your partner just found out that his mother passed away, for example, you would likely react differently than if he just had a wearisome day dealing with an annoying colleague.

In a similar way, understanding *why* your partner is unavailable will give you wisdom in choosing the next steps toward greater connection. My hope is that this understanding will provide you with some relief. Adversity is a little more bearable when you have the why to help you through it.

To do that, let's examine some of the more common causes your guy is emotionally withdrawn.

Perhaps it started with a thought or feeling that your partner may be experiencing, like an unresolved resentment. People often hold on to bitterness or distrust because they were hurt in a past relationship. He could be harboring resentment for a mistake he believes you made in the past, whether it was real or imaginary. He might be reeling from a more shocking trauma like the sudden death of a loved one, being in combat, sexual or physical assault, or a serious car accident. After trauma, people may struggle with overwhelming emotions, haunting memories, feelings of edginess and anxiety, or a sense of danger. Personal trials such as these can create major obstacles to availability.

Or his difficulty to connect might be the result of a damaged childhood. Theory and research on bonding suggest that our approach to relationships tends to reflect the kind of relationship we had with our parents while we were growing up. We learn how relationships work, and what to expect from them, through our attachments with our early caregivers. If those around us were consistent, loving, and available, then we usually learn to expect the same from our partner and we tend to behave similarly. In contrast, inconsistent or unavailable caregivers are more likely to teach different lessons, perhaps instilling an instinct to be wary of trust and intimacy.

Unpredictable or nonexistent patterns of emotional availability might also stem from a neurological condition such as a traumatic brain injury. A condition like this can result in difficulty reading the feelings of others, or in regulating one's own emotions. If a loved one suffers with a traumatic brain injury, their emotions could have more dramatic ups and down, or they may seem more agitated. Disconnection is also linked to depression. Conflict and distance can accompany this condition.

Whatever the root of his disconnection may be, the bottom line is this: In order to deal with his problem, you've got to get a grip on what's behind it. The three types of issues he could be dealing with are:

- **Interpersonal issues:** the kinds of thoughts and feelings he holds on to
- **Personal history:** the way his past influences his present
- **Inner emotional world:** his moods, his level of self-esteem, and his ability to recognize and deal with his emotions

As you read the following sections, you might be tempted to glide over certain issues because at first glance you don't think they apply to your situation, but I encourage you to consider each one. As a therapist, I've learned the human being is beautifully complex and has many layers. Some of us keep layers private even from our loved ones. It's not unheard-of to try to keep painful experiences of trauma, family dysfunction, or upsetting beliefs and feelings to ourselves. You might be in the dark about these kinds of issues when it comes to your loved one, but your heart tells you something "isn't right." In struggling to find the answer, you might start guessing about the root of his unavailability. But without guidance you could end up going down a wrong road.

Of course it's also possible you'll look through the list, carefully consider each one, and still find yourself saying, "Oh, that's *nothing* like him!" Still, it doesn't hurt to be aware of the possibilities. Consider how he does or doesn't fit each one. By noticing which ones make sense to you and which ones don't, you'll be able to devote yourself to the crucial causes.

Interpersonal Issues

This is all about what he's thinking and feeling about you, your relationship, and the world around him. When it comes to interpersonal issues, we need to consider:

- Unspoken resentments
- Negative beliefs about you
- Different theories about relationships
- Difficulty reading or labeling your emotional cues
- Weak social skills
- Hidden emotions
- Fear of being "real"

UNSPOKEN RESENTMENTS

Jack, a sixty-five-year-old businessman, has been married to Maryann for forty years. He's always considered himself a powerful leader in control of his own destiny. But last year Jack sold his company and retired—mainly to please his wife. "We're at that age and financially secure," she said. "Why not travel and spend more time with our grandchildren?" Now Jack finds himself with too much free time on his hands and has a sinking feeling that he's lost his professional edge—*forever*. At loose ends, he's often irritable, even angry. Maryann's mere presence can drive him up the wall. Rather than explore the reasons behind his exasperation, Jack tries to push his feelings away. Yet the more he attempts to tamp down his angry thoughts and emotions, the more he's irritable and short-tempered. Lately, he's been snapping, "Move out of the way!" or "Just leave me alone!" Although Maryann is hurt, she has a sense that her husband is suffering too. But whenever she asks what's wrong, Jack snaps,

"Nothing." When she tries to touch him affectionately, he moves away as if her fingers are poison darts. At the end of her rope, Maryann says, "It's like I'm living with a stranger. A mean and nasty one."

Sacrifices like the one Jack made for his wife have great potential to bond couples. Relationship science tells us that when we can make sacrifices for our partners with no strings attached (the opposite of a tit-for-tat exchange or *I'll do this for you if you do that for me*), it feels good and helps build stronger, happier unions. But there's a hitch: Whether someone suppresses, or expresses, their true emotions when making a sacrifice plays a pivotal role in whether or not their emotional availability will be enhanced. When one partner in a romantic relationship makes a sacrifice and then suppresses their emotions—whether they be positive or negative—the relationship suffers to the point where it would have been better if the sacrifice was never made. But there's a catch here: Science suggests that it also depends on how we see ourselves. If we see ourselves in an independent light, valuing our own individuality and capacity to stand out and be different, then it does hurt the relationship if we sacrifice with a mask on. Although this perspective is extremely common in Western cultures, it doesn't preclude someone having an interdependent viewpoint, which tends to be more common in Eastern cultures. People with an interdependent perspective prize the well-being and goodwill of the group over their own individual needs. If we have an interdependent identity and mask our negative emotions from our partner, we can actually uplift our bond with our partner and benefit ourselves too. So the impact of making a sacrifice and holding in our negative emotions depends, in part, on how we see ourselves.

Let's come back to motive. You might be wondering why anyone would keep their feel-good emotions to themselves when making a sacrifice. Here are a few possibilities: Perhaps you know it's humbling for your partner to ask for help and so, choosing compassion, you don't draw attention to the sacrifice you are making on their behalf. Or you might keep mum about how proud you feel for putting your partner first because you're concerned it might seem unbecoming or "braggy." Or you just might not feel the need, or desire, to express it. You're simply cool with it, as is.

But the motives behind choosing to keep in versus express feelings can also affect your relationship. If emotional expressions are blocked for reasons of self-interest, such as hoping to protect ourselves from an unpleasant outcome—for example, fear of being mocked—then the relationship takes a hit. There's an increase in the number of arguments and how heated they become. Intimacy is also a victim. However, if you're suppressing your emotions in the interest of your mate's well-being (whether it's relieving fear, assuaging guilt, or reducing conflict), then both of you and the relationship will likely enjoy a tighter bond.

So making sacrifices can be a natural and healthy part of a relationship. But as we've discovered, some sacrifices, and the way they're felt and expressed, can perpetuate loving feelings and enhance the relationship's vitality, while other kinds of sacrifice can give rise to resentment and may ultimately add to the erosion of connection.

To gain insight into how sacrifices play out in your relationship, try this:

Think of sacrifices he's made both big and small. Examples of smaller ones could be joining you for an event that's not really to his taste, doing a chore he'd rather not do, or an errand that's a bit of a hassle. Bigger sacrifices could include moving to support your career, making dramatic changes in family plans (welcoming your aging parent to move in), or devoting less time to his personal pursuits or hobbies for the sake of the relationship. Then consider the following:

- Recall how he behaved when making these sacrifices. Did your guy express irritation, anger, frustration, or sadness? Or did it seem like the sacrifice was a conscious choice that helped him feel good about it—and himself?

- Remember how you reacted when he made his sacrifices. Did you find yourself expecting him to make them? Did you heap appreciation on him? Or might these sacrifices have slipped by unnoticed or unappreciated?

- As best as you can, see if you can search back in your mind and get a sense of what your relationship looked and felt like after his sacrifices. Did you both seem to get closer? Or was there a gap wedged in there?

If you felt that gap, there is a possibility he feels it too and that he is harboring resentments against you. Repeat these steps with your own sacrifices. Explore how you felt after giving something up for the sake of your mate. Are you harboring any lingering resentments toward him?

Yet sacrifice isn't the sole reason why we can resent someone. We can also nurse a grudge for a previous perceived hurt, unwilling to let go of the sore spot that nags us. The clincher is that the emotional nick doesn't even have to be something that most people would find troublesome. Our point of view is all that is required for bitterness to blossom. Although virtually anyone can grow resentment within, some of us are more prone to resentfulness than others. Which of the emotional unavailability subtypes are most likely to hold unspoken resentments? Truly, any of them can be privately spiteful, because anyone can be. However, the four types that seem most likely to cradle inner malice are the Critic, the Defender, the Sponge, and the Iceberg. Why these four? you ask.

The Critic sees the worst in everything, and he doesn't hesitate to dismiss or nitpick. Yet these are just the critiques that flow from his mouth. Our minds move far more rapidly than our mouths, which renders him a top candidate for bottling, corking, and shelving daily ill will and resentments, both spoken and unspoken.

The Defender is perpetually on guard, quickly donning his armor and going on the defensive. Although this can happen for a variety of reasons, one possibility is that he's reacting to something in your style, approach, or manner that leaves him feeling defensive and oppositional.

The Sponge depends on you for personal happiness and fulfillment, overshooting the mark of healthy dependence. As a result, you won't be able to meet his standards as they are now (nor should you), and you are quite likely to let him down repeatedly.

And finally we come to the Iceberg. Perhaps your partner started off warm, and then chilled dramatically later, almost to the point that he doesn't seem like himself. In this case, like the Defender, his iciness may be a reaction to painful dynamics or events in your relationship, leading him to pull away. Or maybe he was always removed, and there was something charming and James Bond–ish in his playfulness and indifference at the time. Now it's just heartbreaking. Either way, his tendency to push you away and isolate himself from connection ironically sets the stage for him to experience less comfort, closeness, and fulfillment with you, upping the odds that he'll brew rancor toward you.

No matter which subtype fits your partner, keep your mind open to the possibility that prior hurts, regardless of whether you are aware of them or not, may still be knotted and all too alive in your relationship.

NEGATIVE BELIEFS ABOUT YOU

Now we're going to tackle another why of emotional unavailability that has sizable overlap with resentment: negative beliefs about you. Negative beliefs and resentments aren't exactly the same, because people can nurse a grudge from the past without holding negative beliefs in the present. By the same token, people can have negative beliefs about someone without necessarily holding on to them for the long term. Yet when we allow negative beliefs to grow and multiply, it's hard to imagine resentment not tagging along, closely behind.

How he thinks about you creates the lens through which he sees *all*—or at least most—of your behavior and personality. And not surprisingly, it's nearly impossible for your guy to be emotionally present, warm, supportive, and accepting if he sees you in a bad light. It's completely understandable if you feel defensive, confused, angry, or distressed if your guy has a disagreeable view of you. It's a painful truth to accept. But even though it's not an easy thing to do, let me suggest you try to remove your defensiveness from the situation. Before going any further, take a deep breath. Imagine yourself in a tree house look-ing down at your situation from a wider perspective. Be an observer. You want to watch his behavior without letting it snag you like a bur. Remind yourself the purpose of discovering the root of his problem is to be able to dig it up—and then do what you can to help him.

This dynamic is especially true for Tyrone, whose wife, Aisha, was recently hired as the principal at their town's elementary school. Aisha's new position has her working late, and at times she's forgotten to do her regular chores like putting the dishes away or picking up the dry cleaning. Tyrone views these changes scornfully. "She's too high and mighty now to do anything like housework." In his mind, Aisha is neglecting the housework on purpose because she feels more important than him. Because of his erroneous thinking, Tyrone is distancing himself from their marriage and making snide comments to his wife. Plus he's delib-erately avoiding doing his own tasks around the house. Aisha is picking up on his negativity and they've begun bickering more often. The saddest part of all this is that Tyrone's interpretation is way off base. Aisha is just feeling overwhelmed and honestly for-getting to take care of her share of the housework.

The way your partner thinks about you will affect how often and what he complains about. If he views you in mostly favor-able terms, he'll find fewer reasons to be unhappy about your behavior and he'll nag and complain less. Who doesn't want that? But negative beliefs about a lover can undermine emotional availability and the overall happiness of the relationship, and unfortunately, a pessimistic view holds even more power in a partnership than an upbeat one. So if he sees you in an antago-nistic way (e.g., stubborn versus persevering or selfish versus determined) and he won't work to turn his view around, he'll not only think less of you, but also feel less satisfied with your overall connection.

So, what if your husband views you as the "bad guy" and doesn't make any effort to change his belief? Not surprisingly he'll feel dissatisfied not only with you, but with the relationship. Sometimes his feelings are obvious. He might accuse you of being *selfish*, *clueless*, *nasty*, *unfair*, *high maintenance*, or *manipulative*. What are other clues that he considers you the enemy in the house? He might use hostile sarcasm, make angry accusations about your "true" motives, or make nasty global statements about your behavior, accusing you of *always* doing something *wrong* or *never* doing other things *right*. Nonverbal expressions of resentment and negativity include scowling, eye rolling, contemptuous laughter, cold stares, and crossed arms. Or he may withdraw from you (but not others), offer less physical affection, compare your relationship unfavorably to that of other couples, share less about his daily life, and show little or no interest in yours. Although anyone can develop unfriendly, sour beliefs about others, some subtypes are arguably more likely to do so.

The Critic is particularly likely to display these reactions for the same reason that he's likely to hold on to resentments—your flaws and errors pop out at him like an ink stain on a white shirt. His adverse view of you breeds perennial negativity and ill will, and it shows.

The Iceberg is also a contender to show you these responses. He holds you at a distance with frosty aloofness, setting the stage for him to find the relationship with you less gratifying and soothing, which makes fertile soil for negativity, similar to resentment. The thought of getting cozy and cuddly with some-one who's pushing me away and glaring at me with crossed arms and hostility in his eyes doesn't sound very appealing. His whole attitude successfully creates distance, and that's the way the Iceberg functions.

The Sponge is another subtype who may reveal these reactions, but for a different reason than the Critic or the Iceberg. In the Sponge's case, he's liable to construct an unfavorable frame of mind about you and unveil these kinds of negative reactions when you inevitably disappoint and hurt him for failing to give him the validation he needs.

The Defender is also prone to this type of reaction, particularly as he lashes out at you or pulls away in a self-protective response to something you do or say that feels threatening for him. It's possible that he holds a bevy of unfavorable beliefs about you under the surface, which is propelling his need to erect walls and self-protect, but he also could have carried this style with him into the relationship.

So far, we've been talking about how resentments and negative beliefs can fuel unavailability. But let's stop and address the elephant in the room, shall we? What if he's harboring entrenched negative beliefs or resentment about you and shows none of these signs? Although it's possible, I suspect there would be signs, but they aren't obvious or included in my list above. The truth is, it's tough, if not impossible, to hold on to resentment or budding negativity without it being expressed in *some* way. Of course, it's also quite possible your husband doesn't hold negative beliefs about you and isn't resentful at all, so please don't go looking for something that may not exist! If you do, you'll likely see antagonism where none exists. If holding on to negative thoughts and beliefs about you is an issue for your partner, believe me, he'll probably reveal that to you.

Assuming you do see signs, what's your next move? Well, the best tactic to take is to observe and try to understand what's going on. You don't want to "accuse" your mate of harboring unfavorable beliefs about you, or resenting you or the relationship. For now, keep it simple. Your mantra is simply: observe, listen and understand. Regardless of whether or not you feel as if you've gotten a real sense of why he's combative or unfriendly toward you, or whether you're totally in the dark, the goal is to be able to create a space of greater emotional safety and work toward building a deeper connection and authentic communication with the ultimate aim of uplifting his contentious view of you and releasing his resentment.

DIFFERENT THEORIES ABOUT RELATIONSHIPS

Do you believe in love at first sight? Is Valentine's Day your absolute favorite holiday? Do you think soul mates definitely exist? Can love last forever? Do you agree it takes commitment and effort to keep love alive? Or do you think a lifelong connection is a matter of destiny? And does your guy agree with you? When couples have different theories about relationships, it affects how they respond to each other, especially during a crisis.

For example, if your husband believes there's only one right person on earth for him and you're that person, when he's faced with a threat of some kind to your relationship—let's say someone calls you out on a lie—he'll be able to shift his attention to overlook it and still see the best in you. But if he has a soul mate view and he is now calling into question that you're that one and only special person, well, a mental litany of shortcomings is likely to follow. What if he maintains the belief that couples have to "work on a relationship" and doesn't put soul mates into his equation? Even during a crisis, he's unlikely to change how he thinks about you or the relationship because he doesn't believe there is a "The One" for him. In his view, a search for the "right" partner isn't part of the equation. That's why if there's a threat to your relationship he's more likely to focus on the need to address the problem. This isn't to say that a work-it-out theory is better or worse than a soul mate theory, only that different perspectives will mean a different response to the same challenges.

It's quite tricky to look for signs of these kinds of beliefs, so the best way to understand where your guy is coming from is through authentic dialogue. But he has to be willing to enter into a conversation. Some men find this subject just too romantic or New Agey to be taken seriously, but then some women do too. You might try bringing up the notion of soul mates in general—not referring explicitly to the two of you. However, I advise you to wait to have this conversation until after you've laid the groundwork for greater connection and have moved a bit closer. If he's not in a place to open up to you, it's unlikely you'd be able to explore this more personal subject.

Which of the emotionally unavailable subtypes are you likely to have differences with when it comes to theories of love? That's a tricky question to answer because it depends on the match between you and your partner and your personal thoughts and assumptions about relationships. When you and your partner are hopefully closer and able to reach out to each other more when you're farther along in the book, then you can go back and revisit whether this is an issue that the two of you need to face.

DIFFICULTY READING OR LABELING
YOUR EMOTIONAL CUES

How can your guy respond to your deepest emotional needs if he doesn't recognize how you're really feeling? It's difficult to do. If he can't figure out what's important to you, a wall to emotional availability will be built, brick by clueless brick. The Emotional Silencer is a prime example of this particular "why." He has a flair for being rather unnoticing when it comes to zeroing in on what you're feeling, not to mention either being baffled about what he's feeling or trying hard to dodge inner awareness. Let's look at the recent barrier constructed between Kevin and Lucia.

The couple made plans for a night out of dinner and dancing. But on the afternoon of their date, Kevin's friend Barry called and invited him to a basketball game. Even though Barry is a good friend, the two hadn't seen each other for several months, but as luck would have it, Kevin's favorite team was playing. In his excitement and without thinking it through, Kevin completely blanked on the date night and agreed to go out with his friend.

When Kevin phoned his wife to let her know he'd be out, a tsunami of feelings washed over Lucia. Surprise, confusion, disappointment, anger were all there, but the biggest emotion was hurt. Lucia was so overwhelmed she didn't know what to say or how to react. She stayed subdued, but sounded down when she thanked her husband for letting her know his plans. "Try not to wake me when you get home" were her closing words. Even though this was an unusual request, Kevin didn't pick up on Lucia's deeper reaction. He thought she was just exhausted.

Should Lucia have been more up-front with Kevin? You bet! But her husband's lack of insight is also unfortunate. Being able to tune in to your partner's emotional state is a crucial piece of what it means to be available. This wasn't an unusual instance either. In general Kevin can't "read" Lucia, and their relationship suffers because of it. If his wife smiles while they're discussing a memorable date, he'll think it's because she's remembering something he did that was foolish rather than the pleasure she's feeling. Or he may think her huff of exasperation when he asks about her day (and it's been a bad one) is a sarcastic response signaling that she feels he doesn't have a clue. This kind of misreading takes its toll, but when you become a more effective reader, the benefit is clear. Couples with the skills to read and convey each other's feelings report happier and more fulfilling marriages.

We convey emotions in lots of ways: how we position our body (e.g., arms open and body leaning forward often means we're trusting and connecting versus crossed arms and body leaning backward, a pose that can reflect distance and avoidance) and our facial expressions (e.g., smiling or frowning, brows arched for questioning or furrowed for worry, eyes looking down for avoidance versus looking directly to engage). Our rate of speaking is also an emotional cue (e.g., slow for unhurried, fast for pressured), as well as the use of timing in speech (e.g., leaving space between comments for response or interrupting as a sign of not really listening)—and on and on.

As you can see, this is a complicated process. When a host of other factors comes into play, our ability to express or read emotions can get even thornier. Additional wrenches include efforts to mask what's really being felt, our mood when trying to interpret emotions, or what we're anticipating another person will feel. Even the stereotypes we hold about others influence which emotions we're more likely to see in them.

Is it any wonder we all make blunders in the world of emotional communication? That's why the question isn't whether you or your guy miss or misread each other's emotional signals, or whether unclear messages are sent, but how often it happens. If it happens more often than not, you might be feeling like you don't really "get" or "see" each other, that he has no idea who you are. You may sense a deep, underlying distance that pervades your relationship but isn't directly addressed. You might find your relationship is rife with misinterpretation of what you're each thinking, feeling, or intending. The problem expressing or reading emotions could rest primarily with him, or with you. Or you both need remedial work.

Regardless of who struggles, here are some points to remember:

- No one is perfect.
- We can all improve our emotional communication.
- Emotional miscommunication affects both members of a relationship.
- There are steps you can take to improve the problem, but now is *not* the time to educate your partner on what *he* can do.
- It *is* the time to focus on how *you* can improve the way you read your guy's emotional signals. It will help you release judgment, become more in tune with him, and gain valuable guidance on the best way to relate to him.

WEAK SOCIAL SKILLS

We're so busy yada-yada-ing and blah-blah-blah-ing that most of us don't realize how tricky and complicated communication can be. Let's think about the most recent conversation you had with a friend. First, you took ideas from your head and put them into

TIPS ON READING
HIS EMOTIONAL CUES

✦

Reading silent emotional signals can be a tricky business at first, but with practice you'll be able to pick up nonverbal clues with more confidence. Here's what you can do:

- Look at different parts of his face rather than his whole facial expression. What's his mouth doing? Scowling, frowning, or smiling? What's he doing with his brows? Furrowed (a sign of anger, concern, or concentration) or raised (a sign of surprise or interest)? Is he rolling his eyes at you (a sign of contempt) or is he looking down (a sign of avoidance or sadness)? Is he glaring at you (could be anger) or gazing with a soft expression and a smile (signs of affection)?

- Check out his body. Notice the distance he takes when standing near you. Does he touch you when he speaks (a sign of connection) or move away (a sign of distancing)? Does he keep his arms open (accepting) or closed (a guarded position)? Is he shaking his leg or tapping his fingers? He might be nervous, uncomfortable, or impatient.

- Observe his tone of voice and how fast he speaks. Does he sound calm and friendly, icy, terse, or agitated? How silent or talkative is he? Did he move from engaged communication to prolonged silence? This indicates something has emotionally shifted for him and he's either shutting down or reflecting on your discussion.

Well-read emotions give you crucial information. If you pay attention, you'll learn more about his world and where you stand in it.

words. Then you spoke those words and they slid off into your friend's mind. She responded in a particular way, depending on whether she understood what you were saying or not. With all this uncertainty and room for error, isn't it amazing that effective communication *ever* happens?

Add this to the mix: We need to perform a bunch of different tasks when we interact: from listening and regulating our emotions and nonverbal behavior to deciding on what to say next and reading body language to the best of our ability. If your guy lacks these skills, it will be harder for him to tune in to what you're saying and he won't be able to react to you in a supportive way. These sorts of social skills are usually honed early in life, starting roughly around the age of five or six, when children first go to school.

You may be wondering as human beings why we don't all develop social skills. Well, of course we do, but some of us are better at it than others. It takes good role modeling (usually from our parents), with plenty of practice during early childhood and beyond to sharpen these skills. If your guy's caregivers were socially remote when he was growing up, it likely made learning good communication skills more challenging.

Dot came home from a long day. All she wanted to do was share all of the drama with Godfrey over dinner that night.

"What a day I had. I have to tell you. In the morning, as I was driving to work, a squirrel ran out suddenly in front of the car and I accidentally killed him. It was so horrific. Poor thing. I tried to save him, but when I got out of the car, I knew there was nothing I could do. So I got back into my car and just bawled all the way to work, feeling like a monster. Then, when I got to work, I was so grateful not to have any meetings. I just hid in my office and moped, feeling like total crap. But then, toward the end of the day, I got a call telling me that I got the position I applied for but never imagined in my nuttiest fantasy I'd get.

It's essentially a gigantic promotion and pay raise. So then I was elated. Honestly, what's the matter with me, Godfrey? How can I run down a defenseless creature—causing him at least a moment of agony and terror, I'm sure—and then snap right out of it and feel happy because of this promotion? Ugh. I can see the headlines now: 'Heartless Squirrel Murderer Gleeful at Career Advancement.'"

Just then, Godfrey's phone beeped.

"Wow. That's a lot!" he said, already scrolling through his messages. "Check out what Scott texted me. This is hilarious!"

Godfrey's response doesn't exactly make Dot feel heard and build connection between them, does it? He is completely oblivious to her social cues, dismissing her and leaving her feeling unheard and frustrated. Real communication needs the mastery of important social skills like listening carefully, reading body language, and tuning in to our own emotions. If these skills weren't modeled in early childhood, your guy may have a hard time learning them now. Another factor that can play into the strength of social skills is context. People can show marvelous social skills with strangers and acquaintances, then display careless social skill with their partners, allowing cherished tools such as emotion and body regulation, attentiveness, and caring responsiveness to fly out the window.

So some people can struggle with weak social skills across the board, whereas with others it's more selective. So an Iceberg, a Defender, a Sponge, or a Critic could, conceivably, be quite unavailable to you yet genial and engaging to others. An Emotional Silencer, so long as he's not required to engage in any real personal insight, could thrive and be well liked (e.g., playing on a basketball league, working in a software or accounting firm).

A Fearful Fraud could skillfully display the face that he believes insulates him from the dreaded social thumbs-down, and skirt problems as long as he isn't asked to reveal his true self. In a relationship with you, because social skill is arguably a fundamental component of being able to participate healthfully in a relationship, by virtue of being emotionally unavailable, all of the subtypes are not leveraging social skills, whether they are capable of using them in outside, less intimate relationships or not.

But a lack of social skills is not a hopeless situation. People can learn.

It helps to know the weaknesses and strengths in your partner's social skill set—as well as in your own. Does he have any of the following challenges or gifts?

- Does he pay attention to what people say and understand what they mean?
- Is he respectful and tuned in to social expectations? For example, does he dress for the occasion?
- Does he notice and decipher the nonverbal signs of others' feelings, ideas, and attitudes?
- Can he start and hold a conversation? Does he ask questions to keep a dialogue going?
- Is he able to nonverbally convey appropriate feelings and wishes? For example, does he maintain greater physical distance with people he doesn't know well (if he's in a culture where this is generally the norm), or can he gently convey a lack of enthusiasm for an idea without explicitly saying so?
- Does he have the ability to control and change his comments and personal presentation depending on the situation? For instance, can he choose to behave in a more formal yet friendly

manner at an elegant social function and then drop it all and
be warm and silly at home?

* Is he aware of and able to manage how he nonverbally conveys and communicates his feelings? For example, does he
hold back on the impulse to roll his eyes or scowl?

After going through the list, did you get a sense of your partner's social skills—and perhaps your own as well? One of the
best ways to help him improve is to model the same skills you
would like to see in him. I've had people tell me how much their
partner's words have hurt them and then they engage in the
same hurtfulness. Without fully realizing it, they're sending a
message that hurtful words are okay. If you want your mate to
stop interrupting you, or raising his voice during an argument,
you'll need to resist doing these things yourself.

Another way to help him improve his social skills is by
expressing admiration for what he does well. Highlight his social
strengths by praising them. Maybe you've observed him master-
fully navigating complex social situations at work or with family,
or being a superb listener, or maybe he was astute at knowing just
when you needed a little reassurance; let him know you see and
appreciate this skillfulness. When he shines through and does
better, even a little bit, express genuine appreciation for it. If he's
like most of us, he'll appreciate the attention and praise and be
motivated to do it again.

You can try these techniques now if it seems like your relationship is in a place where he will be open and receptive to it. But
you can also hold off if you prefer. This is a communication issue
and we'll come to communication and how to use it to enhance
connection shortly.

HIDDEN EMOTIONS

There are times when people keep their negative emotions, especially anger, under wraps. A big force driving this kind of secrecy is the hope to avoid hurting our loved one's feelings. This is what I call the "let sleeping dogs lie" approach.

Let's look at Karl, a graduate student in English literature. He's been with Leslie for the past three years. Lately, he's been feeling frustrated because he's preparing to work on his dissertation and needs a few more nights alone in his apartment. Karl would like to be open with Leslie and just tell her, but he's worried she'll feel unwanted. What does he do? *Nothing.* He keeps his desire to himself to avoid hurting her. From this perspective, he's withholding his frustration because he's gone through the thoughtful steps of envisioning what he would say, and then imagining Leslie's feelings. This sounds like a well-intentioned attempt at emotional availability to me. But does this really make him more available? Before we answer, let's imagine that Karl kept mum for less altruistic reasons.

Let's say he wanted to shield himself from a host of unpleasant reactions he fears Leslie will have, such as pity, taking offense, viewing him as weak, or the possibility she won't want to be with him anymore. Bear in mind, in at least some cases, the projected reaction is based in fear rather than in reality. Since it's only Karl's motivation that's changed, not his withholding of information, what difference does it make? Let's compare the two motivations.

When we block expressions of a negative emotion such as anger or fear frequently, irrespective of the intention, intimacy suffers. Bear in mind that even for people who are more focused on promoting social togetherness and harmony than on their own wishes, the benefits of hiding negative emotions only applied to sacrifice. If we wear a mask as a go-to strategy, then the relationship can only ever go as deep as the mask. Not only that, it takes real effort to hide feelings that are naturally expressed through our facial expressions, body language, and voice. It's hard to be intimate when you're wearing a mask. The Fearful Fraud and the Defender are especially likely to construct a false face and duck behind it, but the motive is self-protection rather than to benefit you.

However, in Karl's case, it probably would have made Leslie feel even closer to him if he told the truth about his feelings and the reason for his reluctance to share, since his loving motivation to withhold his negative emotions was for her benefit. After all, it feels good to know our partner has our welfare at heart. Plus, unless Karl has an interdependent view of himself, then while he's trying to inhibit his intention, a taxing and energy-draining endeavor, he's more likely to be out of touch with Leslie's emotional cues and they're both going to feel less connected with each other.

So what to do? How can you help your partner begin to lower the mask, even by an inch or two? Considering that he's holding it up because he's trying to protect himself from rejection or your displeasure, then you could try opening up with a little more vulnerability yourself. If he sees you sharing more, he may open up too. When we share pieces of ourselves with others, they're more likely to share with us. You could also reward any overtures he makes to share. Your receptivity, nonjudgment, and appreciative feedback could push open other windows of opportunity he'll take to share again. For example, let's say that he admits he was a little annoyed when you forgot to do a favor for him. This is an ideal opportunity to thank him for telling you, to apologize, and to clue him in that you actually feel closer to him because he admitted that. Strive to find ways to be a safe space for your partner when he takes risks and opens up, keeping the lines of communication open.

FEAR OF BEING "REAL"

Plenty of guys (but this can certainly come up with women too) view expressing emotions as a weakness. They might also be afraid that talking about painful circumstances in the present or in their past will unearth feelings they've been trying to keep buried. It just seems safer not to feel anything than to allow emotions to bubble to the surface. In other instances, certain emotions are believed to be off-limits. Some folks won't give themselves permission to be sad because "others are so much worse off." Or they may be afraid to express unhappiness because they worry it might grow out of proportion and swallow them. Similarly, we may avoid anger because we believe if we allowed ourselves to experience it, the emotion would overtake us and we would do something harmful to someone else or to ourselves. Or we might avoid anger because we find it too uncomfortable, or because it's tough admitting we're feeling upset with someone we care about.

Whatever the reason, stuffing emotions is not a good coping strategy since it's likely to contribute to problems down the road. When I talk to people about the importance of emotions, I emphasize that we're born biologically ready to experience them. We come equipped with tear ducts and have a limbic system in our brain allowing us to have emotions. If we weren't made to cry and feel fear, anger, and sadness, we wouldn't be built this way. So why put a value judgment on our authentic feelings? Emotions are like a smoke alarm; if an alarm goes off in a building, it's much smarter to heed its signal than to react by wanting to shut it off as soon as possible. A sign of a well-functioning building is a working smoke alarm.

The same is true of our emotions. They're a huge part of being human, and when something powerful is happening, an authentic emotional response provides needed information about what's going on and what to do next.

If your spouse is pushing his feelings away and not sharing genuine emotions, he's working against himself and your relationship. The Emotional Silencer is especially likely to face this problem because he's more disconnected from his emotions. You'll also recognize this issue in the Iceberg due to his efforts to push personal connection away. You may also see this in the Defender if he's feeling emotionally threatened, leading him to evade more intimate, emotional dialogue. Finally, the Fearful Fraud is another subtype who is more prone to this intimacy obstacle, but only if the emotion is one that he is concerned will result in rejection or disquiet. Since unavailability appears in several ways, this might not be his issue. Here are some clues to let you know if this is something your emotionally unavailable partner is dealing with:

- Does he rarely tell you how he's feeling, even when he's talking about a powerful topic such as the death of a loved one, a betrayal, or a job loss?
- Does he speak about these kinds of powerful topics without a notable tone of emotion in his voice? Or does he just mention them casually as though they don't affect him?

- Does he tend to say what he *thinks,* not what he *feels?* For example, if he tells you about an incident at work and you say, "That's awful! How did you feel when your boss did that to you?" his response might be "I think he's a self-important jerk. He does this to everyone."
- Does he deny feeling an emotion despite obvious nonverbal signals to the contrary?
- Does he make disparaging comments about other people's emotions such as "She's a drama queen!" or "He's a wimp!"
- Does he get visibly uncomfortable when others share their emotions with him? Will he try to change the subject?

Even if these clues look familiar (and this isn't a complete list, so you may have thought of others), you won't be able to *make* your guy be more comfortable or willing to express his emotions. That's up to him. However, you can work toward creating a relationship with a solid foundation of emotional safety to help him feel more forthcoming about sharing them. Next, you can build on the progress you've made with specific steps toward greater emotional connection. We'll come to these steps later in the book.

I realize you might think it sounds a little roundabout to focus on your relationship as a key to getting him to open up more. Instead, you may be thinking, "Why not get right to the point and just tell him he's not being as emotionally open as I want him to be?"

I suppose you could try that (and you probably have), but I ask you to consider this first: Think about something you tried that really scared you. When I've gone scuba diving, I considered the risks, but my rational mind told me I'd probably be okay. If I didn't believe that, I would avoid diving. If your partner believes he'll get hurt, judged, viewed as weak, rejected, pressured, or dismissed or that his candor will later be used against him, he may not take the risk. He's probably going to keep his feelings to himself. On the other hand, if he believes he'll be met with acceptance, caring, friendship, love, loyalty, respect, real listening, and patience, he'll be more likely to risk opening up to you—even if he keeps the armor on with others.

It's also possible, even after you've created an atmosphere of safety, that he still won't open up. In that case, when your relationship is on steadier, more loving ground, and he is more receptive, and you're feeling closer, you could approach him and tell him how you're feeling about his reticence. Remember, connection is a process and it needs to happen gradually and in ways that are comfortable for both of you. The capacity to be emotionally in tune is absolutely beautiful, but it's also intricate and multilayered. As we've seen, a variety of interpersonal issues has a powerful influence on how open someone is going to be.

Imagine there are several ropes that pull and tug emotional availability in one direction or another, influencing it in different ways. Some of these ropes represent the day-to-day interactions between the two of you, such as what you say (or don't say) to each other and the obvious or subtle nonverbal messages you both offer. More ropes reflect his emotional style and the degree to which he's comfortable experiencing and expressing himself. How much your relationship factors into his personal identity and how he sees himself are more ropes, twisting either toward distance and resentment or bonding you closer.

But these interpersonal ropes aren't the only ones that tie up emotional availability. Other ropes reflect his personal history and that's where we're turning next.

Personal History

For better or worse, we all bring our past into the present. Depending on what your partner's personal history contains, he may be more prone either to react with openness and authenticity in your relationship or to close down and defend himself. Here are some of the most powerful influences:

- What we learn from our parents
- Insecure attachment
- Trauma and post-traumatic stress disorder (PTSD)

WHAT WE LEARN FROM OUR PARENTS

Tommy grew up in a home in the Midwest where emotions were either denied or swept under the rug. He recalled a time when he became irate after his parents grounded him and his sister for a mistake only she made. "My parents had this crazy rule that we had to be punished together no matter who was at fault." When he got angry and screamed, "Not fair!" his parents reacted calmly. "As usual they were a placid lake," Tommy remembers. "Why are you getting so angry?" they practically cooed. Since his parents never expressed emotions, Tommy started to doubt his own reactions. He wondered whether he was overreacting, but could never be sure.

Even though most of us come biologically "prepackaged" with the ability to experience and express emotions, we start to learn *how* to do it through the examples our parents set. We look to them to see how they respond to certain situations, and we consider whether it matches our own emotional reactions. If the comparison fits, that's great. But if, as with Tommy, it doesn't, we may start to question our own reactions. Tommy also noticed which emotions his parents expressed and which ones they kept inside. As he watched his parents in a variety of situations and paid attention to their statements to him about which emotions were family approved and which were not, he picked up family "rules" about acceptable emotional behavior. It's very possible if your loved one is holding back his emotions that he has his parents to "thank."

In the last section, you read about ways your guy exhibits emotional unavailability through his withholding statements, behaviors, and mannerisms. Now I'm going to build on your awareness with questions you can ask yourself about what *you're* experiencing:

- Do you frequently feel in the dark about what he's feeling?

- How often do you find yourself frustrated by your partner's lack of emotional expression?

- Would you describe him as stoic? At first this might have made him seem strong and resilient, but over time you've noticed that his response almost never changes. You may be wondering if he feels anything at all. The emotionally unavailable subtype most likely to display this quality is the Emotional Silencer. But remember that emotional unavailability is a spectrum, so he may show this trait without being wholly at the level of an Emotional Silencer. For instance, he may have no clue about his own emotions and be unable to talk about them with you, yet he may listen politely while you share your own without withdrawing.

- If he does show feelings, does it seem like he has the same emotional response for a wide range of circumstances? For instance, does he get angry in situations when you would expect him to feel sad or scared?

If your partner grew up with family rules that put potent constraints on his emotions, it's not hopeless—but it can be a tough road to travel. Change will be achievable only if he wants it. But I've seen it happen many, many times. Although none of us has the capacity to completely erase years of learning, we are capable of doing things differently and learning anew. He can come to realize his emotions are healthy and human and not a sign of weakness. He can learn relationships tend to get closer, not hurtful or punishing, when we open up about how we feel.

If he's willing to challenge what he's been taught and try to practice new habits, and he is fortunate enough to have a relationship that supports, nurtures, and rewards these changes, then he really can create different emotional rules than the ones he inherited from his family. But remember, it's up to him to question the lessons of his youth and practice being more emotionally expressive. Fortunately, you have the power to create a new and safer environment for him so that he has an opportunity to embrace these changes.

INSECURE ATTACHMENT

The most famous method of studying attachment is an approach called the Strange Situation. Here's how the experiment was carried out: A mother and child came to a laboratory and met with an experimenter, who escorted them to a room filled with assorted toys. At first, the toddler was recorded while in the presence of his mother. After a while, an assistant (a stranger) enters the room and spends time with mother and baby. Then the mom left the room and observers watched in another room and recorded the child's reaction while he was alone with the stranger. When the mother came back in the room, the stranger left and the toddler's reaction was again noted. After a while, the mother left again, and the toddler was in the room without anyone. Through this exercise, these three patterns of attachment were observed:

1. Secure attachment style: The child playfully explored his surroundings while his mother was present. When his mother left, the child might become upset, but then he enthusiastically greeted her when she returned and reconnected with her.

2. Anxious or ambivalent attachment style: The toddler was highly reluctant to stray from his mother and explore on his own. When his mother left, the child became extremely upset and remained upset even after his mother returned. He desperately reached for her one moment, then angrily pushed her away the next.

3. Avoidant attachment style: In this situation, the child was rather indifferent to his mother prior to her leaving the room and generally didn't appear distressed when she left. He also tended to disregard his mother on her return to the room.

In most instances, our approach to our relationships reflects the kind of connection we had with our parents while we were growing up. That's why the terms "secure," "anxious," and "avoidant" also apply to us now. We can, however, defy the odds and become securely attached even if we were raised by parents who weren't really there for us, so if you notice a discrepancy between your attachment style and how you were raised, don't worry. It's certainly not unheard-of for this to happen.

But let's look at your partner. If he developed a secure attachment style, that's good news. He probably learned he could rely on his parents in times of need. They could be trusted to act in his best interest and to be there if he needed comfort. They provided a safe home base from which he could explore and gave the message that he mattered enough to receive their attention and care. If he carried this into his adult life, he'll believe you're reliable, caring, and trustworthy, and it's safe for him to get close. In this case, you can assume his emotional unavailability isn't caused by early attachment.

I'd like to pause here for a moment and address a common-sense question: "What if my partner had early secure attachment but suffered a bad betrayal by a former girlfriend or spouse? Doesn't that damage him for life?" You would think that, right? Although it's technically possible, believe it or not, the data don't support this assumption. For example, research suggests that when a person is securely attached and they experience a betrayal, they're more likely to be forgiving than someone who's insecurely attached.

So let's move on. What if he developed an anxious/ambivalent attachment style? He learned that sometimes his caregivers would be there, sometimes not. You may not know the reason behind his parents' erratic behavior, and perhaps they weren't erratic at all yet were perceived in this way. What you do know is that, as a result of this kind of on-again, off-again attention, he entered adult relationships straddling both sides of the fence. He wants you close, but he can't trust that you'll stay with him, and he's vigilant for any sign of losing you. The emotionally unavailable subtypes most likely to reflect an anxious/ambivalent attachment style are the Sponge and the Fearful Fraud. That said, almost any of the emotionally unavailable subtypes can wrestle with this sort of insecure attachment.

Finally, if he developed an avoidant attachment style, he

learned it's probably best not to rely on caregivers at all and to go things alone. He's also likely learned to be untrusting and believe you'll eventually leave him in the lurch. An inability to rely on others can also give him the message that he isn't lovable. A mother's depression during early childhood is one predictor of avoidant attachment later in life, but whatever the circumstances behind a parent's neglect, the result is the same. He'll minimize how much he wants to connect with you and he'll push you away. The Iceberg is the emotionally unavailable subtype that most strongly reflects this kind of attachment style.

Some studies have found that people with strong avoidant attachment styles are more likely to cheat on their partners. Sad, but it makes sense since infidelity minimizes connection and creates distance. This behavior may lead to a relationship's end, but this is not always the case. Even if infidelity does occur, there are a number of ways couples can heal from it and come back even stronger.

Let's pause here for a moment and take stock of your guy's history and the kinds of lessons he learned while he was growing up. As you know, the relationships he had with his caregivers gave him his present relationship model, and what he can expect from relationships and from you in particular. Although it's true that caregivers are our original attachment figures and help shape our expectations around connection, it's also the case that long-term romantic partners become our primary attachment figures in adulthood.

That's why you're in a golden position to show him old rules no longer apply. It takes time, but with patience and a gentle approach, it can happen. We'll come to this later as you learn to set pathways for connection. First, though, let's learn more about the old rules that shaped him so that you can be aware of what you're going to contradict. Gaining awareness is also good for your peace of mind. It's easier to deal with a difficult problem and be able to call on compassion when we have an understanding of what influenced our partner's behavior.

To begin to get a clearer perspective, consider the following questions:

- Who raised him?
- What kind of relationship did he have with his caregivers?
- Could he rely on them to be lovingly there for him—or were they dismissive?
- Was there a history of physical, sexual, or emotional abuse, or neglect?
- Was your partner treated with love and consistency, or was his treatment chaotic or unreliable?
- Does he seem to replicate some of the same patterns from his upbringing in your relationship? If so, what are those patterns?

TRAUMA AND POST-TRAUMATIC STRESS DISORDER (PTSD)

If your partner suffered a trauma or is dealing with PTSD, it may be incredibly hard for him to connect emotionally after the horror he experienced. The experience of trauma is disorienting and can affect how he sees himself and the world around him. This can make relationships challenging in the aftermath of a trauma. Of course, it's hard on you too because no matter how much you reach out, your attempts could be distrusted or shunned.

Aaron, a thirty-three-year-old biologist, is a victim of trauma. He was walking to his car after work when an armed robber

grabbed him from behind and beat him with a gun. The assail-
ant took his wallet and gold watch and ran away. Aaron was
found several hours later and taken to a hospital. Although he
eventually recovered from the physical injuries, he was plagued
for months by deeply upsetting nightmares and intrusive thoughts
about the experience. He was also terrified of going out into a
crowd because he never knew when someone would come up
from behind. Aaron felt ashamed for "allowing it to happen"
and thought about how the assault wouldn't have taken place if
only he "had been more careful or fought back." On top of it,
he felt crazy and weak for having these intense thoughts and
feelings.

Although he was able to return to work a few months later,
connecting with friends and dating was a bigger problem. He
described himself as a "nut job" for being afraid of crowds and
unable to stop violent memories from haunting him. Because he
felt isolated and "different" from others, seeking intimacy from
a relationship was no longer on his radar.

Like most of us before trauma, Aaron assumed if he did his
best, was a good person, thought about what he was doing, and
made wise decisions, he'd be okay. He also assumed that he was
generally safe and could trust people not to hurt him. But trauma
can drastically change our perception. Most strikingly, prior to
the trauma, he believed he could take care of himself. Unfortunately, a traumatic event brings on the realization that self-
protection has limitations. If your partner suffered a trauma like
Aaron's, resulting in self-blame for the assault, as well as possible
flashbacks, intrusive thoughts, and other PTSD symptoms, it
may have left him feeling powerless, unable to trust his own
instincts or trust you.

Powerlessness, lack of trust toward oneself and you, loss of a feeling of safety, an internal sense that there's something wrong (many people suffering with PTSD symptoms erroneously believe they're "crazy"), and the determination never to be vulnerable again may lead him to create walls of unavailability.

Trauma and PTSD-related symptoms—such as anger, constant vigilance, intrusive reminders, numbing, chronic avoidance, and lack of trust—can all contribute to building a barrier that separates your mate from you. If you suspect that PTSD is at the root of your partner's unavailability, start by asking yourself whether your loved one has ever had a traumatic experience like sexual or physical assault, combat, robbery with a weapon, a serious accident, witnessing a life-threatening condition, or trauma such as another person being badly injured or killed, or seeing dead bodies.

If your mate has had a traumatic experience and struggles with some of the symptoms I've discussed earlier, he may have PTSD. Fortunately, help is available. You can educate yourself and learn about this very distressing but treatable condition. The National Institute of Mental Health (NIMH) has an excellent website worth checking out (nimh.nih.gov), and if your partner is a veteran, there's also a comprehensive website offered by the U.S. Department of Veterans Affairs (ptsd.va.gov). If you're looking for information on what you can do to help, there are many resources for the loved ones of sufferers as well. But don't stop at researching the disorder; continue following the emotional-safety and connection-building strategies offered throughout this book. Relationship science suggests that a supportive and safe connection is linked to partners sharing their trauma and progressing in healing. If your partner has already spoken about his traumatic event, you might ask him if he'd like to get some outside help for it. If he's ready, provide him with information on treatment options that you found on the websites mentioned earlier.

Inner Emotional World

It's not just the past or communication problems that can affect your loved one's ability to connect; it's also his inner emotional world. This includes how he sees himself in the world, his moods, and whether he can identify his own emotional reactions.

Several factors can affect his inner emotional world:

- Low self-esteem
- Depression
- Difficulty recognizing emotions

LOW SELF-ESTEEM

I always tell my clients the most important relationship we have in life is with ourselves. If we're not at peace with ourselves, how can we be at peace with our partners? How can we let someone get close to us if we believe it's not a pleasant place to be?

Getting close to someone and building a meaningful and rewarding relationship requires some risk. It means letting someone into your emotional world, sharing who you are, and allowing yourself to become invested—to love and to care. If your husband or boyfriend has a strong, upbeat sense of himself, it will most likely give him the courage to move closer to you even if it feels uncomfortable to do it. If your guy has a positive sense of self, he'll have the courage to stay rather than run away if you say or do something that hurts his feelings. And let's be real: no relationship is without its slights and hurts. But the opposite is true as well, as you may have seen in your emotionally unavailable partner.

If a person has a high level of self-esteem and believes his partner is committed to him, he's more likely to reach out when going through a rough patch. But if he has low self-esteem, commitment doesn't matter. He won't draw nearer during tough times. And when it comes to low self-esteem, any of the emotionally unavailable subtypes could find themselves wrestling with it, not to mention those with the many shades of unavailability that don't fit these types.

A couple of years ago Gordon, a twenty-eight-year-old construction worker, was involved with a woman and it looked like they were on the path to marriage. But as he says with a slump of his shoulders, "I knew it wasn't going to last. As soon as she discovered the real me, she wanted out." Since that time, he's been pretty much on his own. One of Gordon's biggest obstacles to availability is that he suffers with low self-esteem. He sees himself as unattractive, unintelligent, and not particularly interesting. When he glances at his reflection in the mirror, he criticizes his physique, thinning hair, and bold features. He blames himself for his failed relationship, saying, "I was boring and stupid." Feeling unworthy of love, he thinks he'll never be able to find a "really good woman again," as he puts it. On the other hand, Gordon has plenty of one-night stands, but figures these women are "just desperate" and he doesn't call them again after they've slept with him.

We all want to feel others "get us," but a person with low self-esteem is likely to push away affection or attempts to nurture intimacy. Why? Because it just doesn't jibe with how he feels inside—unlovable. He may dismiss people who seem to be attracted to him by, for example, viewing them as being "phony," saying they don't know the real him, or calling them "real losers." If he's in a relationship, he could find himself waiting for the other shoe to drop. Or he may sabotage the relationship because he believes it's going to end badly anyway. Why wait?

If your man feels unworthy, unknowable, and insecure, it will be difficult for him to accept and be responsive to your overtures of affection and commitment. Do you hear him uttering self-critical or self-disparaging comments such as "I'm such a moron!," "I can't seem to do *anything* right," or "I'll never get that promotion—so many people are smarter than me"? Does he have a tough time thinking of his own needs? Or when he does, will he dismiss them immediately? Does your guy seem to lack self-confidence, especially in social situations? Does he question why you're with him? These are possible signs of low self-esteem and low self-worth.

If you believe this describes your man, tread carefully. It's an understandable impulse to want to reassure your loved one if he feels terrible about himself. You know he's got it all wrong and he's far better than he thinks he is, but it's unlikely you can talk someone out of self-loathing with simple reassurance. As mentioned earlier, it could even backfire. Your partner may wonder if you're lying, or your words may fill him with further self-doubt as he suspects you really don't know him. He might dismiss you as "clueless." For these reasons, resist the urge to heap gobs of reassurance upon him all at once. It could feel awkward at best and terrifying at worst. It might even trigger him to push you further away.

What to do? Once again, focus on gently creating a stable, loving, emotionally secure foundation for him. This will enhance the odds that he'll open up and connect. Those with an avoidant attachment style or low self-esteem are more likely to come closer to their partners when they're upset if they feel safe in their relationships. In essence, your guy is more likely to jump in the water if he knows it's warm and inviting. I'll help you work on creating these conditions in your relationship. This doesn't mean you haven't already thrown one or several flotation devices in his direction, but now you may be at a loss as to what to do next. The coming chapters will give you additional ideas to help you change the dynamic and increase the odds that your emotionally dismissive partner will drift closer.

DEPRESSION

It's called the "blues," but it's more like living in a state of gray. Life takes on a dull cast and it's hard to see beyond it. Depression is a struggle with low mood and clearly shrinking interest in doing what once made you happy. Concentrating on and making decisions about simple things can be overwhelming. Personal hygiene can be neglected, sleeping and eating patterns can change, and energy and motivation may trail off. There can also be feelings of guilt and hopelessness, even thoughts of suicide. If your guy is in this state, you probably know it.

You can imagine how incredibly difficult it is for him to be supportive of anyone else. People with depression wrestle to care for themselves, much less care for a partner. An analogy I like is to compare depression (as well as other types of weighty emotional hurt) and relationships to the memory of pain right after taking a really bad fall. Remember when your pain was at its worst? At that moment, were you aware of the needs and feelings of anyone else around you? I doubt it. No, I suspect you had a laser focus on your agony and couldn't see past it.

Our culture can also make serious depression difficult to talk about since the word is thrown around so casually. Just keep your ears open and you'll hear people saying things like: "The movie *Bambi* is so depressing!" "This rain is depressing!" "The world situation is depressing!" "All I need is Häagen-Dazs and a glass of cabernet to cure my depression!"

Although these kinds of statements may be referring to valid experiences of stress and sadness, don't be fooled. They're not describing *real* depression, which is a serious yet highly treatable condition. It's also common. The Centers for Disease Control and Prevention (CDC) state that over 350 million people around the world suffer from depression—and that includes approximately 10 percent of the U.S. population at any one time. It transcends all of the emotionally unavailable subtypes too.

How can you tell if your mate is one of the many people struggling with depression? Here are some signs to consider, but keep in mind that he doesn't have to have all of the symptoms listed below. If he has several of these, he may be grappling with depression:

- He has a persistently low mood that lasts for a couple of weeks or longer.
- Activities that were once pleasurable are no longer fun for him.
- He's eating much more or much less than usual.
- There's a dramatic loss of energy.
- He has sleep problems, including troubles going to sleep, staying asleep, or sleeping too much.
- He has problems concentrating. Even making the smallest decision seems like a huge effort for him.
- There's lingering anxiety.
- He harbors feelings of guilt that seem excessive. For example, he might believe he's a horrible person because he simply forgot to call a buddy back.

- He expresses feelings of despair or worthlessness.
- He's spoken about thoughts of suicide or told you that it would be better for everyone if he were dead.
- He's made one or more suicide attempts.

If you believe he's battling depression, seek out information about it including treatment options. The National Institute of Mental Health has an informative website on depression that you should explore (nimh.nih.gov/health/topics/depression/index.shtml).

If your partner has talked about wanting to die, or has told you he's thinking about ending his life, take it seriously. It's a myth that people who talk about suicide aren't really going to do it. Talking about suicide is actually a crucial warning sign, so don't handle this alone. Call the National Suicide Prevention Lifeline for help and guidance (1-800-273-8255). It's available 24/7.

Depending on your situation, the relationship, and your comfort level, you could gently check in with how he's doing and raise the question of whether he might be interested in getting some help. For instance, you might say something like "I've noticed you've been really hurting for quite a while. I care about you so much that I wanted to check in and tell you I support you. Would you be interested in getting some help if it might make you feel better?"

And just as relationship problems can play a role in the emergence and course of depression, relationship improvement can contribute to recovery from it. A recent study found that when depressed spouses entered couples therapy, their condition improved.

DIFFICULTY RECOGNIZING EMOTIONS

We've looked at low self-esteem and depression as parts of the inner world that might play a role in your partner's emotional unavailability. The third one we're going to talk about is an inability to recognize one's own feelings. This issue is particularly relevant for the Emotional Silencer.

Bob and his wife, Ronnie, came to couples therapy at her insistence. When Dr. Myers asked Bob to describe how he was feeling, it was a struggle for him. Although he was able to notice some sensations in his body like his heart racing and his forehead sweating, he couldn't figure out what was causing this reaction—what his emotions were telling him.

This doesn't mean Bob is suffering much. He goes about his business and doesn't think about how he feels. This may work out in plenty of situations, but not when it comes to being able to share more of his internal life with his wife and to emotionally connect with her. His lack of personal awareness erects a wall between them.

People who interact with Bob might see him as unflappable, a private kind of guy who doesn't wear his heart on his sleeve. But his wife has a different experience. She sees him as unread-able. Her efforts to find out how he's feeling are met with either (a) nondescript answers such as "fine" or "good"; (b) a statement that shares what he thinks but not what he feels, something like "I think I'd rather play golf tomorrow than stay home"; or (c) an insightful admission that he's not sure: "I don't know what I'm feeling." It's not that Bob is intentionally responding dishonestly or with cluelessness. He's doing the best he can.

Have you ever had someone ask you how you're feeling and you realize you really don't know? If so, then you have a sense of what it's like to feel disconnected from yourself. If you continued trying to figure it out, you may have found yourself searching for cues such as how your body was feeling (tired, tense, energetic, fidgety) or the thoughts you were thinking at the time (dreamy, focused, nostalgic). If you're usually emotionally in tune, it's likely you'll eventually gain clarity and be able to get at what you're feeling. But does that mean that you'll *never* have a problem recognizing your emotions? Absolutely not! Even the most emotionally connected people occasionally struggle to recognize their feelings. So it's not as if emotional disconnection never happens; the point is to focus on how often it does.

If your guy has difficulty recognizing his emotions on a regular, ongoing basis and doesn't have the tools to tune in to what's going on inside of him, it will have the effect of creating distance in your relationship. How can he connect with anyone if he can't connect with himself? Here are clues your partner might be having a tough time recognizing his own emotions:

- He can't describe how he's feeling, only what he's thinking.
- He may be pleasant but not emotionally expressive. He may smile or laugh easily in some cases, but even if he gets that far, he won't go much further toward expressing more vulnerable emotions. More often than not, he may appear to remain in a neutral mood, telling you about his experience as if he's telling you a story that happened to someone else.
- He has a hard time connecting his physical reaction to any emotional cause. For example, he might complain that he has tight shoulders, a tension headache, or fatigue, but he'll look bewildered when you suggest those symptoms may be related to stress at work.

Your Next Step

Hopefully you were able to identify the reason or reasons for barriers preventing your loved one from being emotionally available, whether they are interpersonal, related to his personal history, or have to do with his inner emotional world. The following exercises will help you move further along.

Mindfulness Training

This exercise will enable you to gain deeper insight into why walls are built and what's hidden beneath disconnection. Sometimes when you're committed to working on emotional unavailability you can be so caught up in how to make changes you get pulled away from seeing the dynamic clearly. This mindfulness technique trains you to wipe away preconceptions and simply be an observer. Here's how to practice:

Step 1. Take a few slow breaths. In and out. In and out.

Step 2. Next, focus on this present moment. Simply notice your breathing. Notice your thoughts drift in and out again. Notice your emotions. Allow them to come in and drift out at their own pace. Gently scan your attention over your body and be aware of any sensations you have. Notice your thoughts, feelings, and physical sensations, but don't try to force your experience. Don't try to forcibly hold on to an experience, but don't push it away either. Your goal is simply to observe, not to judge or label, and not to change. Just be.

Step 3. Now shift your attention. Allow yourself to observe your guy's behavior in the same way—without judgment, without explanations, and without attempting to change anything. Once again, your goal is simply to observe. You may notice strong emotions and thoughts coming up, and that's okay. It's part of the process. Depending on what's happening in your relationship, you may notice that you feel angry, hopeless, sad, hurt, frustrated, or scared that things will never change. You don't have to control your mind. Just be present and notice what's happening without reacting.

Allow yourself to sit for five minutes as you begin this new habit. Start slow. As you continue to progress and you decide you want to add more time, go for it. Mindfulness practices vary, so build up to the time that feels right for you. A recent study showed that people noticed benefits after just two fifteen-minute sessions each day, but more time practicing certainly won't hurt! If you can practice every day, then this is even better. Start with what you know is doable, and you'll find your way from there.

Keep in mind that this exercise may be tougher than it seems. Sometimes certain experiences can come up that we may not want, be it a thought, a feeling, or a physical sensation. If we can remain present and continue observing, such experiences are likely to pass. If they do not and you feel too overwhelmed, you can always stop and bring yourself back to your surroundings. Some people find meditation a little frustrating because their mind seems to flutter around too much, or they find themselves momentarily getting wrapped up in their own tangled thoughts. If you find yourself feeling frustrated with your own brain's stubbornness against slowing down, take heart. That's what healthy brains do: They flitter and create. With practice, meditation will get easier. What's more, there are various forms of meditation. I invite you to try different kinds and use the ones that feel like the best fit for you.

CHAPTER FIVE

Respecting Boundaries, Setting Ground Rules, Creating Goodwill, and Building Trust

❖

I never understood why Clark Kent was so hell-bent on keeping Lois Lane in the dark.

—FROM *THE TIME TRAVELER'S WIFE* BY AUDREY NIFFENEGGER

What if, at the very core of your guy's being, he's unable to trust that you truly love him, will always be there for him, are capable of staying the course, understand him, and are willing to make a devoted effort to work stuff out? Imagine how that would make him feel. Or what if he doesn't trust that he's truly lovable and deserving of love? Remember, even Superman feared Lois Lane would reject him if she discovered his alter ego was mere mortal Clark Kent.

Then again, what if along the way in your relationship you or your man has done some things to erode your commitment? Maybe your connection was driven off the road by betrayal, anger, or neglect. Whatever caused this atmosphere of distrust, your relationship may now be mired in a lot of difficulty.

In this chapter, I'll not only help you navigate through fear, one of the most powerful dynamics behind emotional unavailability, but also help you lead your guy toward the territory of trust. You'll have a much better chance of assuring and guiding him as long as you honor his personal boundaries, while continually offering him the security he needs to express his true self.

The Importance of Trust

Trust is absolutely crucial for an emotionally close relationship and that fact is backed up, not only by my experience as a therapist, but by several studies. From our infancy forward we search for and need relationships in which we feel we will be cared for, are able to express our true selves, and feel safe.

Imagine asking someone to walk across a high wire two hundred feet in the air with no safety net below. It would be pretty scary and very few people would agree to do it. The brave souls who did would most likely still approach the task with tremendous trepidation. Now, let's change the scene and imagine there's a sturdy safety net not far below the wire. It would certainly require less daring and the task could be approached with more sure-footedness.

Similarly, revealing more of yourself and allowing strong feelings to develop and grow toward another person can feel as if you're walking a high wire without a net at times. It entails a certain amount of vulnerability and risk. There's the risk of being abandoned, rejected, or betrayed. Your partner may leave you because he stopped loving you, so there's the possibility of great emotional pain. But if you trust the other person, you believe he's a source of safety and genuine caring, and you trust he'll take care of your heart, you're in essence envisioning a safety net. This makes it less scary to take the risk and be vulnerable, love deeply, and express your authentic emotions despite the possibility of loss. And even though you know loss awaits if he eventually dies before you do, you're willing to take the leap because it feels worth it to keep your heart open and love him immensely.

Sadly, when a person doesn't have trust, it can feel too frightening to move closer. He doesn't have confidence in his own sure-footedness and can't see a safety net below. In reaction, he may push you away, steer clear of sharing his inner thoughts and feelings, and try to minimize your importance in his life.

Let's look at Mark, who suffers with deep trust issues. He's a strikingly handsome sixty-year-old restaurant owner with a shock of wavy gray hair and oceanic blue eyes. Not surprisingly, he's had plenty of women coming on to him, but the mistrust and fear of intimacy he has developed recently are holding him back. The prospect of opening up emotionally just feels too unsafe for Mark, leading him to erect walls. Of the different subtypes, he most closely resembles the Defender. Mark was happily married for three decades to his wife, Carmela, but two years ago she left him for someone else. Ever since, he's felt his own heart die too. "I'll never be close to anyone again. I won't do it," he vowed. That is until Ellen, an attorney, walked into his life. Although they've been regularly dating, Mark is terrified of being hurt again. Ellen, on the other hand, feels deeply in love with Mark and wants to be close to him. She insists, "If I do all the 'right' things and show him unconditional love, Mark's heart will fly open." But for every step Ellen takes toward Mark, he retreats with two steps back.

Mistrust is the culprit. No matter what triggers it, the result is often emotional distance. How can you deal effectively with this problem? A good first step is to try to understand the basics of trust. Trust takes two forms:

Reflective trust: This form operates at the level of conscious awareness and refers to the expectations about how much your guy really believes you're committed to and care about him. He'll make a deliberate choice to be vulnerable and share difficult experiences that may come up in his life because he has faith you won't reject him or respond in a hurtful or dismissive manner. When you say you're working late, he trusts it's true rather than suspecting you're out on a date with someone else.

Impulsive trust: This form is unconscious and that's why it's often more of a challenge. This is the type of trust people feel, or don't feel, instinctively toward another person—especially a romantic partner. It's an immediate, automatic response signaling that their partner is trustworthy or, on the flip side, untrustworthy. By definition he's not likely to be aware of the automatic ways he evaluates you or the relationship, yet it impacts his behavior and his reflective trust in you. Imagine you mistakenly made a comment that hurt his feelings. If he has low impulsive trust in you, not only will he have unfavorable automatic associations toward you, but he'll have a tougher time consciously recalling all of your kind, trustworthy qualities. On the other hand, if he has high impulsive trust, he'll still be able to see your goodness and know you didn't intentionally want to hurt him.

Yes, trust really is the net allowing us to walk the wire of vulnerability, openness, and love. This is especially true of the deep, impulsive trust we feel that acts as an automatic green light in a relationship. Trust allows us to retain faith in our partners and maintain a desire to be close, even in those moments when we might feel challenged.

While trust promotes actions that foster connection and advance intimacy, spurring us on to take risks and be open, distrust shuts us down, closes the gate in our heart, and makes it difficult, if not impossible, to move closer. Since distrust is the enemy of intimacy, it's worth exploring the ways it feeds emotional unavailability.

The Assumption Trap

Before I dig into distrust, I want to take a moment to look at our very human tendency to make assumptions. Assumptions can be trust's public enemy number one. They can damage or even destroy feelings of security and well-being. I'm talking about what goes on in the mind, not what's actually happening in your relationship. There's a saying I love (not mine originally—I wish it were!) that states, "Don't believe everything you *think*." Yet people often do believe what they think. Our minds have a funny way of convincing us that our beliefs about ourselves, or others, as well as about our future and the world around us, are spot-on.

Now, don't get me wrong. I'm a huge fan of the human brain. Arguably, your brain is your best buddy. It helps you make really quick decisions in a pinch, grasp highly complex and subtle problems and situations, communicate, and create new ideas and concepts seemingly out of thin air. But ideas aren't the only things we can create out of thin air. Our minds are also masters at inventing future scenarios. There's a pretty good chance your guy (and probably you as well) is embracing a view of your relationship that may not truly exist and in the process he might be distrusting you and the strength of your connection.

Primo sat down for a session with his therapist, Dr. Hastings, who could tell that he looked distraught and unsettled.

"How are you, Primo? It seems like something's on your mind."

He slightly chuckled and gazed down, holding back tears with considerable effort.

"Yeah, Doc," Primo said. "Something is definitely on my mind, and it's going to sound completely crazy to you."

"Try me."

"All right. I'm so deeply in love with a woman that I can't stand it, and the problem is that she tells me she's really devoted to me too. That's why I need to end it. Crazy, right?"

"Not crazy, no. I am waiting for you to fill in the gap though."

"The gap of what?"

"The gap between you loving her, her loving you, and the decision to end it," Dr. Hastings said. "Something's missing here."

"Oh, well, because it'll never last," he said. "Amabel loves me now because she thinks I'm this easygoing guy who can make her laugh and likes to have fun. But if we stay together, one day she'll see behind all of that. She'll see my angst and my foibles and then any allure I ever held for her will be gone—*bang.*"

Here we witness how Primo, a Fearful Fraud, was silently waiting for "the other shoe to drop," expecting that it's just a matter of time before Amabel loses interest. We don't know why Primo foresees such a grim future. Maybe he feels terrible about himself and doesn't see why anyone would accept him wholly. Or perhaps it reflects gender-role messages about how vulnerable he should be as a man that he received and carries with him. He may be drawing from past hurts, presuming that Amabel will betray him, just like every other woman has done. Someone who makes this assumption and anticipates betrayal is highly resistant to being open and emotionally available and to allowing a partner to truly get to know him. Unfortunately, this is likely to become a self-fulfilling prophecy. If he believes that you'll eventually jilt him, the emotional connection between the two of you is likely to erode, leaving him at greater odds of losing exactly what he's afraid to lose.

It's not just big events like inevitable betrayal that we're good at imagining. Our brains are also adept at fantasizing endless scenarios. Some fantasies depict passion or romance in a relationship, while others? Not so much. We might envision how a difficult conversation is going to play out, or mentally rewind an interaction, berating ourselves for not handling it differently. On the other hand, we might imagine a happy scene such as Sunday breakfast in bed with our loved one, or a good deed that left us feeling like a better person.

Happy, sad, or angry, it really doesn't matter. Our minds enjoy creating new scenes and re-creating past ones. When we repeatedly envision a certain emotional interaction, we'll end up believing it's going to happen in real life. Let's say your guy thinks you're not listening to him, or you're going to leave him; the more he thinks this way, the more he actually believes it's happening and the more likely he'll pull away and stay distant based on his mind games. Depending on your partner's personal history, or his history with you, he may also create scenarios in his mind about how you're likely to react to him in different situations. For example, he may expect if he tells you he feels upset with you about a particular situation, you'll react by getting defensive and verbally attacking him in return. This expectation may be true or not. You might blow your gasket, or you might stay chill.

But here's the snag: It doesn't matter what you actually do. His perception creates his reality. As long as he expects you to get upset when he shares his real feelings, he'll act on this belief and stay mum. And just a gentle reminder: You're not immune to making assumptions that affect your behavior either. Don't worry—everyone does it. If you find yourself starting to act on what's going on in your head and not on the facts, just take a breath and ask yourself: "What assumptions am I making?"

A prediction doesn't have to be real to have a powerful impact on your relationship. It just has to be believed. I've spoken with many people who made predictions about what someone else will say or do in response to a feeling, idea, or experience they merely imagined. These thoughts end up shaping their next move, and not always for the better of the relationship.

Although plenty of us can make hopeful, trusting predictions about what our partner might say, or how he will act, others may find it a struggle to stay in the positive zone. Instead their predictions are laden with distrust and anticipation of hurt, disappointment, lack of understanding, hostility, or abandonment.

As you recall, our expectations and beliefs form our reality and influence how we feel and how we behave. This means if your partner doesn't trust you to be there for him, to be loyal, to accept him, or to be honest, he'll treat you accordingly. He'll hold back and won't reveal significant information, like we might witness in an Iceberg or a Defender. Akin to the Fearful Fraud, he may put up a false front and present what he thinks you want to see. If you're away for any length of time, he may become suspicious. You get the idea. And as you may already know, it's an unpleasant kind of relationship to be in.

This picture is a reality created in the mind, which may have little to no basis in fact. Yet these distrustful beliefs become fact in his mind, influence his choices, and create distance. And here's another snag: It also perpetuates itself and may also infect *your* trust. When someone believes their partner is keeping something from them, they trust their partners less and they conceal pieces of themselves. In return, the partner feels less trust and becomes more secretive too. And the cycle plays over again and again.

Here's what the distrust cycle looks like:

- We don't trust our partner and create stories about why and how our partner can't be trusted.
- We act based on those beliefs and tend to interpret what our partner says and does in ways that are consistent with what we believe.
- Our partner feels distrusted and unable to reach us emotionally, struggles to get to know us better, and is hurt.
- Our partner may persistently encourage us to open up, question why we're so distrusting, become angry and express frustration, withdraw, and emotionally close up in an attempt at self-protection.
- We trust less. We move away more. Emotional distance widens.

But even if this cycle sounds familiar, don't give up hope! At any point, it's also possible to make choices that prevent the cycle from getting worse. We can even reverse it and build trust and closeness. This means even if your guy is distrustful now, you can remain steady and present in the relationship. You can continue to respond in ways that invite openness, trust, and connection without demanding it, withdrawing, or expressing frustrated exasperation.

Your side of the relationship involves the choices you make. You don't possess power over his mind to make him trust you, but you do have more power than you probably realize. What you manifest on your side of the relationship creates conditions from which he'll respond on his side, and this influences the likelihood that he'll behave in ways that promote connection versus distance.

It's like a game of tennis. When you serve a ball to your partner, you can't actually force him to do anything in particular from his side of the court: If you hit the ball to the left side of the court, he could just stand there and not hit it. He could run to the right of the court, or he could leave the match altogether. But none of this is likely to happen. Odds are, if you hit the ball to the left, he'll run there. In other words, you have influence over the environment your partner encounters. You're on the same court and you can increase the chances he'll move toward you rather than away from you by your intentions and actions.

So what can you do to create an atmosphere of safety and pave the way for greater connection? You'll find out as we work on the steps you can take to halt, and ideally reverse, the cycle of distrust. These steps are about acknowledging his distrust, regardless of whether it's warranted, stopping the cycle, and creating an atmosphere of trust in your relationship. Please have patience. Behaviors don't change overnight. It's a gradual process.

Now let's take the first step.

Building Trust

Step 1: Respecting His Boundaries

Boundaries are healthy limits we set between ourselves and other people. They help define who we are and who we are not, what we are comfortable with and what we are not. A healthy relationship is one in which our boundaries are strong, yet flexible enough to allow each partner to feel secure and flourish within their own uniqueness. There's a sense of respect on the part of both partners, allowing each to live as full a life as possible and to explore their own personal potential. Healthy boundaries allow trust and security to develop within your relationship.

Trouble can occur when boundaries either don't exist or are too rigid. If they are too rigid, the relationship can get stifled. With rigid boundaries and a lack of trust, couples are unlikely to be comfortable being honest about sexual desires and sharing personal information, or trusting their partner can have a positive influence that won't erase their own identity. (Case in point: The reason you see golf and tennis mentioned in this book is thanks to my husband, Guille, who lovingly exposed me to these sports.)

Conversely, weak or absent boundaries can feel threatening and/or smothering and can also erode trust. It may include discouraging privacy (insisting on knowing about personal emails, texts, phone calls) or not allowing partners to have their own interests, hobbies, or friends. Balance in boundaries allows couples to grow individually as well as together. Partners feel respected and trusted. In this kind of atmosphere, it's more likely trust and respect will want to be returned and the couple will feel the desire and safety to move even closer. Even if you desperately want to connect with him, to know him more deeply, and to enjoy greater emotional intimacy, it's important to respect his boundaries—and this includes allowing him to open up at his own pace.

Here are important boundaries to respect:

1. Let him make his own decisions. Contrary to what you might expect, supporting your guy's sense of independence (or autonomy) is an excellent way to draw him toward you. Dr. Martin Lynch, psychology researcher at the University of Rochester, conducted a 2013 study on how a sense of personal autonomy impacts our willingness to emotionally rely on those who are close to us. Dr. Lynch describes autonomy as being able to make our own decisions without feeling pressured. He found that the more we support our loved one's ability to make his own choices, respect his right to have his own opinions and feelings, and hold back from trying to direct or control his actions, the more he'll emotionally reach out to us for support. Interestingly, this happens regardless of how secure he feels in the relationship. As paradoxical as it may seem, if you want to set the stage for your partner to turn toward you and emotionally connect, honor who he is as an individual. Even if he doesn't have trust in you or the relationship right now, if you respect his decisions and allow him to have his own opinions, he'll be more likely to reach out to you. This doesn't mean you can't disagree and debate, but when you're presenting your side, be sure you're not putting down his values, ideals, and beliefs. This also means letting him have his own style of living his life, including the personal goals he strives for and how he handles his daily tasks or challenges. Of course, there are exceptions. You don't want to support your partner if he's doing something that's dangerous to himself or others (e.g., drinking and driving) or that's abusive or profoundly dishonest or disrespectful toward you (e.g., emotional abuse or infidelity). These exceptions are essential for healthy boundaries. You can respect someone's right to go swimming in cold water if they want to do it, but if they're about to dive into the sea despite a warning by the Coast Guard of dangerous riptides, it's not disrespectful to try to stop them. It's called looking out for someone. Similarly, if someone tries to pull you into the wild water, it's not disrespectful to object and refuse to be swept up in the tide. It's about looking out for yourself. If he's engaging in behavior that's harmful to him or you, it's healthy to refuse to reinforce that.

2. Release your perfectionism. How often have I heard people criticize their partner's ability to do something "the right way"— whether it's managing finances, taking care of household chores, child rearing, or driving? Of course, countless times. But if you find yourself doing this too, try to let go of your perfectionism by realizing there are multiple "right" ways to do most things. Show respect for his approach and you'll help him gain the confidence to be emotionally honest with you.

3. Give him space and privacy. From sneaking peeks at emails or text messages, signing on to a partner's Facebook page without permission, or going through personal belongings, a good deal of couples are invading one another's privacy, and they're finding plenty of ways to do it. Why does this happen? Results from the same study show that mistrust and an inability to exercise self-control are the biggest triggers. To add another layer, one study found that people are more likely to snoop on their mates if they perceive them as tight-lipped and withholding. And that intrusiveness actually hurts intimacy. Not surprisingly, if you honor his privacy and refrain from digging around in his business, he'll be more likely to feel you're respecting him.

Now you understand that respecting his boundaries is essential to creating emotional safety and building trust. It takes the air out of the cycle of emotional withdrawal and increases the likelihood he'll move closer.

In the next step, you'll learn how to build on respecting

boundaries along with practical tips on how to continue improving your relationship's environment. As I've said before, but it's worth mentioning again, you can't change your partner. But you can increase the chances he'll feel safe enough to make different choices. With that understanding in mind, let's move on to Step 2 of building trust.

Step 2: Setting Behavior Ground Rules for Disagreements

The focus in your relationship needs to be about what's under your control. You have the power to make choices that increase trust and connection, or choices that tear them down. When communicating with your guy, in any given moment, you have a choice about how you're going to respond. This may be tough to imagine when you're involved in a heated argument, but remember—the ball is in your court.

Disagreements are a normal part of all relationships, and in some cases, arguing can actually help couples learn about each other, resolve differences, and break down barriers. But there's a difference between healthy disagreements and destructive, distancing ones. Lots of couples get caught in a cycle in which they look for who is wrong or who is to blame. This dynamic can be corrosive to trust and security, and it definitely won't help you lay the foundation for the kind of emotionally snug, joined environment you want in your relationship.

If you want your partner to be able to stay open and to hear what you're feeling rather than both of you resorting to a litany of perceived failures or faults when you're having one of those inevitable arguments and emotions intensify, try approaching him in the following ways:

1. Tread softly. Forget the hard sell. Use what are called "softening" approaches to keep the disagreement from spiraling out of control. Examples of softening approaches include:

- Communicating upbeat views of your partner. For example, if your partner makes a particularly perceptive remark that illuminates a part of your disagreement that you had previously not seen, say something like: "You're so insightful and smart. I've always admired that about you."

- Expressing points using a humorous or playful approach. If you are butting heads over something that really doesn't matter—like who should take out the trash—and either or both of you are beginning to realize that the argument is not worth your time or energy, instead of letting the fight wander from the original issue or allowing yourselves to stew in combativeness, you might say: "How about we settle this in the bedroom with awesome makeup sex?"

- Conveying appreciation for his values. If you are fighting about wanting him to spend more time at home, say something like: "I really understand how important staying physically fit is to you and why the gym is a nonnegotiable in your life." Then you are letting him know you are hearing him and you are not trying to force him to give up something that he feels is important.

- Minimizing levels of concern about the problem. Defuse a silly argument as soon as you realize how solvable it is and say: "It's a minor blip. No biggie at all. I'm sure we'll be able to come up with a solution."

- Validating his points. When you realize you are wrong, say something like: "You know, you're absolutely right. I didn't handle it well when you said you wanted to go away on a camping trip with your buddies. I get it now and I'm really sorry." It's not worth getting overly defensive, or going on the attack and opening up old wounds when you realize that you overreacted. This is also one of the most potent ways you can show your partner that you are emotionally safe. Think about it. If he knows that you are invested in hearing him and being fair to him rather than in being right, you are showing him that you're on his team and that he can let down his guard more when you have friction or differences. After all, he won't have to brace himself for a battle in which you are determined to win.

- Recognizing his effort, progress, or growth. Say something like: "Thanks so much for texting me when you realized you were going to have to stay late at work. I know how busy it gets there and it was sweet of you to think of me," when he does what you ask and shows he respects your point of view.

When you use these softer approaches, the research shows you can reduce defensiveness, withdrawal, and anger during conflicts; as a result, you'll enhance the likelihood of intimacy. What's especially notable about this research is softening approaches were successful with partners who had an avoidant attachment style. Remember, these are the guys who are usually the most challenging to reach. Of the emotionally unavailable subtypes, Icebergs are most likely to have an avoidant attachment style.

2. Don't guess what he's feeling. You may have a habit, like a lot of us do, of thinking you know what your guy is feeling. Guess what. There's a good chance you're off the mark. You may be overlooking his fears and insecurities. Women tend to be significantly less accurate in gauging how anxious their mates are feeling about attachment. In other words, they're more likely to miss seeing their partners' fears and insecurities. And the realization that your partner may be vulnerable can help you approach him with gentleness and care. Isn't it a lot easier to reach out to someone you believe may be hurt or frightened rather than someone you think is dismissively trying to push you away?

3. Avoid anticipating a response. You may also find you have predictions about what your guy is going to say. This may come from past experience. I know this is tough to do, but as much as you can, try to resist investing a lot of confidence in how you imagine he's likely to respond, particularly if you're thinking he'll only react in the same old way.

4. Ban blame. While we're talking about negative communication, expressing blame to a partner is a common tactic among couples. However, blame doesn't help anyone. For example, one study found that blame toward one's partner for financial problems is associated with lower relationship quality for both the person doing the blaming and the person being blamed. But even if you aren't pointing your finger at your partner for financial problems, a good approach is to guard against blame across the board. But what if the problem really is your partner's fault? Blaming him isn't likely to accomplish anything except causing you both to feel bad, undermining good feelings, and increasing emotional distance. Instead, see if you can set aside blame and come together as a team to work on the problem. Not only will this approach create an emotional bond and build trust and goodwill between you, but you're being a good role model. Down the road when something is *your* fault, he'll be more likely to show you similar magnanimity.

5. Share agendas. When there's a joint decision to make, respect his perspective. Try to reach a decision that feels agreeable to both of you rather than trying to enforce your agenda on him. Couples who face greater conflict over their individual goals are more likely to have poorer, more distant relationships.

Thankfully, there's a safety switch when it comes to conflict and power struggles. Both people have to participate in the "battle" in order for it to happen. So if you don't engage, it can't get off the ground. To prevent yourself from getting fired up, remind yourself that you're on a team—and there's no need for a captain. Focus on ways to make decisions, especially the big ones, together. As a couple you can make team decisions on just about anything. A good place for teamwork is in areas you both care about: how you'll support each other's personal aims and goals, making decisions about your shared social calendar, where you choose to spend holidays or vacations, hobbies you'd like to pursue together, how you want to decorate your home, or how you want to spend your money.

A note about money: When it comes to frivolous spending, plenty of us don't want to tell our partner when we've made an irresponsible purchase out of embarrassment or because we suspect it might start an argument due to a clash of values. If this is true in your relationship, I encourage you to muster courage. See if you can change this pattern and have an honest discussion with your mate about spending and work together to develop a strategy that includes a shared vision. Admittedly, money can be a hot-button issue. Discussing it honestly can help it stay chill.

So far we've learned when boundaries are respected and communication guidelines are followed, even during times of high tension, trust can bloom. The point is to try to consistently send the powerful message that you respect your guy's individuality, care for his well-being, and honor his needs, preferences, and values. When you do this, you convey that you're motivated to walk beside him as a friend. His wants and needs do not need to overshadow your own as a hard-and-fast rule, nor should they. It's crucial to take proper care of yourself to be your best self in the relationship. That said, at times you may choose to give his needs or wishes priority over your own. There is nothing wrong with that. Actually, it's quite loving and beautiful to do this when you feel moved. However, what is an immovable rule is that his wants and needs do need to be given consideration and respect. You're not going to pull him along and coerce him into doing what you want. This message is about safety, loving-kindness, mutual respect, and friendship.

In the next step, you'll explore ways to build on this message and enhance crucial trust by bumping up feelings of goodwill. Relationships are like banks. When there is a high reserve of warmth and friendship saved, it can better withstand a hit, whether it be a hurtful argument or a thoughtless or harsh comment. Or to put it another way, it's easier to be charitable and offer the benefit of the doubt when we're wounded if there's an extended history of love and devotion. So how do we build goodwill?

Step 3: Fostering Goodwill

There are countless ways to bump up goodwill and we'll cover the ones I think are most effective. You'll see that all of them embrace the elements of friendship. It makes sense, right? Goodwill and true friendship nurture trust in a relationship, which in turn cultivates more friendship and goodwill, each positive quality bolstering the others. That said, the door swings both ways. If you don't trust your guy, he'll be much less likely to trust you and the goodwill and friendship you have between you will erode as well. So, as much as you can, try to hold on to trust in this process, in your relationship, and in your partner. This crucial factor involves a degree of vulnerability as you share personal details of *your* life and *your* feelings with your partner. But I need to stress again how important it is to adhere to the boundaries and ground rules discussed earlier. Without them a relationship will struggle with unnecessary stress, anxiety, and reduced intimacy. That said, goodwill is part of the foundation of trust and any solid relationship, and the following techniques will help you gain it:

1. Allow yourself a minute. One thing we tend to forget is that it is perfectly acceptable to take our time when we're communicating. We can pause and take our time as we collect our thoughts. Prior to a conversation, we can also think about how we would like to approach it and what we want to say. Simply giving yourself a little more time to think about your approach can help you communicate in a more positive and effective way. Rehearse what you are going to say ahead of time, or during a conversation, you can say, "Hold on a second. I just need a minute to think things through." Speak slowly or pause before you utter the next phrase, taking time to ask yourself questions such as "Do I really want to say what I'm about to say? What will the impact be? Can I say it differently to achieve a more productive, connected outcome?" You can always change words in your head, but once they leave your mouth, you can't take them back.

If tensions are escalating, you can also take a step back by just honestly saying that you need to take a break from the conversation and asking if you can reconvene later.

2. Have fun. Studies have shown a boost in trust when couples had fun together. A genuinely positive environment not only feels happier but also feels safer. Who wants to take a chance when you're not enjoying yourselves? So give yourselves permission to have a good time together. Go to upbeat movies, walk in nature, take a drive to your favorite park, or just stay home and have a romantic dinner for two, or try cooking together. Whatever you choose to do, the aim is to keep it stress-free and fun.

3. Offer assurances. Another approach associated with more secure attachment, goodwill, and trust is assuring your mate that you're there for him, you value the relationship, and you want to be together. These kinds of assurances let your partner know your relationship has a solid foundation to stand on. This knowledge is likely to enhance a sense of safety by reducing fear. When one partner uses assurances, the other comes closer. What does this look like? The exquisite part about offering reassurance is that there are untold ways to do it. You could say: "I'm so sorry that it's all been so hurtful for you. I understand that you don't want to talk about it right now—just know that I'm always here for you anytime you want to talk, okay?" "You are simply amazing." "If I could go back in time, I'd marry you all over again."

4. Share tasks. Why have him take care of particular chores all on his own? Sharing responsibilities can provide a layer of comfort and intimacy. Offer to dry the dishes when it's his turn to wash, or replace the trash bag in the bin while he is bringing the full bag out to the curb. It's a way of showing your mate that you want to cooperate and help in concrete ways. He'll gain a feeling of reassurance when he realizes he needn't shoulder responsibilities all alone.

5. Pay attention to timing. If you're a woman reading this, you need to pay particular attention to your menstrual cycle. Okay, I'm aware that this sentence might not be popular, but hear me out. I'm most definitely not a fan of the stereotype that women are overly emotional creatures who lose it and can't think rationally during their period. That's ridiculous. But it is true that many women notice an increase in negative emotions at certain points in their cycle, and this isn't at all abnormal. It also doesn't mean you're at the mercy of these emotions, especially if you're aware of them. One study found that when women were in the late follicular phase of their cycle (i.e., shortly before ovulation), the volume of neurons in the amygdala (a part of the brain associated with processing emotions, including negative feelings) increased. This change was linked to feelings of being stressed and negative emotions. What can we take away from these results? Well, definitely not that you need to lock yourself away like Rapunzel. The study merely suggests there may be times of the month when your brain is going through changes linked with feeling more stressed. During this time, the process of laying the groundwork for connection and building goodwill may feel more challenging; it's important to consider the possibility.

6. Be mindful. This approach, which you hopefully practiced in the exercise on pages 150–51, has been associated with less storminess and emotionally charged reactions. Mindfulness, as you may remember, is the practice of noticing and paying attention to what is happening in the present moment without judging it. The present moment includes your environment as well as your thoughts, feelings, emotions, and physical sensations (e.g., muscle tension in a certain part of your body). There are fewer ups and downs in our emotions when we practice mindfulness. It keeps us steady and more aware of what's *really* going on. For example, let's say that your partner comes home in a bad mood and doesn't say hello to you. He goes directly to the bedroom to change. You feel hurt. If you're not in a state of mindfulness, you might not even notice your reaction. Or you might get sucked up into blaming thoughts ("I can't believe he didn't even say *hi*. How dare he treat me this way!"), or you might be controlled by the hurt by acting out (coldly withdrawing or wielding sarcastic, biting comments). On the other hand, if you're mindful, you're more likely to be aware of how you feel and to take responsibility for your own reactions. Ultimately, you'll be less controlled by your reactions, probably less likely to blame, and more able to see there's a better way to think and respond. This is an important skill to develop, especially as you strive to increase good feelings in your relationship and meet the challenge of reaching out for connection and building trust.

7. Celebrate good news. Speaking of reactions, you might be thinking a great way to create goodwill and set the stage for trust is to be available to your partner when he's upset or when a stressful and difficult event has occurred in his life. I can definitely see why you would think this. It just makes sense on the face of it, right? Of course we're going to value those who are there for us even when life hands us lemons. And we're going to reach out and trust them too, right? Well, there's actually more to the story. When people get support for positive events from someone, they are actually more likely to believe that this person will be there for them at a time of stress than when this same person gives them support during negative events. So as you strive to offer a well of comfort to your partner when hardship looms, take every opportunity to celebrate his accomplishments and good news too!

Now that you've covered the steps in building trust and goodwill, it's time to do some self-exploration exercises. When we're more self-aware, we're better able to recognize and manage our impulses and motives. Ultimately, this leads us to greater freedom by giving us more control over how we react.

Facing Your Own Fear

It's important to understand your partner's fear of being in a close relationship. One way of doing this is to try facing a fear of your own. Create a list of five things you feel afraid to try and select one or more of these to conquer. Importantly, the fears you select must be related to objects, places, situations, or experiences that leave you feeling frightened or extremely anxious, but are actually *safe*.

To get the most out of this exercise, make them all similarly anxiety-provoking. Examples include public speaking, skydiving, bungee jumping, joining a new social group, and introducing yourself to new people.

When you're finished, allow yourself at least ten minutes to reflect on the items on this list. How does each one make you feel? See if you can connect these feelings to how your partner might experience taking a chance and moving closer to you. And the next time when he seems to be evading emotional intimacy, try recalling the feelings you imagined during this exercise. Hopefully, this will help you empathize with him during frustrating or discouraging moments.

Crossing the Line

We often assume people will think and respond to situations the same way we do, and our loved one is no exception. These situations can be big (e.g., reacting to the death of a friend or relative) or small (e.g., choosing what to eat for breakfast). When our assumptions are proven wrong, it's not uncommon to offer our own two cents' worth with utterances such as "How can you like *that*?" or "It wasn't polite of you to say that! I would have kept my mouth shut!"

In this exercise, you're going to note at least ten times when you find yourself, even for a moment, judging by your own standards and expecting your partner to feel or act like you do. When this happens, write down:

1. The situation
2. How you expected your partner to think or act like you
3. A new, more accepting statement in which you imagine why your loved one said what he did or behaved in a particular way from his perspective—not yours.

An example of an entry might look like this:

THE SITUATION: *My husband came home from work and looked upset. When I asked him what was bothering him, he said, "I don't want to talk about it."*

HOW I EXPECTED MY PARTNER TO THINK OR ACT LIKE ME: *I expected him to come home and immediately share what was bothering him. I expected him to need me to listen and help comfort him.*

A NEW, MORE ACCEPTING STATEMENT: *He might have felt overwhelmed and just needed some time alone to think about what happened before talking to me about it. Or he might have been trying to protect me if he thought it would worry me.*

My advice at this point is to practice the steps involved in respecting boundaries, setting ground rules, and building goodwill. These steps will help increase trust in your relationship. Over the next four weeks, track your efforts and progress by writing in a journal or on an electronic device. Review this chapter from time to time to remind yourself of what you've learned and for help with approaches you might not have tried yet. If you need more time, take it. Hopefully, during this time you'll experience an increased closeness or relaxation in your relationship. Perhaps there's less stress or more cuddling. Are you experiencing more intimate conversations? Pay attention to changes and embrace gratitude along the way.

Once you feel comfortable and you experience your relationship moving closer, by all means turn the page and let's break those barriers to intimacy.

CHAPTER SIX

Breaking Barriers

❖

Love recognizes no barriers. It jumps hurdles, leaps
fences, penetrates walls to arrive at its destination full
of hope.

—MAYA ANGELOU

Arnaud and Svetlana have been in a cool and distant marriage
for three years. Frustrated and dissatisfied with her life, Svetlana
began therapy and, with the help of her counselor, began to
explore her relationship. She realized the emotional and physical
distance from Arnaud, an Iceberg, was playing a major role in
her overall discontent and that it was time to mend the rift. For
a very long time, her husband was a bit on edge and seemed
nonplussed by her warm advances. "What's going on? You know
I'm not touchy-feely! Is it that preposterous therapy you're
doing?" was his reaction. In the past, Svetlana would have merely
shrugged her shoulders and walked away; no longer. "I realize
I'm missing out on being close to the man I love," she whispered
to him tenderly. Despite Arnaud's tendency to snub her time
after time, Svetlana held herself steady. She didn't push him, but
she didn't retreat to her corner, erecting her own walls either.

Now, Svetlana's warm approach is beginning to melt Arnaud's heart.

After doing the work in the previous chapters, you've hopefully gained an understanding of your partner's distancing behaviors as well as your own. You've set healthy boundaries, and perhaps, like Svetlana, you're now willing to try to break the barriers and move toward greater trust and connection.

But I want to keep it real. Removing emotional barriers isn't a simple, straightforward task. It's not like breaking a brick wall. Once a brick wall is down, it's down. When it comes to relationships, barriers can be broken but then pieces of them may be put back up. If that happens, and it certainly can, you'll need to chip away again . . . and again. Change is rarely a straight line. Often we take a step forward and two backward. Or our progress slows and then leaps ahead. We might be diverted or distracted and then a time arrives when we have super focus. Take a common example of opting for a healthier lifestyle. You might vow to eat a healthier diet or exercise more regularly, and then you hit a snag. Maybe you forgot what a difference a change in diet and exercise can make in your life. Maybe you lost focus on why you wanted to make changes in the first place. Perhaps other obstacles arose such as longer work hours, fatigue, or the irresistible call of sugar or fast food. Happily, it doesn't have to stay this way. You can get back on track and your progress will continue. Ideally, you might have learned what snagged you so you can avoid temptation the next time it rears its head.

The same principle applies to your relationship. There are lots of reasons why progress may falter. As your mate is gradually lowering his defenses, a strong wave of vulnerability and fear might hit him for any number of reasons (e.g., he hears about a friend who was hurt by his partner) and he might decide it's not worth allowing himself to open. Or *you* could find yourself feeling more comfortable with the relationship the way it is now and lose sight of the changes that helped you get there. Exhaustion; strong emotions that make it harder to interact; external stresses such as financial, family, or work problems; or a major loss can cause either or both of you to lose motivation. Please don't panic or get complacent. Re-center yourself and focus on what really matters to you so that you can continue forward.

Also keep in mind that it's not uncommon to feel anxiety while you're baring your soul and letting someone back into your heart. This dynamic can be true for you *and* your partner. When we try something uncomfortable, we may hesitate or waver; we can jump back momentarily or run the other way for a while. Please, if this happens to you or your guy, be easy on yourselves and try not to get discouraged. Think about it this way: Have you ever seen a child attempt to take an escalator for the first time, or the second or third time? In many cases, they approach and then hesitate, slowly reaching a foot out before cautiously pulling it back, then waiting for another fresh stair to emerge and then, at the right moment, reach out again. Eventually the child masters the task, but it can take a few tries. You may want to keep this image of courage and forbearance in your mind whenever you hesitate.

Unfortunately, I can't guarantee that you, or your guy, will definitely be able to ride a stairway to heavenly love, but I'm willing to bet it will take at least a few tries, even missteps, before you get near the top.

A long time ago, my lovely godmother, Helga, wisely told me, "Every day is just another chance to try again." Her words stuck with me, and they apply here too. If you don't get it the first time, hit the reset button and take the opportunity to try again.

• • •

So now it's time for you and your mate to make the next move toward emotional availability. I'll offer tips and exercises based on my clinical experience to help your loved one open up and express his authentic feelings. And I'll include exercises to enable *you* to receive and embrace your new intimacy.

Let's get started.

Communication

Communication isn't simply a matter of how we speak with one another. And often, what we don't say speaks even louder than our words. Nonverbal messages play a huge part in a couple's communication. A person's smile, for example, can convey many different emotions. A smile with the eyes crinkled? Genuine positive feeling. A smile with no eye crinkling? A more neutral place or negative feeling. And couples who are experiencing stressful feelings look at each other more, but this is especially true of women who were probably trying to get their husbands to change.

What else is nonverbal communication? It's basically *any* way you communicate that doesn't involve actual words. These examples all count:

- Your facial expressions (e.g., smiling, scowling, frowning, playful)
- Where you direct your gaze and for how long as well as how you move your head (e.g., nodding versus shaking your head, looking directly at someone versus looking the other way)

- How you position your body (e.g., having an open and forward posture with your arms leaving your core exposed versus leaning back with your arms folded across your chest)
- Your paralanguage (e.g., utterances such as "uh-hum," "mmm-mmm," "hmph!," and "ooh!"). These expressions reveal what you're thinking and feeling without having to explicitly say it. Other examples include how loudly or softly we speak, our tone (e.g., loving, soothing, agitated, sarcastic), and our pitch (e.g., changing from low to high pitch can be used to ask a question, express enthusiasm or surprise, or convey disappointment or anger).

Research shows humans are adept at reading nonverbal communication and we do it at breakneck speed. Our brain's premotor cortex can put together different pieces of nonverbal communication to read the underlying intentions and emotions of others in just 200 milliseconds. That's 100 to 200 milliseconds faster than our eyes can blink! Incredibly, other parts of our brain's amygdala can read the emotion behind nonverbal cues even faster, at a speedy 170 milliseconds. And while we're congratulating our brains for a super job, add this to the accolades: The human brain is even faster at recognizing that someone else is feeling an emotion just from their facial expressions, albeit without being able to classify the exact emotion. How quickly? Well, studies show it takes just 10 milliseconds. That's five times faster than it takes a Lamborghini to change gears.

But here's the hitch: Nonverbal expression is only one of several clues to what's going on. You also need to pay attention to the situation and decide whether you believe the expression matches it. These two pieces have to fit together. Let's say someone is smiling while they're cuddling a puppy. This registers as authentic. But what if someone is smiling while being robbed? We can make sense of the first situation, but not so much the second. What relevance would this have to your relationship? Perhaps you've been in situations when it seemed like a happy time and everything was going well, only to see your mate's face not quite as positive, or maybe there was a moment of calm and yet you sensed a look of tension. Or perhaps there was a heated argument and you sensed your partner was enjoying it.

These are moments of mismatch, and if you can catch them, they can help you become more attuned to your partner on a deeper level and break down obstacles of misunderstanding and disconnect. His nonverbal communication (facial expressions, body position, etc.) gives you important information into what he's feeling in a situation. When something doesn't sit right, most of us show it. Let's say you're together in a movie theater on a beautiful day. You notice he's fidgeting a lot. Even if the movie is a great one, he might be itching to get out of there and into the sunny afternoon. Or the movie's theme may be making him uncomfortable. Or the mismatch could be a sign that his mind is somewhere else and what you're seeing is not a response to what's happening in the moment.

Regardless, if you pay attention to his nonverbal signals and the extent to which they mismatch or fit (pay attention to matches, too!), this will give you a greater understanding of what he enjoys (romantic nights at home with you) and dislikes (noisy restaurants) and who he is as an individual. You can use this awareness to enhance your sensitivity to his needs and be a better friend and partner. This builds goodwill and connection.

Nonverbal behavior also impacts the depth of communication. Researchers have discovered nonverbal behavior helps the listener connect more intensely to the speaker's message. But when listeners stop themselves from showing any emotion, it interferes with their ability to empathize with the speaker.

When your guy is trying to tell you something, keep this in mind: It doesn't help to offer him a stony expression. Allow yourself to react honestly and from your heart.

A reaction from your heart isn't the same as one that's shot from the hip. The latter can be a terribly bad move. So I'm suggesting you pause, center yourself, and give yourself a moment to consider what you really want your message to be. Often the message will be more loving and vulnerable than the impulsive one.

For instance, in anger your partner blurts out: "You don't care about me at all!"

Hearing this, you can have any number of reactions, but let's say in this case your first one is: "What?! I bend over backwards to make you feel loved. I bought this freakin' book about emotional unavailability—and you don't see any of it! You ungrateful jerk!" Pair this reaction with a sarcastic laugh and a nasty stare and there it is: You've laid down the gauntlet—and it's not a pretty one.

Clearly, you don't want to go that route. It's not only destructive, but you probably don't mean it anyway. Perhaps your more honest reaction is vulnerable and tender, like a look of quiet sadness or disappointment or a sigh of caring desperation. Maybe at your core there's something like this: "It's heartbreaking for me to hear you don't feel cared about. I've been trying so hard to show you I care. I feel (lost, frightened, sad) now." This is an example of what it means to respond with heart. It allows you to be more authentic while minimizing hostility and building warmth, openness, and connection.

Another surprising aspect of nonverbal communication is how closely our expressions match our partner's when we're face-to-face. We often tailor our emotional expressions to those of other people, and we do this to greater or lesser degrees. How much we decide to amp up or dial down our emotional mimicry depends on the context of the situation and what we want, either consciously or unconsciously, from our interaction. We tend to mimic other people as a way of getting closer to them and, conversely, when we want to create distance, we mimic less.

Does this mean you should become Marcel Marceau, mirroring every expression he makes? No, definitely not, unless you want to drive your partner insane. But it does mean that if your partner is excited about something and smiles, it's helpful to join him in the excitement. If he's concerned about a problem or is annoyed by something that happened, express concern or reflect annoyance too. It's a way of showing him you're in this life together.

Tales We Tell Ourselves

In earlier chapters, I discussed the dynamic of creating stories about ourselves, others, and our relationships, but it's worth a bit more discussion because it's particularly relevant when it comes to breaking down barriers. That's because the stories we tell ourselves about our partners and why they do what they do (or don't do) can contribute to whether the bricks get knocked down or cemented securely back into place.

Women who tend to create an unfavorable explanation or story for their guy's actions (e.g., he's selfish or doesn't care) are more likely to be unhappy with their relationship and less apt to communicate in a positive and effective manner.

Try to be aware of whether you're creating negative stories to explain your guy's behavior. Switch it around and try giving him the benefit of the doubt. It will really improve your relationship!

Another story that we tell ourselves revolves around our notion of the "ideal" partner. This story may be hiding in your subconscious—you may not even realize it's there. If you doubt you have one, just ask yourself this question: "How would my perfect man look and behave?" If you're like most people, your mind will start to paint a picture of Mr. Perfect. You might also be able to imagine Mr. Wrong.

On one level, it's healthy to know what you want in a partner. We should know what type of mate will fit in our life and meet our needs. And we should be discriminating and have certain standards. But if those standards are unrealistic and if your current partner doesn't meet those standards, it could spell trouble for your relationship.

A recent study has demonstrated that people are actually pretty accurate at detecting from their partners whether they come close to meeting their ideals or not. In this study, the ideals were about warmth and trustworthiness, attractiveness and vitality, and how much status and how many resources the person had. The study also revealed that when people get the message that there's a sizable discrepancy between them and their partner's ideal, it has an adverse effect. They report feeling overall less satisfaction with their relationship.

In other words, we tend to feel happier in situations when we believe we're doing a good job. Intuitively, that just makes sense.

So your partner is likely to feel more satisfied with and connected to you if he receives the message "You're getting it right." You needn't say it literally for him to get the message. When you point out ways you appreciate him, share more happy moments, and express gratitude for what he does for you, these are subtle ways to get the same point across. Of course, if you want to be absolutely direct and it's true, you can certainly tell him how happy he makes you. It's as simple as that.

Comparisons

It's also common for us to think if we point out what our partner isn't doing, and compare him to how he used to be, or to how someone else's partner is, or to some other comparison point, it will help motivate him to change. Regardless of whether or not this approach works (and my guess is it probably won't), it's giving your man the message he doesn't measure up, and not surprisingly, this conclusion creates distance.

It's also important to be mindful of the kinds of expectations you're setting for him. If they're unreasonable, you'll be placing the bar out of reach, which will leave both of you feeling dissatisfied and likely resentful and less trusting.

Relax your standards. Be sure that your expectations are reasonable. Is it humanly achievable for him to give you a foot massage every Saturday morning? Yes. But is it reasonable? Not even close. If your expectations are unreasonable, take them down a few notches. If he's aware of your extremely high standards, and it's been an issue in your relationship, I'm willing to bet you'll get relationship bonus points (remember the bank in the previous chapter?) and a lot of credibility if you apologize and admit that you were wrong to hold him to such over-the-top standards.

But what if your expectations are reasonable? And what if he isn't living up to them? In this case, you might want to step back and consider whether these particular unmet expectations are on your must-have list of partner attributes or if they fall on your would-like-to-have list. If they're on the former list, you can't compromise those standards. Perhaps he's willing to change and meet your expectations. But what if he's not? Then it might be time to reevaluate the relationship and decide whether he's the right match for you. I'm definitely not suggesting you slacken important standards, such as expecting your guy to be faithful to you, but I might advise you to relax certain other standards, such as listening to every word you say, always wanting to cuddle whenever you do, or earning a six-figure salary.

What if you have an entirely reasonable expectation (e.g., that he stop buying so much food because it ends up going to waste and being thrown out) that likely falls onto the would-like-to-have list? Now you have a different kind of choice to make. You can:

1. Make a request for change, explain why, and offer a solution that works for both of you, or

2. Accept this shortcoming as part of an overall package of qualities you appreciate about him.

It also helps to focus on what he does right. Remember, we see more of what we're looking for, so look for all the good he does. Like what? Smiling at you when you walk through the door, giving you a hug, taking the trash out, sexually satisfying you, and giving you a compliment are all examples.

Speaking of where we place our focus, emerging research shows the memories we hold of our intimate relationship in the past predict our relationship in the future. There is a link between good memories of your partner meeting your needs in the past and how satisfied you both are in the present. For example, let's say that Hester started reminiscing about times when Serge listened to her when she really needed to talk, offered soothing words of comfort, passionately attended to her sexual needs, went out of his way to help when she faced a predicament, and set about errands that she loathed. Not only will she feel more fulfilled in the relationship, but Serge will too—Hester's happiness will rub off on him.

So just as you pay more attention to what your partner does right in the present, it's also worth taking a stroll down memory lane and reflecting on all the times he's been good to you and he's met your needs in the past.

A Word About Projection

Although as a human race we're generally impressively accurate in our capacity to read one another, we can also make mistakes. Sometimes we project onto others emotions that aren't there and these mistakes can bias our understanding of a situation. An illuminating example of projection happened to me while I was teaching a class. Let me begin by saying that I genuinely love teaching. It's one of the things I do that brings me tremendous pleasure and being kind to my students and forming caring, authentic relationships with them just comes naturally. People who know me best can see this. My husband once observed a talk I was giving on relationships at Harvard University, and afterward he remarked about how clearly I loved teaching.

So I was quite surprised when I read a student's evaluation of my class. This student made it very clear she didn't like me at all. Her comment was that I was obviously being "fake" because I was always smiling and nice. "No one is *that* nice," she wrote. Initially, I remember feeling perplexed because I was only being myself. But then I realized her comment wasn't really about me.

She was projecting her own skeptical view about kindness onto me. Ultimately, I was saddened for this student. And I was also a bit wiser in the ways that we can sometimes be off the mark when it comes to reading others.

Perhaps your partner is projecting his feelings onto you and, in the process, distorting what he sees. If he's afraid he's going to lose you, your assurances of love may be seen as pity, or your wish to have a girls' night out as a clear sign to him that you're not interested and you're on your way out of the relationship. His anger, fear, or resentment gets placed onto you and seen as irritation, insensitivity, or ingratitude. It's a pretty common dynamic and we all have to watch out for it.

Projection can also come in a different guise based on our experiences in past relationships. Perhaps you were in a bad relationship and your last boyfriend was fickle, hurtful, inconsistent, and on an apparent campaign to change you. Even though you know your current boyfriend is definitely not your ex, you may nonetheless project those same attributes onto him. You may have grown accustomed (perhaps understandably) to looking for signs of anger, boredom, fear, or other pessimistic reactions like those you often recognized in a previous partner. Instead, try turning what you're looking for on its head and seek out signs of interest, happiness, love, and playfulness. You'll see more of it when you look for it.

In a different vein, you may find your partner often misinterprets what you're really feeling (kind of like what happened with my student). If you haven't given him any feedback about what's really going on with you and instead you remain silent, now might be a good time to let him into your inner world too. For example, let's say you accompany him to a party and he says something like "I know you really don't want to be here." If that doesn't match how you're feeling, tell him in a kind and upbeat way: "Actually, I'm really looking forward to spending time with you and our friends tonight. I'm sorry if I'm giving the impression I don't want to be here. That wasn't my intention."

If he says he thinks you're feeling one way and you're not, give him a window into what's really happening for you.

If he doesn't ask about your feelings, there's still a way to do this with ease. Let's go back to the party. You might notice him looking at you in a concerned way or joking to a friend that he had to drag you here, so say to him casually, "I'm so glad we came tonight! I'm having a blast hanging with you and our friends."

Brain Games

Have you ever felt anxious and then, as if on cue, threats pop up and take over your attention? A late-night solo stroll to your car, for example, turns into a parade of shadows in your peripheral vision. Your body tenses as you scan for looming danger. Or perhaps you're unsure if a new group of people likes you, and you start noticing the social missteps you make—or at least you interpret them as missteps. Or, on a more intimate level, reflect on a time when you felt uncertain about how your mate felt about you. Did the "signs" of disconnect suddenly get bigger while the ways he showed you how much he loved you seemed smaller?

Anxiety isn't necessarily a bad thing. In fact, it has a very useful purpose; it helps us become more attuned to threats and marshal an appropriate and adaptive response when necessary. In one study, researchers assigned some subjects to be faced with a threatening, anxious situation (in this case, a foot shock that came at random times) and others to have the ease of no threat (meaning no shock) while looking at pictures of faces and deciding whether the person in the picture is feeling happy or frightened. They found that the brains of folks threatened with shock showed a stronger neural connection between the brain's prefrontal cortex and its amygdala, which was linked to being able to more quickly read fear and anxiety in a person's face.

But what if the switch for anxiety is chronically flipped? This most likely applies to the Fearful Fraud, the Sponge, the Defender, and the Iceberg. Then we're likely to notice threats even when the threat is only in our imagination. As we've talked about before, and as I suspect you've experienced, this can happen between two people who love each other but are frightened of being abandoned, hurt, or betrayed, just to name a few triggers.

Basically, when we're anxious and fearful ourselves, we're much quicker at spotting the same in our partner. This means that if your mate is feeling fearful or anxious, not only is he more likely to project it onto you even when you're not feeling it, but also he's primed to see it when you are. If he sees you as frequently fearful, it could promote distance. Research reveals when we're shown pictures of angry or fearful faces, we're more apt to avert our gaze and avoid eye contact.

That said, if you're feeling anxiety or fear, don't habitually hide it from your partner, or chronically evade these feelings. This could just make it worse. Instead, work on acknowledging these feelings, managing them, and finding ways to soothe yourself, such as regular exercise, hanging out with close friends, or watching a comedy, all of which can release anxiety. You can also help your partner reduce the fear or anxiety he sees in you—whether it's real or not—by helping him turn down his own fear or anxiety.

If your partner seems to jump back as you begin to break barriers, be aware he may be feeling anxious, and he may react by keeping you at a cooler, less threatening distance. Ease up a little and give him some time to relax and adjust. Continue to project a warm, friendly attitude toward your partner by greeting him, smiling, being polite (e.g., using "please" and "thank you"), and expressing interest in what he has to say. If you find that you tend to tell him what to do rather than politely request, or you frequently find yourself trying to have your way, this is a good time to work on letting up.

Stress and Emotions

At the same time, let's not forget about *you* in all this. It's not easy to make yourself vulnerable and allow for intimacy after it's been missing for a while. As I mentioned at the start of this chapter, it's a process, and the journey forward is not always a nice, clean, smooth one. Your brain could go on high alert too, and that's okay. Thankfully, you don't have to stay there, devoid of options for how to cope. There are plenty of ways to reduce stress. In a later chapter, I'll be offering more stress-reducing solutions, but in the meantime, let me just suggest that you engage in activities that are emotionally soothing or that calm your body. This could be doing something pleasant with a trusted friend, being in nature, exercising, or practicing a fun, enjoyable hobby.

While we're touching on the subject of finding ways to reduce stress, it's worth mentioning a closely related subject—emotion regulation. When we regulate our emotions, we're not just passively sitting at the receiving end of a feeling. Instead, we're responding to our emotions in an active way, using strategies intended to reframe an emotion that may not be serving us in the moment to make it more desirable or useful. For example, you might try turning one emotion into another. You may try to change sadness into desire when, say, you fail to achieve a certain goal. Instead of feeling hurt, you channel your desire for the outcome to motivate you to try harder next time. Or you may intentionally enhance or tamp down the intensity of a feeling in order to make it more manageable. Say you are in a meeting and your boss takes credit for an idea you brought to her; it may be beneficial for you to tamp down your anger so that you can get through the meeting without exploding in front of clients and losing their business. Some people are more skilled at doing this than others, but don't fret if this is hard for you. And remember: This section is not meant as a lesson in bottling your emotions, but as a lesson in being aware of how you handle these emotions, which will help you more effectively express them to others and manage those outward reactions. Emotion regulation skills can be learned.

To start, ask yourself throughout the day: "How am I feeling right now?" If you can, keep a journal. Write down those situations causing you to feel strong emotions. This technique can help you pinpoint the moment feelings appear instead of letting their origin slip away.

This can give you helpful insight into the kinds of circumstances that bring up certain emotions. You can use this knowledge to not only understand yourself more deeply, but also help you deal with problems more effectively as they arise in the future and as you find yourself in similar situations. For example, back to your idea-stealing boss: You will now be prepared for this rush of anger when she swipes another idea and you'll be more prepared to respond coolly, maybe even figuring out a way to subtly take credit for your own idea! Or let's say that it makes you positively fume if you notice your partner looking at another woman. In the past, you became sullen and berated him for it.

But when you realize that your anger flares up in these moments, you can take stock of it and think through a plan to calm yourself and react more effectively in the future. For example, you might reassure yourself that it's normal to notice other attractive people, and that you're the one he loves. As you soothe yourself, you find that the flame of your anger gets extinguished. If you don't know what caused you to feel so strongly, that's fine too. You don't have to dedicate yourself to understanding every single reaction you have. That would drive most people bananas!

This brings me back to our friend mindfulness (quite a multi-talented approach, isn't it?). Just as a little refresher, mindfulness allows you to observe what you're feeling without judging whether it's good or bad. Simply watching it, without reacting or creating a story around it, allows you to gain valuable perspective on your thoughts and feelings. As a result you'll be less likely to buy into the story you would normally tell yourself. With mindfulness, you're less likely to be triggered. But this approach takes practice.

Changing how you talk to yourself is another strategy. We blame and judge ourselves in ways we would never accept from another person. These inner conversations are not productive and can only make you feel worse. If you catch yourself being self-critical, switch a mental lever. Remind yourself it's not helping and instead turn your inner dialogue around to be encouraging and comforting. For example, if your guy doesn't want sex one night, instead of thinking, "Who can blame him? I'm a big fat turnoff," switch it around to: "I don't know why he doesn't want to have sex, but I'm proud of myself for initiating. What a hot minx!" It might feel awkward at first, but it works.

Another method is to write down your personal strengths. You can go back and review this list whenever you find yourself falling into a pattern of self-criticism.

Arguably, the most effective way to regulate your emotions is by living a healthy lifestyle. This probably isn't news to you. We've all heard about the importance of exercise, eating a diet rich in fresh fruits and veggies, and steering clear of processed foods as well as getting a good night's sleep. And despite the warnings about sun exposure, getting a little each day can boost your mood. If you are healthy physically, you will most likely be healthier mentally as well.

I'll be covering more tips on this subject later in the book, but I'd like to offer one more bit of advice now. It's about your perspective on *your* emotions and how it can impact how you see your partner and how you choose to communicate your feelings to him.

Rather than blaming your emotions on your guy, try to take ownership of them. Accepting full responsibility helps you hold the reins of your own emotions. It's a powerful way of confirming to yourself that no one can make you feel anything. I'm not talking about self-blame, but rather self-empowerment. Thinking erroneously that he can control your feelings means you're relinquishing your own force. Believing someone else is in control of your emotions leaves you feeling powerless and probably resentful.

Is it true that he may be behaving in a way that triggers a certain reaction in you? Absolutely. But there's a difference between a trigger (something that your partner says or does) and a reaction (your interpretation and emotional response). As you read earlier, shoot-from-the-hip reactions come up. Sometimes these reactions are exactly how you really want to respond. They're genuine, they're heartfelt, and they offer openness. But hold on. Other times, especially when you're tempted to give what feels to be a witty, sarcastic retort that will put your partner in his place and prove just how right you are, a knee-jerk response won't give you the result you want. It won't bring him closer. It won't help him feel safe. It won't help him listen or open up. It will do just the opposite.

On the other end of the spectrum, your initial reaction may be to clam up. Again, ask yourself: "Will this help him open up or get me closer to what I want?" Maybe it will if what you want is space and time to see if feelings shift. But it probably won't help if the problem needs to be addressed sooner rather than later.

I want to be clear about something before moving on. Every time you express an emotion, you have a choice about how you're going to do it. It's generally not the emotion that's the problem. It's *how* it's expressed. We can express anger by calmly telling someone we're feeling angry and why, or we can yell, make sarcastic, biting comments, and engage in name calling. It's okay to show that you're angry, but it's how it's expressed that's going to make the difference.

Complaints

Let's assume you've been scanning diligently for all the things your partner does right. Fabulous! But what if you or your partner find there's a real complaint—something that isn't quite working for either or both of you and that needs to be addressed? Thankfully conflict and barriers don't have to go hand in hand. In fact, if they're dealt with in the right way, conflict can actually help the health of your relationship. The way couples behave during a conflict is connected to their relationship satisfaction. Specifically, couples who discuss concerns with fewer antagonistic emotions, and who look at each other while they're talking over issues, experience greater intimacy. So if you raise a concern with your partner, keep the negativity low, remain physically connected, and allow him to speak more than you. Keep in mind, when it comes to complaining: Less is more.

Sex

Have you been assuming that barriers need to be brought down before you can be physically intimate again? Well, the reverse is actually true. When it comes to repairing emotional rifts, sex is a plus. Although people with an anxious or avoidant attachment style tend to have more problems and disconnection in their romantic relationships, sex protects against the damaging effects of their attachment insecurity on the relationship. For couples who have sex more often, the link between attachment avoidance and relationship unhappiness actually dissolves. In fact, people with an anxious or avoidant attachment style who had better or more frequent sex were more likely to view their spouses as emotionally available. This is especially true for the Sponge, the Fearful Fraud, and the Iceberg subtypes, as these most closely resemble the anxious and avoidant attachment styles. But any of the emotionally unavailable subtypes can struggle with attachment insecurity, so the advice ultimately applies to all of them. Let's take a look at Blanche and Lou, to wrap our minds around what all of this would actually look like in a relationship.

Blanche decides to come on to her husband, Lou, more often by seducing him with sexy outfits and researching new sex positions. It pays off, and their sex life skyrockets. Not only is Lou more likely to feel sexually gratified as a result of Blanche's efforts, but he'll also see Blanche as more emotionally available for him. This makes him less likely to protect himself by being on alert for rejection or seeking too much closeness, such as with the Fearful

Fraud or the Sponge, or to retreat to a faraway, cool distance, like the Iceberg.

Clearly, sex is one way of creating greater security while working on availability issues. But you'll want to tread lightly, especially if your guy's been battling depression or if you've both had conflicted discussions about sex in the past. Although couples generally handle conflict around sex in a constructive and connection-building way, when husbands struggle with depression, discussions around sex are more likely to involve anger and depression for both spouses.

If this sounds like your situation, the next time you approach your partner sexually, be ready to respond to any expressions of anger or depression with as much calmness and kindness as you can. If you find yourself tempted to match his pessimism or antagonism, give yourself permission to pause, take a slow breath, and remind yourself of your goal: connection.

The World Beyond the Two of You

Relationships don't exist in a vacuum; social support matters. A study on patients with prostate cancer and their spouses illustrates this point. Researchers found that couples who had more support from their social network tended to experience more openness in their communication with each other. Social support is an emotional stress buffer for the cancer-free spouse, and probably helps her be more constructive and available to her spouse when he opens up. The bottom line is this: If you nurture your friendships, you'll nurture your ability to be there for your partner.

We sometimes believe our friendships with other couples are separate from what goes into making a great relationship, but relationship science suggests otherwise. The more friends a couple jointly shares, the happier they are together. Nurturing these social connections by regularly going out on dates with other couples, having them over to your place, or joining in hobbies or activities together will give your relationship a happiness boost.

But give some love to your single friends too! Although it's wonderful for couples to go out together, it's equally important to socialize with your own friends separately. The benefits to your well-being are numerous, including reducing stress, building trust, even improving immunity.

Friends can also be an invaluable source of emotional intimacy, but you don't want to turn to them to meet all your needs for emotional connection at the exclusion of your mate. This isn't as much of a concern if you're in a close relationship with your partner. However, if there's distance and strain, you may be at risk for confiding in your friends and shutting your partner out. Let me put it this way: It's certainly okay for buddies to seek each other out for relationship advice and support to a degree, but be careful. Sometimes we can make the mistake of venting, sharing highly personal or unflattering information, even exposing super-confidential secrets. This isn't helpful for several reasons, including:

1. It can prevent you from opening up to the person who matters most—your guy—because there's no need to if you are already having all of your emotional needs met.

2. It will likely cause your friends to have a one-sided and negative impression of your man, so they won't support your relationship.

3. You're not respecting your partner's privacy. Before revealing all, try to think about how comfortable you would be if your

guy were talking to his friends in the same manner. If you wouldn't like him dishing on you, don't do it to him. Similarly, be mindful about what you share with your family.

And keep in mind, there may also be a more complicated side to our friendships. As in any relationship, when we allow ourselves to be vulnerable and open and care for a friend, there's the possibility of getting hurt. Even friends make mistakes, say hurtful comments, argue, disappoint us, or choose to no longer spend time with us. Friendships involve conflict and differences and strong emotions can arise.

In this chapter, we've explored strategies that you can use to start dismantling barriers that stonewall emotional connection, as well as considerations to keep in mind on the journey. Barriers don't come down automatically and they can't be forced down, but with patience and gentle persistence, it is possible to topple the divide. The exercises that follow will help you get started in practicing some of these tools.

As we end this chapter, please give yourself a hug. No doubt you've made a tremendous effort and it deserves to be acknowledged and celebrated. Just as when you concluded the previous chapter, focus on practicing the skills you've learned. Continue respecting your partner's boundaries, follow behavior guidelines, and build on the foundation of goodwill.

Now add to this your new skills that you're about to practice of speaking with your body, reflective listening, and making "I" statements. They'll not only dramatically reduce tension and defensiveness, but can promote greater mutual understanding, growth, and connection.

If you want to take two weeks to a month to practice these skills before moving on, that's perfectly fine. If you do, just remember to go back and revisit this chapter for a refresher. Also remember to keep a journal to track your efforts and progress. It can help sustain you during tough moments along the way.

Once you're feeling more confident using these skills, you'll be ready to take another step and move forward to Chapter 7.

Speaking with Your Body

Without meaning to do it, you can shut down dialogue with just the shrug of your shoulders or the roll of your eyes. In contrast, encouraging nonverbal behaviors increases the odds a conversation will keep going and flowing. Here are ten nonverbal cues for better communication. Try practicing these while your guy is talking to you, whether you agree with him or not. Gradually add more upbeat nonverbal cues to your repertoire. To master physical reactions, you might want to practice in front of a mirror. These behaviors include:

* Nodding

* Open posture (arms open rather than folded in front of your chest)

* Making eye contact

* Facing him

* Mirroring body position (e.g., if his right leg is crossed over left, do the opposite and cross your left leg over the right)

* Leaning forward to show you're engaged in what he's saying

* Using excited gestures such as a thumbs-up or smiling when he's sharing good news

* Mimicking his facial expressions if he's happy, but avoiding doing the same with an angry or sullen face, unless he shared something that made him angry that had nothing to do with you. A relative's insult, a coworker's deceitfulness, and a

friend's betrayal are all appropriate examples of this. In that case, go right ahead and show him you're right on board with his anger!

* Moving in closer

* Using touch. When comforting your partner, reach out and gently stroke his arm or hold his hand.

Listening Reflectively

The goal of this exercise is to fully tune in and "get" your guy's message.

Step 1. Listen carefully to what he's saying and gather meaning.

Step 2. Once you think you grasp the essence, check in to verify. You might say something like "Okay, let's see if I've got this right. You're saying you feel _____ because _____. Is that what you mean?"

Use your best judgment about when you want to use this technique. You don't need to do it with every interaction. But I would recommend trying it when you're having a serious discussion with the potential to escalate into an argument, or one that involves sharing sensitive emotions or experiences.

Owning "I"

For this exercise, face your partner with a warm and open expression (check previous exercise) and be prepared to communicate using only "I" statements. This approach limits defensiveness and supports communication. For example, if your partner ne-glects to tell you he's staying late at the office, instead of saying, "You're so inconsiderate!" try this: "I felt hurt when you didn't call to let me know. I know that's not what you were trying to do. Would it be easier for you to text or email me the next time you have to work late?"

CHAPTER SEVEN

Securing Your Connection

✧

Pay attention. It's all about paying attention. Attention
is vitality. It connects you with others. It makes you
eager. Stay eager.

—SUSAN SONTAG

Kudos for your courage! You've taken the tough steps of facing
your partner's issues as well as your own. Now you're standing
in a place where it's possible to imagine what lies ahead. It's natural for anyone doing this kind of heart-centered work to set
their focus firmly on the goal. You might be thinking, "Okay,
we're close enough—let's just get on with it." Or you might feel
energized and anxious to throw caution aside and prematurely
bump intimacy up to a new level. Or maybe things haven't gone
as you hoped and you're ready to just give up.

*Before you let your thoughts run on, I'm here to say please slow
down.* Try not to look ahead. Stay in the present, in the here and
now. This very moment is the exact one to make a conscious
effort to build an even stronger connection before moving on.
Why? Because when the walls come down, it's human to feel

more emotionally exposed and vulnerable. You might be thinking, "What if he rejects me after I've bared my soul?" Or you've vowed to reach out just this one last time and now you're waiting anxiously to see if any change is taking hold. That's why I suggest before going forward, you follow a few tips to help you stay centered:

- Stay mindful of the present and what's happening in the here and now rather than projecting to a future you're hoping for or fearing.
- Notice small signs of progress rather than getting caught up in the finish line and feeling discouraged by progress that hasn't happened yet.
- See the value in making changes for your own self-improvement, even if your relationship or your partner hasn't changed. One of the beautiful aspects of this process is that it helps *you* be a more emotionally available person.

As you work toward securing your connection, I'm going to ask you to keep these three rules in mind. Notice the ways in which he's expressing intimacy. Even the slightest shift toward communion is worthy of appreciation. Just as importantly, notice changes in yourself, the ways in which you've become a more attentive partner and a more conscious person.

In Chapter 6, you worked to break down the walls and now you're working on building the connection. Ideally, this step involves your partner's enthusiastic involvement, but he doesn't have to be 100 percent on board to try these approaches. He just has to have a willingness to attempt something different. What if he totally scoffs at some of these approaches? That's okay too. It doesn't have to stop *you* from doing them on your own. Keep in mind when one part of a system changes, it ups the odds that the whole system will change. And if you move forward, he just might inch ahead along with you. This was the dynamic experienced by Stan and Lisbeth.

For the past year, Stan had been slowly distancing himself from his girlfriend, Lisbeth. He confided in her less, never held her in his arms, and spent long hours playing video games or watching television during time they could have spent together. Lisbeth was dumbfounded and tied up in knots. As she was running errands, her stomach ached and a pang of hurt ran down from her chest. Sometimes the sadness felt so heavy that her chest would heave and tears stung her eyes, but she didn't dare cry in front of him. Engagement at work turned into going through the motions, as her mind inevitably drifted to trying to sort out why Stan seemed to be distancing himself. Gradually, she felt more wary around him, frightened to make a misstep that would push him farther away, but unsure how she could avoid that. She didn't even know what she was doing wrong. If she ruffled him in some way, she bent over backward to make it up to him. For a while, Lisbeth resolutely reached out, unflagging in her belief that he would eventually come around if she just persisted, but after being consistently stung by Stan's rebukes, she felt a part of herself giving up on regaining his affection. She began to immerse herself in outside projects, trying to push the hurtful chasm out of her mind. She stubbornly refused to make any more overtures and the icy distance grew over the next six months. But one night alone in her room, she panned back on the problem and realized that if she continued to give up and allow the gap between them to widen, she would eventually lose him. Armed with an awareness that she was unwilling to let the relationship die without giving her best effort, coupled with the belief that she had nothing to lose, she vowed to give their relationship one more try before calling it quits for good. "He's worth it. *We're* worth it," she told herself.

Initially, her renewed efforts to hug Stan were met with a stony turn. In the past, she would have angrily huffed and demanded that he tell her what's wrong, but this time, she tried a novel approach. She accepted his dismissal, reminding herself she was taking a loving action. She also got strategic, expressing love to him in other ways like running errands for him, making him lunch, or leaving a sweet note tucked inside his pocket. She would occasionally try to hug Stan, and if he turned away, she told him she understood. "No biggie." She calmly shared with him her wish to make things right if she did something to upset him, and reminded herself that she could not literally prevent him from getting upset; she could only strive to be the best person and partner that she could be. At first Stan didn't respond, but she kept at it. She kept her focus on becoming a new kind of partner and having empathy for him. One day, Stan cracked a casual joke with her. Stan hadn't joked with her in months. A few days later, she was surprised to come home to his inquiry about how her day had been. She felt his presence at home a little more, his video games captivating him a little less. A light of clarity flashed on as she realized that the tide in their relationship was starting to turn.

Boost Self-Esteem

The most important relationship you'll ever have in life is with yourself. Okay, I know you've heard that one a million times, but it's a diamond-shining truth; you truly are the foundation of all your relationships. Psychology researchers conducted a study using data from the Longitudinal Study of Generations, a project following people across four generations over twelve years. The study shows a person's self-esteem powerfully predicts several aspects of their life over the years, such as their overall mood, how much they like their jobs, and how happy they are in their relationships. So when we cultivate self-confidence, we're actually moving toward the possibility of more connected relationships.

Does each person in the relationship need to have equally high self-esteem? Relationships are at their best when both partners possess strong self-confidence and high self-esteem, but you needn't be in exactly the same place. If one person in a relationship has high self-esteem and it's enough to carry the needs of the relationship, then the couple will do just fine. So even if your partner lacks self-confidence, by cultivating your own, you'll be boosting the health of your connection.

What does this mean for you? If you had to choose one thing to work on in your relationship, choose *your* self-esteem.

Content and Process

When I was doing my therapist training, one of the lessons my clinical supervisors taught me was the difference between content and process. And now, dear readers, I'm passing this wisdom on to you.

Content is basically what you are saying to someone else. Depending on what choices you make, you can always change content. For example, let's say Maria asks her partner, Jesse, to

SELF-ESTEEM HELPERS

✦

Improve how you treat yourself. We sometimes think we have to feel better about ourselves before we change how we behave, but sometimes feelings follow behavior. Examples of this include getting regular physical activity, eating healthy food, getting enough sleep, soaking in a little sunshine (not too much!), quitting smoking, and keeping an eye on how much you drink. Additional ideas for treating yourself well are taking yourself (literally) to a serene place such as a hiking trail, making time to relax and enjoy yourself with others, setting limits on when you can be reached by email or text, and practicing the art of being yourself rather than trying to please everyone.

- Make an effort to challenge critical and perfectionistic self-talk. Our brain becomes better at doing whatever we train it to do. Just as we can train our brains to think more self-critically, we can also learn to question our own excessively high standards and hurtful self-talk. For example, let's say that Jane had promised Collin that she would pick up his favorite dinner on the way home, but after an extremely busy day, she completely forgot to do it. As she walks through the door, she immediately realizes her error. At one time, she would have said to herself, "Oh no! You moron! If you weren't so absorbed in yourself, you'd be a much better wife. It's amazing that Collin sticks around, because he could do much, much better." Today, even though she's not ready to be the picture of self-graciousness, she's willing to try something just a little kinder. "Oh no! I can't believe I forgot! Well, I can't get too upset at myself, I guess. People forget things, especially when they're busy. I suppose this just proves I'm human. I'll turn around and pick it up now."

- See yourself as others see you. Try checking your own negative beliefs about yourself by remembering positive remarks that people have made. You can even keep a list. For example, you could take your notebook to a relaxing, mellow place (e.g., a favorite room, a pretty outdoor spot, or a café) and spend some time jotting down the favorable observations people shared with you over time. If you struggle to summon these to mind, keep at it. You may find that the cheerful gems people offer you aren't always going to trot out as typical pats on the back. To illustrate, recently my husband, Guille, called me "kooky," and my parents, Dennis and Terrie, called me "a badass." Those aren't the first words you'd think of as kudos. Yet that's exactly how they were intended and they made me feel great.

cuddle with her and he says, "I don't feel like cuddling now, honey." She could respond in any number of ways. She could say:

- "No problem—we'll do it another time."
- "Are you all right? Is something bothering you?"
- "Of course—you never want to cuddle!"

Process is the overall pattern of communication and it's usually less transparent than content. It's kind of like looking at the surface of a lake; you can't really see what's going on until you swim under the surface. Process is the message people send beyond their words. One process is often referred to as "pursuit-distance." It's a dance between two people in which one person moves toward and the other moves away, toward, away, toward, away, and so on. There are actually two kinds of pursuit-distance dynamics: "pursue-withdraw" and "attack-withdraw."

In pursue-withdraw, one partner approaches the other and the other responds by moving away. In attack-withdraw, the partner approaches but in a more verbally aggressive fashion, such as complaining, fault finding, shunning, acrimony, criticizing, nagging, ridiculing, and blaming, to name a few, and the other person moves away even more. In this process, each partner is hitting a soft spot and pushing a button in the other, and each partner's response to his/her button getting pushed actually makes the cycle worse.

Let's go back to the cuddle with Maria and Jesse and look at the attack-withdraw dynamic . . .

Maria approaches Jesse to cuddle.

Jesse tells her, "I don't feel like cuddling now, honey."

Maria reaches out again to Jesse to try to convince him to cuddle with her, but he keeps saying no, at which point Maria feels hurt and rejected. She falls into an attack-withdraw pattern, and criticizes Jesse. "When we first got together, you used to cuddle with me all the time, and now it's like you can't be bothered! You never touch me anymore. You're so cold!"

Feeling overwhelmed, hurt, and defensive, Jesse withdraws, walks into another room and slams the door.

What is another way she could have handled this? She could have worked to use an "engage-engage" process. In this kind of interaction, one person reaches out for connection and the other partner wants to do the same. The result is what I like to call a beautiful snowball—as the process reinforces itself it continues: Both people feel closer and more connected rather than hurt, defensive, frightened, resentful, and disconnected.

What kinds of actions reflect an engage-engage cycle? Here are some choices:

- Confide
- Admit

- Listen
- Reassure
- Disarm
- Comfort
- Open up
- Be vulnerable
- Give the benefit of the doubt
- Offer empathy
- Be consolatory

So let's look at how Maria could initiate an engage-engage process in her interaction with Jesse . . .

Rather than continuing to persist or criticizing Jesse for not wanting to cuddle, Maria doesn't take it. She checks in with him calmly and affectionately.

"Okay, no problem, sweetheart. By the look on your face, it seems like something is bothering you—are you all right?" Now, she is in an engaging stance, and Jesse opens up.

"Yeah, I'm okay. It's not you—I've just been so stressed at work and it's on my mind. I just need some space right now, I guess."

Maria expresses empathy and compassion. "I'm so sorry things have been rough at work. Sometimes work has a way of following us home, doesn't it? I get it—I've been there myself, and I'm here for you if you need anything. For now, can I get you your favorite cup of tea?"

Jesse turns toward her and reaches out to grab her hand and softly smiles. "Thank you so much, sweetheart—that would be really nice."

Instead of attacking, Maria engaged, and even though she didn't get the cuddle she originally reached for, she did get exactly what she was truly looking for: a connection.

Catch Your ZZZZZs

It's worth noting that if you get enough sleep, you'll be better able to use the connection techniques I've laid out in this book. People who have poor quality of sleep (e.g., often waking during the night, not going to bed at a timely hour, having difficulty falling asleep) are less able to change their perspective and look at a situation in a more optimistic way than are people who have better sleep quality.

So what does that mean for you and your relationship? If you or your partner don't get enough quality sleep, you'll be less able to reframe a situation in a helpful way. Your emotions are also more likely to run wild. Make it a priority to catch enough ZZZZZs.

Of course, with the hectic lives that people lead, with work schedules, children's activities, hobbies, and social commitments, that last tip might sound pretty challenging. That's okay. Challenging doesn't mean impossible. If you want to make changes to improve your sleep and your relationship, remember to start small and doable. See if you can spot areas of wiggle room in your evening schedule. Does the laundry absolutely have to be done tonight, or can it wait until the weekend? Can you save a favorite TV program on your DVR and watch it the next night? Can you create a ride-sharing system with other parents to pick up the kids from after-school activities? Can you personally challenge yourself to go to bed (with no TV and lights off) 15 minutes earlier? Thankfully, your menu of possible changes is a very long one, so pick what feels manageable and right for you.

TIPS FOR A GOOD NIGHT'S SLEEP

⬥

- Avoid watching television in bed. The flicker of light from the television can be highly stimulating for your brain.

- If you wake up in the middle of the night and it's hard for you to go back to sleep, don't lie in bed and watch the clock. It just prolongs the onset of sleep and then you'll link bedtime to being awake. Instead, get up and try a relaxing activity in another room, such as reading or listening to relaxing music.

- Give your body time to wind down from the day before you get into bed. Try not to engage in physically or mentally demanding pursuits (e.g., exercise, complex problem-solving for work) or stressful activities (e.g., responding to a taxing or contentious email, watching the news) within two to three hours of bedtime. As much as possible, try to reserve the very end of the evening for light reading or other relaxing activities.

Invest in Your Relationship Account

I often tell my clients that we're like mini emotional bank accounts. From the situations we encounter to the feelings we have or the choices we make, we can experience, think, feel, or behave in ways that nurture us, lift us higher, and leave us feeling better. Or we can react in ways that drain us, create more stress, and leave us feeling down or weary. I don't have to tell you which is a deposit and which is a withdrawal.

If you keep a large sum saved in your emotional bank account, then you'll have a plentiful reserve to draw from when there's need. How do you bank positive emotions? The options are virtually endless. Just a few tweaks in your lifestyle can make a major difference in your emotional reserve, such as (you guessed it) getting more shut-eye, being more physically active (if you can aim for thirty minutes of moderate physical activity, five days per week, beautiful!), and eating more fruit and vegetables. These are great places to start.

You can also bank positive emotions by treating yourself with the same kindness and consideration that you would show a dear friend, even if you don't feel like you deserve it right now. For example, rather than buy into the same self-defeating, self-critical stuff you've been telling yourself, begin to question the reality of those negative words, even if they feel really compelling. If you find you are tearing yourself down, think, "I've been calling myself a failure, but that's just me telling myself that. It may not even be true." Look for the best in who you are and what you do well and don't hesitate to make a list of all of those positive qualities! Don't get me wrong: I'm not telling you to look into a mirror and tell yourself what a magnificent person you are (although you could—I certainly wouldn't object to it if you truly feel that way!), nor am I asking you to force-feed yourself any compliment that you don't believe. This is just an invitation to open up your mind to the following:

1. Looking for what you do well (e.g., your talents and skills)

2. Recognizing your personal character highlights and good points (e.g., honest, funny, creative)

3. Questioning some of your self-criticism (e.g., is it really true that you're unlovable?)

4. Accepting your imperfections (it's okay—we all have them!)

You can also bank positive emotions by pursuing goals that are personally meaningful for you, like identifying ways you want to grow as a person, engaging in volunteerism for a cause you believe in, creating a personal challenge for yourself (e.g., to run a marathon), or seeking out a new career or opportunities in your current job that will imbue your work life with a greater sense of purpose. Watching, listening, or reading a little comedy never hurts your emotional bank account either.

Just as you have your own emotional bank account, you and your partner also have a joint account. This shared account is partly made up of the individual accounts you each bring to the relationship. However, it's also true that two people create a relationship that is its own living system, greater than the sum of its parts. And this living system needs to bank positive emotions to thrive, just as we do individually. So how do we stockpile a wealth of good feeling in our relationship? Your creativity is the limit. Although it may be tempting to think that building relationship wealth would involve extravagant romantic trips that drain your actual bank account, don't be fooled. It's really the everyday little things that can fly under people's radar yet make the biggest difference. You can build emotional capital by having fun and trying new activities together, telling each other how much you love each other, being generous with compliments, making plans together, and having close, personal conversations. Those inside jokes you have, the cute names you call each other that no one else knows, and the moments of silliness? Yep, they all boost the account. Couples who have a wealth of investment in their shared emotional bank account have more restrained and level reactions when they encounter a threat to their relationship, compared to people who have less emotional reserve. This is another example of a beautiful snowball: Couples who have built this kind of connection are more likely to show a sense of resilience and maintain their connection when they experience a stressor to the relationship.

EASY EVERYDAY INVESTMENTS

✤

- Ask about his day.

- Show him that you're interested in listening to him. You can do this both nonverbally (e.g., eye contact, facing toward him, nodding) and verbally (e.g., asking follow-up questions, expressing genuine enthusiasm).

- Look for ways to make your partner's life a little easier. Volunteer to do an errand or a chore for him that you know he doesn't like or make an extra effort to give him words of encouragement, reassurance, and support after a tough day.

- Notice what he does right. Watch out—this may include things that you may not think are special or have been expecting him to do already, such as take out the trash. The bottom line is: Look for anything positive, big or small.

- Find little ways to bring love and romance into his day. Try a note, a text, a card, an unexpected phone call, a small gift, a love letter, a romantic or loving sentiment that you share with him, an evening stroll together, a low-lit dinner you prepared just for him with mellow music, or a massage to help him relax.

- Find ways to sexually turn him on and surprise him. It feels good to be pursued, so show him that he is desirable and sexy to you. Most women don't initiate sex, but that doesn't have to be the case in your relationship. Is he really into lingerie, or does he have a fantasy that he's shared with you? Are there new sexual positions or techniques that you could bring into the bedroom? If you're looking for ideas, the Internet is a treasure trove.

- Reflect on and share what you admire and love about him. Are you struck by how intelligent he is, what a caring father he is, his athleticism, his courage, his sense of determination, his handsomeness, or the sexy way he moves in a room? Don't just keep that to yourself. Let him know you see it too.

- Validate his point of view. Too often, couples engage in power struggles, putting their pride ahead of their relationship. It's as if people have an allergy to saying "you're right." Instead, many people are hesitant to admit to their partner that they're in the wrong, or they poke holes in their partner's viewpoint with an unfortunately placed "yes, but," a "you're wrong," or even a "that's ridiculous!" This doesn't build an emotional reserve. Instead, it's likely to put your partner even more on the defensive. But effort to see things from your partner's point of view, even if you don't personally agree, does stock emotional wealth. I'm not suggesting you say it without meaning it, but a little "that's a great point," "I can see why you would feel that way," or a "you're right" can go a long way.

- Assuming that you are in a nonabusive relationship, when in doubt, give him the benefit. View him in a charitable light. For example, if he forgets to do something that he promised to do, like picking up milk on the way home from work or cleaning the gutters, try not to assume that he did it on purpose to spite you. Make your starting assumption a merciful one, like he forgot because he has a lot on his mind.

- Play and be good friends. Part of what we love about our friendships is that they are infused with so much positive energy and fun. Well, in the wise words of Ann Landers: "Love is friendship that has caught fire." So remember that your relationship with your partner is a friendship at its foundation, and this friendship must be watered to thrive. So do what BFFs do: Be playful, joke around, let your silly side out, try to engage and entertain your partner, share adventures, and explore new sights and places. Faraway travel isn't necessary for this. You can even search TripAdvisor .com for undiscovered fun gems in your local area.

- Be polite. This is probably the most fundamental, underestimated, and sadly underutilized relationship wealth builder. It's pretty basic, but worth a pause to contemplate the implications of this for your relationship bank account. Would you rather hang around

continues . . .

with rude people or polite people? Yeah, I thought so. I rest my case . . .

Most of these are deposits you can make daily. If your guy isn't willing to contribute, try as best as you can (and I know it's tough!) not to let it discourage you. After all, as a couple dealing with emotional unavailability, you're coming from having a pretty low balance, so it may take time to build up trust, goodwill, positivity, and connection. But don't give up. Start your savings today.

Embrace Gratitude

Gratitude reminds us to value and appreciate what we have and what others give to us. It's also a deeply bonding emotion. One study showed that when gratitude is expressed, couples report feeling closer. Six months down the road, couples who experienced expressions of gratitude were more likely to report having a healthier, happier relationship than those who didn't experience it. That's a powerful result.

Now as you read about this study, you might be wondering *why* gratitude brings two people closer. Well, gratitude enhances the desire in the grateful person to spend time with the person toward whom they feel gratitude and to be more helpful and generous toward him. This makes sense but there's also surprising research suggesting gratitude impacts our relationship in ways we might not expect. A group of psychology researchers conducted a study on the effects of gratitude among couples who have been together for approximately twenty years. There were two main results. The first is that the more people felt and expressed gratitude toward their spouses, the happier they felt in the relationship. But it was the second finding that was particularly eye-opening.

It wasn't the gratitude people expressed that predicted their partners' happiness in the marriages. It was the gratitude that a person *felt*, even if it wasn't expressed outright. Pretty amazing, huh? This suggests the gratitude we feel leaks out and impacts our behavior in ways that we may not realize—whether we come out and say it or not—but in a manner that our partner notices and feels.

Even though you're facing emotional unavailability and disconnection right now, if you can seek, find, and share the good in each other and express what you admire, respect, and appreciate about each other, you'll reap the benefits.

Cultivate Optimism

Focusing on the sunny side of life has innumerable benefits, including increasing feelings of intimacy. An overall optimistic outlook toward life, which is also called "dispositional optimism," is beneficial in strengthening relationships. Optimism is the belief that life will generally have good experiences in store, and any problems that arise will be relatively few and surmountable. Couples who hold this generally sunny view of life are better equipped to behave in constructive ways when conflicts arise.

Interestingly, that's not the complete picture. Couples who are *only* optimistic about their relationship, such as expecting their sweetheart would always be considerate or communicative, but not about life in general, which is called "situational optimism," are less successful in working out conflict. Why would this be the case? Well, it's possible that when we hold a broadly optimistic mind-set about life, such as that things will turn out favorably for us, this sunny attitude is so shapeless and leaves so much room for interpretation that it would be a hard expectation to overturn. It is vague enough to leave room for problems, because we can

INCREASE GRATITUDE

❖

- Choose an everyday moment that would typically pass you by unnoticed, and look for what you can appreciate in it. My realization of the power of gratitude first hit me when I was stuck in traffic. I felt eager to be out of the gridlock, until I thought about how fortunate I was to have eyes that could see the cars, a mind that could grasp my situation, a healthy body that was sitting in the driver's seat, the use of a car to drive in, and a beautiful sky in my view above the traffic. Taking a quiet moment like this can help us get better at spotting moments that we should be grateful for.

- When you start to think about what you don't have, remind yourself of what you do have. It's a subtle change in perspective, but it's powerful.

- We all have different tendencies to feel grateful, and we are also unique in how often we say "thank you." If you want to practice sharing your appreciation with others, start by telling others what you value about what they do and who they are, and over time it will become a habit.

encounter obstacles and overcome them, which still confirms that life will lean in our favor generally. When we have cheerful expectations and they are either confirmed or at least not disconfirmed, we are more likely to be motivated to persist in trying to effectively overcome the problem and to cope well as we do so. On the other hand, if we have optimistic expectations only in a specific area such as in our relationship but not in general, then it would be much easier to have experiences that contradict our expectations. For example, if we expect to never feel hurt in our relationship or to always communicate well, then all that would need to happen to belie this expectation is an argument that proceeds less constructively than we intended, or for our partner to follow through on a thoughtless comment or hasty action that pains us. Unfortunately, when we have hopeful expectations that are contradicted, we are actually less likely to behave in productive, connection-building ways, and less motivated to persist in the face of difficulty. So a potential downside to holding optimistic expectations about our relationship, in particular, rather than about life more broadly is that the expectations are more specific and therefore easier to refute.

These concepts don't just apply to romantic relationships, but to other domains of life, such as our health (i.e., general optimism versus health-specific optimism). However, there is a little caveat here. There is nothing inherently wrong with feeling optimistic about your relationship. If anything, the opposite is true: Relationship science tells us that bleak expectations about relationships are not exactly linked with connection and blooming intimacy. The key here is whether the optimistic expectations that we have are specific enough to be refuted and whether we possess the ability to make our expectations a reality. If you are a person who is able to communicate constructively and make charitable assumptions about your partner, then you are more likely to be able to confirm your own positive expectations. People who hold optimistic expectations about their relationship— for example, they believe their partner will always be available in times of need or will make few errors—and who also communicate constructively and make charitable assumptions about their partner have a steadier degree of satisfaction in their relationship.

So what's the take-home message? We should all try to cultivate optimism. A life of gratitude will make us happier and more emotionally available, plus this will have a positive effect on others; our sunny outlook can be contagious, and who wants to hang out with Debbie Downer? We can certainly have optimism about our relationship more specifically too; it's just important to make sure that both partners possess the skills to live up to the expectations.

On the other hand, if you generally don't have an optimistic attitude but you're optimistic about your relationship and you think that either you or your partner do not have the skills to make your expectations a reality, that's okay! Arguably, some expectations are so unrealistic that they are just beyond anyone's abilities and they should be modified. For example, if you think that your partner will never, ever say anything to hurt you or do anything that will upset you, try loosening this expectation a bit and giving him leeway. Remember that we're all human and we may do or say things that unintentionally upset others. Keep your unrealistic expectations in check and you'll avoid setting yourself up for disappointment.

Enjoy Yourselves

This probably seems like pretty simplistic advice, but in our age of hyper-accomplishment and maniacal multitasking, a lot of estranged couples neglect playtime. Yet without a doubt just having fun and enjoying yourselves will promote connection. Studies have shown that when couples complete a new and exciting task in just seven minutes, their closeness increases from before they tried the task to afterward. We're talking just *seven minutes*! Another study showed that when couples engage in exciting activities for ninety minutes a week, their intimacy and happiness increases after four weeks. Not only that, but they hold on to their increased closeness and positivity until four months later.

This increased closeness has a positive ripple effect on the rest

TO ENCOURAGE OPTIMISM

✦

- Remember the good stuff. When people entertain fond memories, they feel more connected to other people, which raises self-esteem and fosters optimism. Try remembering the good times, and a cascade of benefits will likely result.

- Envision a best possible you. Imagine a future in which you've reached every goal you've set and have arrived at your dreams. Next, think about what this future life would be like on a general day and then write about a usual day for this future self for fifteen minutes. After you've finished writing, try to envision your description of a day in your future life for five minutes.

of your life as well: A study found men and women who view their relationship as emotionally close are also significantly more likely to perceive their job as rewarding, to have fewer concerns about their employment, and to experience less conflict between work and family demands.

So if you want to increase your connection, go for it! Have fun and try something new. It can be big or small. Skydiving? Chess? You could try those, or you could just make a date with your partner and have some fun out. If your partner seems hesitant to try new things, resist the urge to try to convince him to do it, to reason with him about why it would be a good idea, or to get frustrated if he's not as on board as you would like. He has a right to his feelings just as you do to yours, and it's a beautiful thing that we're all different and have unique preferences. Instead of trying to change him, seek instead to try to understand where he's coming from. Express appreciation that he's telling you what he wants and doesn't want (remember, that's much better than holding it inside and seething), and ask him if there are any small activities that he would be willing to try together, such as going for a walk, trying a different local restaurant, or seeing a new movie together. Another solution is to try something that he is already familiar with, but that you have not been exposed to as much. For example, if he enjoys bowling or astronomy or a great Thai restaurant near his office, ask him to introduce you to his world. Not only will this be an avenue to enjoying a new activity as a couple, but you'll be showing him that you're interested in what he loves, which he'll really appreciate if he's like most people.

Boost Oxytocin

Oxytocin is a hormone that scientists have discovered is linked to bonding and positive social behavior among mammals (non-human, that is). But research also shows that we humans are no exception. How can oxytocin strengthen your emotional connection? Couples who got a nasal shot of oxytocin during one study communicated more effectively and less antagonistically while they discussed a conflict between them compared to couples who got only a placebo nasal shot. Other research shows that oxytocin increases the strength of the neural connection between the amygdala and the rostral medial frontal cortex, an area of the brain that scientists believe helps us to regulate our emotions and to manage our social dealings with others, including with our partner. Oxytocin also seems to tamp down our brain's response to stressful situations.

Of course, there is certainly still much work to be done to fully understand how oxytocin helps us act in bond-solidifying ways, but these results give us a helpful clue. So it's safe to say that you'll feel closer to your guy and he will to you if the oxytocin

WAYS TO GIVE OXYTOCIN A BUMP

❖

Studies show that you don't have to have sex to boost oxytocin. Affectionate but nonsexual moments have the same effect for both of you. Here are a few examples:

- **Hold hands.** This is a great one because, unlike sex, you can do it anywhere (and with no legal penalty whatsoever!). You can hold hands when you're out with friends or at home. Enjoying a night in with the television? Why not turn it into a romantic date night and hold hands at the same time? Even better, pair it with fond memories about a time when you bonded while you sit together and hold hands.

- **Cuddle.** Speaking of a romantic date night, if you want to take your touch up a notch, by all means do. It feels wonderful to curl up on the couch with your partner, and it deepens your connection and good feelings without the two of you having to say a word. Now *that's* multitasking at its best.

- **Spoon.** Who says touching has to be done while you're awake? Add more intimacy and oxytocin to your nighttime hours by snuggling against your partner in bed as you both drift off to sleep. Believe it or not, you can get pretty creative with it too. For ideas, check out *The Art of Spooning* by Jim Grace and Lisa G. Grace.

Science also gives us nonintimate ways to elevate oxytocin, which is pretty cool considering that it will actually help you be more intimate (and your partner, if he does these things too):

- **Try listening to soothing music.** A little soft jazz or Handel, anyone?

- **Enjoy a nice meal.** Research shows that our oxytocin levels rise when we eat food.

- **Consider adding a canine to your family.** When your dog looks at you or your partner, oxytocin levels get a hike. Not only that, but when you pet your dog, you both get an oxytocin boost. You might be wondering whether this works for other animals like cats or

continues . . .

guinea pigs. Unfortunately, with a lack of research on this question, the jury is still out, but if you prefer a guinea pig, a hamster, or a cat to a dog, go with your gut and do what feels right. As you can see, simple actions can foster intimacy. Regardless of whether your relationship actually becomes more emotionally available or not, you'll reap the benefits of trying. Any kind of self-improvement is a win-win for the relationship. Keep your eye on the process, not the destination.

hormone is triggered. But how do you do that? Sure, we know that oxytocin is released during orgasm and couples who are sexually satisfied are more likely to be happier and experience greater emotional availability, but this could be a challenge when sexual desire isn't at its peak, especially when you're feeling emotionally disconnected from your partner. However, there are actions you can take to boost oxytocin in yourself and your partner.

Take a Stroll Down Memory Lane

Yes, you are capable of time travel. Well, in your mind, at least. Our minds have a tremendous ability to revisit the past, but as numerous studies show, we're also somewhat biased time travelers. We don't always remember events exactly as they happened, and we can choose where and when we want to visit. In other words, we don't look at everything in our past. We're a little selective. But not to worry: relationship science also tells us that we can use this to our advantage. What we choose to remember about our partner in the past can also help us forge a stronger relationship in the present. When people recall times when their partner praised them for an internal quality, like an admirable personality characteristic (e.g., courageous, caring, outgoing, conscientious), they feel more positive in the relationship and respond to their partner in more connection-building ways. Importantly, this boost doesn't happen when people are praised for external reasons, such as a recent achievement. And the biggest boost in good feelings doesn't happen for couples who were already very happy and connected, but for couples who are less bonded and content. In other words, this technique works best for couples who need it the most, couples who are feeling disconnected, just as you may be feeling now. So if you want to enhance the connection with your partner, try this:

- Recall a time when your partner commented on what he admires about you. Try to focus on what it is about you as a person that he appreciates, not what you've done.

- Increase the times that he'll be able to recall hearing you share your admiration of him. To do this, try looking for not just what he does well, but what is good about him. You get to send loving words his way, and he'll be more likely to feel happier and more connected in your relationship. It's fun, sweet, and connection-building—a clear win-win.

- If your partner reacts negatively, because not everyone responds positively to compliments, try not to get discouraged. Instead, at another time, try giving a smaller, more toned-down compliment. Meet him where he is, see what he can handle, and go from there.

Sometimes it can be a real challenge to continue trying to foster connection when you're bumping up against a wall and not getting a response. It's okay to feel frustrated or discouraged, or to have thoughts of how much better it would be to just back away and show him how lame it feels when no one is reaching out to show appreciation and love. In those moments, take a step back and focus on soothing your own stress level through some of the mood-boosting activities we've talked about in this book (and we'll go into more of them later). Then remind yourself why you're on this journey in the first place and go back through old entries you've made in your journal, marking progress along the way. When you're in a calmer place, check in with yourself about whether this is a journey you want to continue. What would be the benefit of this? you ask. Sometimes we forget that we have choices in many of our circumstances in life. By reminding yourself that this is what you *want* to be doing, you'll likely feel greater empowerment and resolve.

Accentuate the Positive

You know how incredibly uplifting and encouraging it is when someone notices what you're doing and expresses appreciation? Well, it's no different for the man in your life. Feeling gratitude for him also makes you feel good. Instead of looking out for what he does "wrong," focus on what he does "right." Choose the same two days a week (so you won't forget!) to write down one thing about him that brings up gratitude. And remember to say "thank you" or comment on his many endearing qualities.

Play the "Know My Partner" Game

Back in the 1970s, there was a popular television quiz show called *The Newlywed Game.* Contestants tried to guess their partners' preferences, and winners were rewarded with a great vacation, a living room set, or a year's supply of frozen dinners. Well, this is a quiz just like it—without the cameras and competition, and the only prize you get is satisfaction. Even better: You take it privately—just the two of you. In this version you needn't be married either. If you keep your answers honest, you'll discover not only just how much you really know about each other, but how much more there's still to learn. Make up at least ten questions in advance. Don't get too deep. This is supposed to be lighthearted fun. Here are some examples:

1. My partner's favorite TV show is _____.
2. When we go out to eat, my partner is most likely to want these types of cuisines: _____, _____, or _____.
3. If your partner was a cartoon character, which one would he/she be?
4. What did your partner get you for your birthday last year?
5. Who is the safer driver?
6. How many cousins does your partner have?
7. What's your mate's favorite restaurant?
8. What would be your partner's dream vacation?

CHAPTER EIGHT

Forgiving the Past

❖

Without forgiveness, there's no future.

—FROM *EXPLORING FORGIVENESS*
BY DESMOND TUTU

Amaya and Ben, both in their thirties, have been dating for three years. Afraid of his vulnerability yet feeling increasingly needy, Ben started reacting irritably whenever his girlfriend was around. He picked fights with Amaya, ignored her calls, said hurtful things to push her away, and eventually as the distance grew greater, broke up with her. But with time on his own to think about what had gone down, Ben admitted to himself it was the intimacy and possibility of getting hurt that was really at the deep root of his actions. Along with this insight came a desire to work out his underlying issues. With help from a therapist, he began to focus on understanding his reaction and learning how to release fear and open his heart.

A few months later and while still in therapy, he asked Amaya to forgive him. He knew this much: Nothing was worse than losing her forever. He desperately wants to be back in her arms. But Amaya is having a hard time letting go of the pain and anger over Ben's hurtful actions. She doesn't like the bitterness, anger, and revenge fantasies flooding her brain and wants to be able to forgive him. But *how*?

I've included a chapter on forgiveness at this point in the book, not because you're necessarily feeling more connected and emotionally available to each other, or even that you "should" be. Your renewal is unique to your relationship and *you* have to determine when the timing feels right. But if you decide to remain together and move toward greater communion, forgiveness is essential. Couples who try to move forward while still tethered to anger and resentment are basically running on a treadmill. They're going through the motions, but not really getting anywhere. The fact is this: *If you make a commitment to hold on to your relationship, you can't hold on to your resentment.* You can choose one, but not both.

What may not be so clear at this point is whether you're ready for a close relationship if resentment is still lingering. Well, you don't have to know yet. The key, in my view, is to make a commitment to work toward one, while trying to let go of the other. If you want your relationship to heal and for it to be its best, then forgiving is a must. Resentments can easily rip a connection apart or prevent it from re-forming. If you have, in fact, come to realize you just can't forgive him and move beyond the hurts of the past, then it may be a clear sign to let the relationship go. Either way, the first step is to come to a resolution: Move toward the direction of forgiveness—or just move on.

Let me stress this again: sitting somewhere in the middle, bitter and distant, is not an option.

. . .

Another important step in the forgiveness practice is to recognize that, in many instances, it's a two-way street. Of course, this isn't true for all couples; there are plenty of cases where there is a clear transgressor. But I suggest you hold open the possibility that your partner may also be clinging to acrimony and also have some forgiving of his own to do. Also keep in mind forgiveness isn't only directed toward super-dramatic, thunderbolt-from-the-sky kinds of events. The list of grievances can build up over time for small hurts or minor slights.

It isn't even necessary for either one of you to have done anything "wrong." When it comes to hurt, perception is all that matters. An action that one person could easily blow off might deeply upset and hurt someone else. And here's an even trickier part: At some level it doesn't really matter whether the hurt "makes sense." The emotional pain is a fact. It's also true while some people can forgive a particular action, others would find it intolerable to extend an olive branch over the same issue.

Keeping all this in mind, here's what I'm *not* going to do:

• Tell you which actions do or don't deserve your forgiveness.
• Make a case that if you achieve forgiveness you should stay in your relationship.

But I *am* going to:

• Support working toward forgiveness so you can become happier as an individual.
• Help you let go of resentment if you've decided to stay with your mate.

The Past Can Still Hurt

Getting to forgiveness can be a challenge. There are myriad feelings swirling around you and your relationship, and it can be difficult to wade through them all. So many questions to be answered: Can I get over the hurt? I know that forgetting is impossible—memories can't be wiped away—but can I forgive him? Does he *deserve* to be forgiven?

We'll take it one question at a time. First, let's acknowledge that you have been hurt. Your partner said or did something that hurt you. Why did he do it? Did he mean to hurt you? Will you be able to forgive him? Should you? The hard part is getting past the pain in order to view the situation with a bit more objectivity.

Have you ever scraped your knee badly? I mean, *really* badly? It hurts. I remember running a marathon, and when I was about a mile and a half from the finish line, like the graceful gazelle that I am, I tripped over my own feet and I suddenly became intimate friends with the pavement. With gravel embedded in my hands and knees and blood streaming down, I braced myself through the pain and went on to finish the race. But in that moment of falling, I was only focused on the very painful result of the fall and the seconds taken off my marathon time. In those immediate moments, I was completely unconcerned with what caused me to fall, only the damage that was done.

This is a lot like what happens when we get emotionally hurt. When you're personally impacted by something, such as your guy's wrongdoing, your mind tends to focus on how badly you feel. Most likely you won't be considering what caused the misdeed in the first place. But if you can take a step back and wait to think about what caused the hurt, you'll be more likely to consider the entire picture of cause and effect, and thus you might be able to decide if forgiveness is warranted.

Getting hurt is not a rare occurrence. Almost half (42 percent) of us have been badly hurt in a relationship. Twenty percent say they suffered in an existing relationship due to a previous relationship. But what if you were to imagine a situation in which either you were hurt by your mate or you did the hurting, which reality would leave you feeling sadder? Over one hundred couples were asked this very question during one study. The couples were followed over ten weeks during which time researchers checked in every two weeks to see when any transgressions were committed. The study revealed several enlightening results:

- We tend to imagine we would feel sadder if we commit the transgression rather than if our partner does.
- We're right. We actually do feel sadder when we're the transgressor.
- We tend to imagine our partners would feel sadder if they were hurt by a transgression—rather than if they had been the transgressor.

We're wrong. According to the study, everyone experiences greater hurt in the transgressor role. So chances are, if he's done you wrong, he's hurting even more than you. And that's probably a surprising and huge point to digest because of how badly you are feeling.

I know it's especially challenging to consider your partner's suffering if you've endured long-term emotional neglect or pain. The task of forgiveness can be exceedingly hard and ultimately its success may depend on the underlying strength and resiliency of your relationship. Even if your partner apologizes sincerely, it won't necessarily be easy to accept his overture if your relationship is on shaky ground.

And what if he has done something hurtful but you haven't heard the words "I'm sorry"? Does that mean he's not deeply upset about what he's done? If this is something you have experienced, keep in mind that some people are just better at apologizing than others and sometimes we avoid addressing issues head-on out of a sense of shame. So maybe he's feeling too ashamed to say he's sorry. And as hard as this may be to imagine, he may not even realize that he's hurt you.

If someone is truly sorry, we may understandably be more likely to forgive them than if we know they are not. Unfortunately, it can be challenging to tell the difference between indifference, shame, and a simple lack of awareness. For example, let's say that your partner lied to you to get out of a charity or work function that you asked him to attend with you. Consider that shame involves a desire to hide and cover up the mistake. People who feel ashamed are less likely to apologize than people who feel guilt, which involves a greater tendency to apologize and make amends. But a person who has a total lack of remorse may also not apologize. Similarly, if he doesn't know that he did anything to hurt you, he certainly won't apologize.

So what are we left to do? How do we know how he feels? Your only choice may be to talk with him about what happened and your reaction to it, and see how he responds. His reaction may tip your scale of forgiveness in one direction or another. When you share with him what happened and how you felt, you may even realize that he is completely unaware of your hurt feelings or that there was any harm done. The only way to know is to be honest and talk with him. Later on in this chapter, we'll go over how you can maximize the odds that you'll have a constructive conversation with your partner and be in a place to decide whether you want to let resentment go.

Depending on the severity of the wound, forgiveness can be quite challenging. As C. S. Lewis once said, "Everyone says forgiveness is a lovely idea, until they have something to forgive." And in the end, you may decide not to forgive. But if you can cultivate this ability to have empathy and care even when you've been wronged by your partner (again, assuming you are motivated to remain in the relationship), you'll be better able to let go of resentment and to communicate in more constructive ways. This will move you toward healing and strengthening your bond.

Forgiveness for the Right Reasons

Honestly, if I had a dollar for every person who has equated forgiveness with giving a partner a "pass" and saying that what happened was "okay" or "not really so serious," I'd be rich. And this is unfortunate because neither response is beneficial. Forgiveness doesn't excuse an action. It doesn't mean it was okay. You can forgive and still know your guy did something wrong.

The story I'm about to tell you is a true one and helps describe my point. It involves Gary Weinstein, a man who lost his wife and two sons in a drunk-driving accident. The drunk driver was Tom Wellinger. In court, Wellinger asked the grieving husband and father if he could ever forgive him. In return, Weinstein asked a profoundly powerful question: "Can you forgive yourself?"

TAKE A MOMENT

✧

It's a good idea to take a deep breath here and devote a few quiet moments to contemplation. Forgiveness tends to open slowly, petal by petal. You've been familiar with the hurt you are carrying, and now you've learned he may be feeling pain as well. Considering this, I'm going to ask you to take a break before reading further and reflect for a few minutes on the following:

• How much you care for him

• What you love about your relationship

• A time when *you* transgressed in some way and hoped for forgiveness from him

At the end of this chapter, you'll be offered an exercise to help you explore these issues further.

Keep in mind: It's highly doubtful that Weinstein condones what happened in any way. But as this example illustrates, you can make a choice to accept the reality of an event without excusing it. In this case, Gary Weinstein forgave Tom Wellinger despite undoubtedly being highly aware of the profound wrong of the loss of his entire family. So forgiveness does not involve pretending that no harm was done. In fact, it's quite the opposite. When we choose to forgive, we make a conscientious decision to accept the reality of what happened without excusing it, and without allowing resentment to burn within us, which only cultivates the stress and pain we carry. And remember, it's also true that your choice to forgive and your decision to remain in the relationship are related, yet separate, choice points. You can decide to acknowledge that a wrong was done and then focus on using it to learn, heal, and grow as a couple. Or you may choose to forgive to spare yourself the pain of resentment, but decide that because of what occurred you cannot trust your partner again. You could also choose not to forgive and remain with your partner, holding on to a bitter wound. I completely respect your right to decide what will be the most authentic choice for you, but I would respectfully caution you against the last option. It leaves you with a painful lack of resolution and closure in any direction you turn: no ability to move forward united with trust and no way of healing from the acrimony.

As an incentive, it may be helpful to learn that true forgiveness can also be a healing balm within you. Research has pointed to its mental and physical benefits. When one spouse takes forgiving steps toward the other for a past hurt, blood pressure actually lowers in both partners. How long did it take for blood pressure to go down? Just forty minutes! It's also been shown to boost mental health and well-being, though not directly. Instead, it looks something like this:

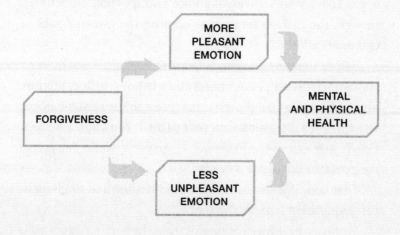

What's more, forgiveness may also lower your pain—and not just the emotional kind. According to a study of sixty-one subjects who suffer chronic back pain, those who are more likely to forgive were also more likely to report lower levels of pain. This led researchers to conclude "a relationship appears to exist between forgiveness and important aspects of living with persistent pain." Forgiveness is good for us, both emotionally and physically.

The Power of Communication

Thus far, we've been talking about forgiveness only as a solitary journey—a path of introspection and personal reflection. And it can be at times. Let's say after a hard day at work, your guy gets snappy and voices a slew of hurtful comments, on par with the Critic, needling you about the mess in the living room, the food you worked hard to prepare, and how you haven't gone out together for a long time. Instead of stewing over it, you forgive him, justify it by telling yourself he's had a bad day, and let it go. That's your individual choice and it's cool. Sometimes, though, the path to forgiveness requires the give-and-take of communication.

Before I go any further, it bears repeating: If you're in an abusive relationship, communication is not worth exploring. There are certain transgressions that point to the need for an exit strategy, not a discussion with your partner. You know your relationship. If any of the following suggestions would put you in danger, *don't attempt to try them.*

That said, if you're working toward healing and forgiveness, communication is a valuable tool.

To foster healthier communication, be sure to watch your

delivery. The way a couple communicates sets the stage for the success of forgiveness. To do that effectively:

- Trust your partner wants to make amends.
- Stay calm.
- Take your partner's perspective into account and reflect it back. Say something like "I know that you weren't trying to hurt me."
- Show your partner that you recognize how his situation could have led to the transgression. For example, you might tell him that you know he's had a lot on his plate lately.
- Try to convey an emotion of sadness rather than anger. Often, when someone hurts us, the surface emotion is anger, but the underlying real emotion is sadness. Convey the more vulnerable emotion that you feel.

Take some advice from the police in the old TV show *Dragnet* and use "Just the facts." Describe the events that led to your hurt as you understand them. Resist the urge to add any interpretation to it that could be inaccurate. For example, "When you didn't call me to let me know you would be home several hours late from work, I felt so worried and hurt" states the specific behavior of concern and does not draw any conclusions about why the call from work didn't happen. In contrast, "When you casually decided to forget about me and carelessly disregarded how worried you knew I'd be, I felt so hurt" contains the assumption about what the partner was thinking and feeling. The challenge is that not only could these assumptions be wrong, but their inherent cynicism is likely to put most people on the defensive, reducing the odds of an effective interaction.

Also, remember the "I" statements you learned earlier and use them.

Forgiving Yourself

Guilt is one of the most gut-wrenching burdens you can carry. Perhaps you ache over those cruel words you spat out in a rage at your partner that one night, intending to wound him, yet ultimately wounding yourself in the process. Or maybe you reproach yourself for offenses that were more subtle or drawn out, like all of the times you took him for granted. And, if you're like most people, you even have the capacity to harbor remorse when there was no misdeed at all, such as guilt for having had a happy, fortunate childhood while he did not. You can spend your whole life beating yourself up and stewing in self-loathing over a wrong you've committed. Or you may spend your lifetime trying to atone for what happened by denying yourself uplifting experiences or by punishing yourself in some other way.

In fact, according to one study, the desire to atone can be so great that people will self-inflict physical pain to make it happen. In this study, people were asked to write about a time when they committed a hurtful deed and were feeling guilty, a time when they felt sadness, or a time when they felt neutral. Then everyone was asked to give themselves electric shocks. Each participant could decide how intense the shocks would be.

The study results showed people who were asked to write about their guilt-ridden actions gave themselves bigger electric shocks compared to folks who were writing about the other two topics. Tellingly, those who gave themselves the most powerful shocks also felt the most unburdened of their guilt afterward. Guilt creates a compelling need to punish ourselves to "balance the scales."

In line with this dynamic, you might also believe if you forgive yourself you'll undeservedly be let off the hook. But this isn't true. What you can do is feel upset with yourself for a wrong you've committed, and then without denying your wrongdoing, realize you can't go back in time and change anything. This will help you accept responsibility for your mistake, let go of self-loathing, and move forward.

In my work as a therapist, I've found there are two simple yet powerful questions you can ask yourself:

1. *"How long do I think I deserve to be punished for what happened?"* This provokes a lot of thought and reflection. It highlights the reality that the past can't be changed, and self-punishment is a self-imposed sentence with a self-defeating outcome.

2. *"What have I learned from my mistake?"* By reflecting on how you can make something good come from your error, you take a sure step toward changing the future. It can lead you to help others, improve yourself, and enhance your relationship.

It turns out self-forgiveness isn't just good for you as an individual, but it's healing for your partnership too. When we forgive ourselves, we feel happier in our relationship. Not only that, but when we forgive ourselves and let go of thinking about ourselves in antagonistic ways, our partner is also happier in the relationship.

But this strategy isn't foolproof. Although you can forgive yourself for your misdeeds and let go of guilt, you can't make your partner do the same for himself. As the old adage goes: You can take a horse to water, but you can't make him drink it. However, if you hold out refreshing, clean water, he's more likely to drink than if you offer muddy, toxic water or no water at all.

You can try:

- Extending an olive branch
- Sincerely expressing forgiveness for his wrongdoing
- Embracing the desire to move forward

If you really want to build a deeper connection and a happier relationship, guilt will need to be released on both sides.

This chapter isn't about pretending something hurtful didn't happen or that it was okay; it's about a willingness to let go of resentment while embracing hopefulness about the future. If you don't achieve forgiveness, there's a good chance you'll leak out comments about the past that will contaminate the relationship as it is now. What's more, whether you stay together or not, holding a grudge can swallow you up with bitterness or a sense of injustice. Below are a few exercises to help you let go and truly forgive.

Wear the Other Shoe

When you're angry or hurt about something your partner did, it can be easy to forget you make mistakes too. Taking time to recall your own wrongdoings counteracts this common defense. Make a list of five times when your mate forgave you, or when you did something that was a mistake in the relationship. To get the most out of this exercise, write down:

1. The biggest mistakes you made in your relationship

2. The times he forgave you (or if he doesn't know about a particular transgression, the response you would hope to receive if he did)

Switch Focus

When you're upset with a loved one, the transgression can eclipse all his other acts of kindness, thoughtfulness, and generosity. If you can step back from how you're feeling now and remember his many good deeds, it allows you to see his behavior through a broader perspective. Make a list of twenty-five thoughtful and positive actions (or more) your guy has done or repeatedly does for you. This can be a great way to zoom in on his pluses and help to put bad behavior to bed.

CHAPTER NINE

Healing Your Emotional and Physical Self

✦

Happiness depends on ourselves.

—ARISTOTLE

And now we've reached the "end" of our excursion together. I put "end" in quotation marks because working on relationships and all aspects of ourselves is never truly over. That's what our lives are about—finding ways to be connected and content; relieving anxiety and stress (including the kind that can emerge when we take chances in our life and step toward what we want); turning down the volume on worry, self-criticism, and dissatisfaction; and experiencing flow and pleasure, perhaps even ecstasy. There's no simple way to get there, no snappy point-A-to-point-B formula. Just like within our individual lives, relationships at their most sublime are growing, changing, and evolving. The quest to be the best possible person and partner is never-ending and ripe with potential for growth and beauty, even as you face challenges. With this in mind, my sincerest hope is that you successfully achieve restorative transformation both in yourself and in your relationship.

If you haven't found connection with your mate, please don't be discouraged. When we first started working together, I wrote about the possibility your partner may not open up and become more available, but it's one thing to acknowledge this possibility, and another not to experience improvement. If you still have some hope and want to keep trying, hold on to that. Just because he hasn't opened in the time you've worked with this book, it doesn't mean he won't become more available. Try not to let what you've read here be the be-all and end-all of your decision to stay or leave. Let your own gut decide that for you.

Regardless of where you may find yourself right now— whether you've forged a stronger bond, or he hasn't opened up but you want to keep trying, or you've decided to let go of your unsatisfying relationship—you've been through major changes. And this process can take a lot out of you. No matter where you're standing in the moment, this chapter is for you. It will help you take care of yourself individually, and if your partner is more connected, offer healing techniques to experience together.

I have no doubt you probably already have healing tools in your coping toolkit. After all, you've been through some real challenges in your relationship, and I'm willing to bet that you've tackled pretty difficult situations in other aspects of your life as well. And yet here you are—still standing. So you definitely have approaches you've used that work for you. In light of these impressive self-care skills, you may find you've already tried some of the approaches I'll be suggesting. In that case, I'm going to validate what you're doing already; by all means, keep doing it.

But there are probably several techniques you haven't tried yet. Give them a chance. I guarantee there's still room in your toolkit for more.

Let's start with something most of us suffer with regardless of our relationship status, and that's stress.

Stepping Out of Stress

Before rolling your eyes and muttering "Stress—what a no-brainer!," hear me out. I bring it up at the start because in my experience (and this includes clients and other mental health professionals alike) we humans are notoriously good at acknowledging the importance of stress management and notoriously bad at actually dealing with it at the level, or with the consistency, most helpful for us.

If you're already optimally dealing with your stress, good for you—and please bottle whatever you're doing and send it to me so I can give it to others and try it myself! On the other hand, if you're like most of us, you could probably handle your stress at least a little bit better than you are right now.

Stress management isn't something you either do or don't do. It's on a continuum from no stress management to optimal stress management. It takes conscious effort. And believe me, upping our capacity to take care of stress is a worthy investment of time and effort. Maybe you take walks to release tension or you relish taking relaxing bubble baths with a book, but lately you have had trouble fitting your me-time activity into your busy schedule. It may be time to recommit yourself to that de-stressing time! It pays off not just in our own well-being, but in our relationships too because stress is an intimacy killer. As you may have experienced in your own life, when people get highly stressed in their daily lives, they bring it home and take it out on their mates. For example, that meeting you had to suffer through or that stressful traffic jam that held up your commute? Those moments can limit whether or not you can be patient and understanding when you get home. And the same goes for those moments in your partner's life. This dynamic is called "stress spillover."

Also stress management and regulating your emotions will keep you around to enjoy your partner longer, because stress is not just an intimacy killer—it's a killer. As you have undoubtedly heard, stress is detrimental to our physical health. Epidemiology and psychology researchers have examined the impact of two kinds of coping strategies on our health. One of these strategies is "emotional suppression," which involves preventing yourself from expressing an emotion you're feeling. The second strategy, called "cognitive reappraisal," is a way of changing the emotion you feel in response to a touchy situation by changing the way you think about it. The study's results show use of cognitive reappraisal as a coping tool is linked with lower stress and lower resulting inflammation, whereas emotional suppression—or as it's commonly called, bottling your emotions—is associated with more stress.

What is inflammation? Quite simply, inflammation is part of our immune system's defensive reaction when our body encounters harm of some kind, such as an injury or an infection, or even stressors such as too little sleep. It is even possible for it to become chronic, however, as inflammation spurs on the body's need for further inflammation to take care of the original inflammation. It is our body's natural healing response—our personal corporeal cleanup crew. But it can get out of control, which is why it is linked to stress and coronary heart disease. By managing stress and keeping it in healthy limits, you can spare your immune system the inflammation and likely reduce your risk of heart disease, the number one cause of death in the United States, according to the CDC.

However, I don't want to oversimplify coping, because our efforts to regulate our emotions don't happen in a bubble. It occurs in a rich, cultural context, and our culture influences us. A recent study compared the same coping strategies we just talked about—emotional suppression and cognitive reappraisal—in women from Germany (an individualist culture) and in women from Turkey (a collectivist culture). The study revealed that the women from Turkey had greater flexibility than those from Germany in how they coped, using emotional suppression and cognitive reappraisal as needed. So, as the study's researchers observed, emotional suppression may not be harmful in and of itself, as people from collectivist cultures may see constructive results in their everyday lives from suppressing their emotions at times, such as feeling fewer saddening emotions, a lessened sense of loneliness, and a decreased amount of counterproductive attitudes and beliefs. From this study, we can see that there is not a one-size-fits-all way to cope. Arguably, our culture, our personal preferences, and our unique circumstances impact the strategies we choose to cope. A coping tool that works for one person may not work for another, and we won't want to use the same coping strategy at all times, across all situations. For example, if you find heat relaxing and you're fortunate enough to live in a home and have access to running water, then a shower or bath could be just what you need. Or perhaps your family raised you with the value that personal problems need to be kept within the family. You agree with this, but at a time when you're highly upset, you also happen to be at work. In this case, you might choose emotional suppression during the day, and then reach out for support from your family later. The key is in having flexibility with our coping tools and being willing, like a painter filling a canvas, to swap out our brushes to fit our needs and the situation at hand.

And while I'm talking about how we think about events, have you ever heard the saying "The devil is in the details"? The big moments in life, such as a death in the family, job loss, or moving, are much easier to spot as triggers for stress overload. It's the daily hassles of life (rush-hour traffic, anyone?) that can fly under our radar. But they matter too. One study's results suggest when we have stronger emotional reactions to minor everyday hassles, it predicts more emotional distress and an increase in odds we'll struggle with depression ten years down the road.

These results are in line with how our minds operate. Our brain gets better at whatever we repeatedly do, and what we repeatedly do becomes its default. It's like a hiker who comes to three possible directions to take. One is a well-worn path that many other hikers have clearly taken. The second is a weak grassy indent where a few people have ventured. The third is just meadow, and a place where no one has walked. If you were that hiker, would you opt for the first well-worn path? I certainly would. That's exactly how our brains work, with the result that our habits, reactions, and ways of thinking become more entrenched the longer we do them. This is the reason why working with emotional reactions and learning to soothe yourself when encountering even minor stressors is important. With diligent practice and repetition, you'll become a master at it and your brain will learn to choose the calmer, more even path more habitually.

Hang a New Frame in Your Mind

Now I'm no interior designer, but in my humble view, the right frame can transform a picture and do wonders for it. It can change the whole tone of the photo, and the right frame can change the tone of how we experience stress. In a study on the effect of how we perceive stress, people received information about stress that portrayed it either as being damaging or as being a robust force for self-improvement. The results showed that when people viewed stress from a self-enhancement perspective, their bodies released only a moderate amount of cortisol (the body's stress hormone), which also suggests that they actually felt less psychological stress. And this from just suggesting a different way of thinking about stress. In other words, whatever we think stress is, we have the power to make this come true. Are your deadlines at work making you nuts? Try to think of them as a way to prove your value in the job and as a step in the direction of a promotion instead of a barrier or an annoyance. Your little one's hectic schedule making you feel like you live in your car? You might decide to reflect on the reasons that motivate you to do this. For example, you might think about the hope you hold that your child will benefit developmentally from these activities. So the next time you encounter stress, look at it as a way to make you a stronger, wiser, better person, and you can turn down the dial on stress.

Steer Toward Happiness

There are many things in life that we can't control, but thankfully one of the things that we can determine is the choice to move toward happiness. Cultivating uplifting emotions is one of the best ways that we can nurture ourselves and manage stress. So how do we do it?

Here are a few ways to boost your mood individually and as a couple:

- **Savor the enjoyable moments of life.** A researcher asked people to select two enjoyable moments in their day, and then focus on stretching out those moments to about three minutes. Examples of this would include a moment of gazing lovingly at your partner's sleeping face; noticing the wind brush by your skin; savoring the light, warm taste of green tea; relishing the texture of your favorite food; or enjoying the lilting sound of classical music.

- **Commit random, and planned, acts of kindness.** There really is something magical about simply being kind to others, isn't there? Happiness research tells us that the types of good deeds we can do are as varied as our imagination. We can do something minor and relatively immediate, like greet someone and hold open the door for them, or a little more involved, such as volunteering your time at a local animal shelter or helping a relative repair a broken fixture in their home. If you buy your partner a present, it will boost your happiness too, even more than if you bought a gift for yourself. Interestingly, researchers find that even just reflecting on times when you've been good to others leaves you feeling more cheerful.

- **Strike up a conversation.** People often mistakenly assume that they'll be better off by themselves while riding public transportation and not chatting it up with strangers, but in reality, we enjoy talking more. This makes sense considering that having a connected social circle boosts our cheerfulness in life. So the next time you're out and about, try envisioning people not as strangers, but as potential good friends you just haven't made yet. The cool thing is, even if they remain strangers, talk with them anyway. Just a simple hello or a smile is all it takes. You'll be happier in the long run for it.

- **Sing a happy song and try to lift your spirits.** One study asked: What would happen if people tried to intentionally lift their spirits while they listened to music? Over the course of two weeks, people tried five times to boost their mood with music in the background. Some of the people in the study were asked to try to feel happier while they listened to music with an upbeat sound, and it was only in that situation that happiness-boosting worked. If you want to feel happier, listening to cheerful tunes will help. If you want a great modern example, try checking out "Happy" by Pharrell Williams or "Uptown Funk" by Mark Ronson.

- **Accentuate the positive.** Even back in the 1940s, Johnny Mercer and the Pied Pipers really knew what they were singing about when they encouraged people to "Accentuate the positive . . ." The beauty of this advice is that not only can we accentuate the positive for ourselves, but we can accentuate the positive for our partners when they share something happy and joyous with us. It's a process called "capitalization," and it happens when we share good news with someone and they react in a very delighted, engaged, excited, and animated way. Their enthusiastic response fills our good-news joy balloon with air, whereas a muted or disheartening response has a way of letting the air out of that balloon, deflating some of the merriment we were feeling about our good fortune. What's funny is that we might not even be conscious of how we respond to our partner's good news. You might just say, "Oh, that's nice," after good news is shared and move right on to the next topic, completely unaware that you might have just burst your partner's bubble or denied him a swaggering moment to share his pride. He may have been looking forward to telling you all day! We tend to think about the

importance of being there for our partner in bad times, but
being there for him in good times is at least as important, if not
more so. The next time he shares good news, genuinely celebrate
it and show your sincere enthusiasm. Not only will it give him a
happiness boost, but it will for you too—fun!

- **Get random (with rewards anyway).** The couple that shares
  together stays together, and one of the many aspects of life that
  you can share involves joint tasks, projects, and goals. It could
  be a shared financial goal, a relationship improvement goal, a
  personal improvement goal (e.g., eat healthier foods), or a project you decide to take on, such as a home renovation, learning
  a new skill, or starting a shared business. It's completely up
  to you both—there are no right or wrong answers. But whatever you do, as you pursue a shared task or goal, don't forget to
  give yourselves a reward for benchmarks reached from time to
  time. I am a huge fan of people rewarding themselves. What
  kind of rewards to give yourselves? Well, according to one
  study, you are better off giving yourself rewards from random
  categories. Their results showed that when people separate possible rewards for tasks into various categories, their motivation
  to complete the task is heightened, even when the reward categories are totally made up and random. So call the rewards
  you give yourselves anything you want. Say if you are learning
  a language together listening to CDs, reward yourselves with
  a celebratory root beer float every time you complete a lesson.
  Hell, get festive and make up funny names for the type of
  rewards you get. Call it a One-More-Step-to-Fluency Float if
  you want! It will keep you both motivated and you'll have fun.

- **Make time for play.** Who said playing is just for kids? Speaking
  for myself, I'm having way more fun playing as an adult than I

did when I was a kid. I wasn't against playing as a child, but as an adult we have so many more possibilities, don't we? Think about it. There's no curfew, no parents telling us what to do (sorry—I love you, Mom and Dad!), we're more able to get around on our own, and we can leave the neighborhood if we want. However, adulthood is also a time of increasing responsibilities that we didn't have as a kid. No mortgage, no kids to raise, no pets that we assume total responsibility for, and no job (and no, second-grade homework does not count as a job!). When the time that we can play the best and the time that we have the most responsibilities coincide, many of us just stop playing. We look at our lives and believe our best years are behind us, but that's usually because we're looking back to a time when we tended to do, what? Oh, you see where I'm going: play! The reality is that our best years aren't behind us, or at least they don't have to be if we don't let them. If we reinvest our energy into having fun like we used to, give ourselves permission to throw caution and concern about what others think to the wind, and allow ourselves to be downright silly, we can create a life where our best years are before us. Buy a snow tube and tackle that hill together, go camping and play hide-and-seek in the woods, go miniature golfing and make up your own scoring system, make absurd movies with your smartphone, go dancing at a club even though you feel like you have no earthly right being there. Why not? Go wild! Allowing yourself to have fun will help you build a better life not only for yourself, but for your partner and your relationship too. The enjoyable times couples share enhance the overall quality of their relationships.

• **Tickle your funny bone.** I have to tip my hat to stand-up comedians. You really do make people's lives better. Few things have the power to simultaneously bring people together, break the social ice or tension, lift people's spirits, and ease stress as well as humor. Humor is so powerful that, in my view, it's an essential component of a healthy, well-lived life. Research shows that humor that is not derogatory to others or self-deprecating is quite good for you! So crack cheerful jokes and make light with abandon; just be sure to do it in a way that leaves you and others feeling all warm and fuzzy inside!

• **Mind your p's and q's . . . and your verb usage.** Our life is essentially a story, and language frames our thoughts. The words we use affect how we process events in our lives, and believe it or not, the language we use to recount a past event affects how we feel in the here and how. One study examined how our use of imperfective verbs and perfective verbs to describe beneficial or upsetting experiences in the past affected our mood later. Now don't worry if you didn't retain your middle school grammar lessons: When we describe a past action or event using the imperfective tense, it has a spirit of being ongoing and continuous. The sentence "I was rejoicing" is an example. In contrast, when we describe an event using the perfective tense, we describe it in a way that shows our action or the event ended. "I rejoiced" is an example. The study showed that when people described past positive or beneficial experiences as if they were still going on, they experienced greater happiness compared to people who talked about the events as if they had already ended. The opposite was true when the subjects talked about their negative experiences. So when you're recalling the past, talk about the good times in a way that reflects that event continuing over time, and talk about the unhappy times in a way that puts the period on them. "I was dancing that whole night at the wedding," instead of "I danced," and "I cried when I got the bad news," instead of "I was crying." Language matters.

Sometimes all it takes to boost your mood is to decide to boost it and take action. Your decision to be happier and practicing these tips will reduce your stress and—perhaps more importantly—it will be fun!

Go Easy on Yourself

Striving toward becoming the best we can be is a beautiful way to live. But let me add a cautionary note: Even though striving toward self-improvement can be invigorating, inspiring, and buoyant, it can also have a dark side. It all depends on your inner voice. If you have a reasonable, accepting, and sweet inner coach motivating you toward reaching your goals and your coach offers comfort: hallelujah. It means those times you fall short, you'll still feel supported and in balance. But if your inner coach is a rigid perfectionist, exacting and harsh, then you're probably going to end up feeling bad about yourself, and also set yourself up for failure. People who create personal standards that are virtually unreachable and who give themselves a hard time if they don't meet those standards are more likely to develop depression over time. If you find yourself with a not-so-nice coach on your shoulder, shrug her off.

The view that you have to adhere to unattainable standards or else you're a failure doesn't define reality unless you give it permission to do so. If your inner voice sounds like Judge Judy, put the gavel down and hand over a sentence to lighten up.

Here are other ways to get a confidence boost:

- Remember that simply thinking something doesn't make it so. Your thoughts are just that—thoughts, not necessarily reality. So if you can remember that and give your thoughts a little less credibility, they'll have less power over you. To illustrate this point, I often encourage my clients to imagine me as a six-foot giraffe. Despite all their mental efforts, I haven't transformed into a giraffe yet.

- From personal and clinical experience, I'm aware that many people hate writing for lots of reasons. But writing down your thoughts is inexpensive and simple to do and can be accomplished almost anywhere. Expressive writing in particular is a form in which you record your emotions, thoughts, and experiences around a particular emotional event or situation. A lot of research has been done on the benefits of expressive writing, and although not all researchers come to exactly the same conclusions, they agree it's a healing exercise, which is why I encouraged you to keep a journal from the beginning of this journey. One study suggested that expressive writing can refill our emotional gas tank when we're depleted. In this study, people engaged in expressive writing over the course of three days. Those who had a tendency to worry about others and take care of others at the expense of themselves, *and* who also had low levels of social support, went on to feel less discouraging emotion and anxiety after their expressive writing exercise. The content of what they wrote about, whether it was neutral, happy, or bleak, didn't matter. It was healing regardless. And the benefits of expressive writing don't just stop with your own well-being. It can also affect your relationship. When partners write about their most profound, authentically held thoughts and feelings about their relationship they're more likely to stay with their mate. The pen is mighty!

. . .

Well, there is no doubt that you've put an astonishing amount of effort into your relationship over the course of these chapters. Always keep in mind that even though you've been focused on repairing your relationship, the most central figure here is actually you! After all, you are your own best tool in the relationship and this is your life, right? So it feels fitting that we end with a chapter that is all about you, and the myriad ways you can treat yourself the way you deserve to be treated—superbly! We explored strategies such as stepping out of stress, switching your frame of mind, choosing happiness and seeing it in the little moments, making time to play and laugh, and using our language to uplift ourselves. We also covered strategies that you and your partner can use to heal together. You might gel with some of them immediately, while other ones could seem like a stretch. That's great! Allow yourself to experiment with the tools in this chapter, practicing them in your daily life and discovering which ones fit best for you. As you move forward, I hope you'll know that no matter what happens in your relationship, you will never regret the work you put into your own well-being and personal growth. Trust me!

I wish you every happiness . . .

Get Your Mojo Working

If you do nothing else, exercise. There's an ever-growing body of research supporting the mental-health benefits of exercise and its stress-relieving, anxiety-reducing, mood-enhancing benefits. You can exercise on your own or with your partner. FYI: Studies show motivation stays stronger when you make a pact to exercise with others.

Make a list of five to ten kinds of physical activities you enjoy. This could be walking, running, swimming, basketball, biking, weight lifting, etc.

Set a plan for how often and how long you'll exercise and where. The American College of Sports Medicine recommends 150 minutes of moderate exercise per week (approximately thirty minutes of exercise five days per week). If you can't make this commitment, pick the number of days per week that you can. With any luck it will be at least three days.

Set Playdates

When you're stressed about your relationship, it can be hard to pull away from a cycle of bad vibes. Having fun together is part of the antidote. For this exercise, sit down with your mate and agree on ten fun things you'd like to do together. You can experiment with each other's interests, or try something completely new. If you're running out of ideas, ask friends or look online. Then make sure you enjoy at least one playdate a week.

Affirmations

Affirmations can help you approach problems with more open-ness and zeal. Personally created affirmations are optimal but the ones listed below are also strong and effective. Here are a few to get you started:

* *I care about what my mate needs.*

* *I will listen without judging.*

* *I will be my best self.*

Final Note

❖

It's hard to believe we've reached the end of this book. Truly, it's been profoundly rewarding for me to be able to accompany you while you explore intimacy and connection. It takes fierce courage to devote oneself to personal growth.

I wrote this book because I'm unendingly passionate about being present for people as they strive to make their relationships and their overall lives better. Because of this sincere caring for what happens in your relationship and your life, I'll be thinking about you and earnestly hoping you find genuine, deep, passionate, and secure love. You certainly deserve it.

As you move forward beyond this book, you're welcome to contact me. I'd love to hear from you. My website is DrHollyParker.com.

I also have a blog. You can post comments there, or you

can submit a question to my "Ask Dr. Holly" column on my website.

No matter how we communicate, my goal is to have a conversation with my readers, and I look forward to hearing from you.

ACKNOWLEDGMENTS

It's hard to find words to express the full gratitude I feel to those who guided me along the way through this remarkable journey. I want to begin by offering you, Dear Reader, profound gratitude for reading this book; you took the time to allow me into your life, which is humbling and amazing. Dr. Shelley Carson, my dear friend and colleague, *thank you* for believing in me and throwing my name into the wind; this book would not be happening without you. Thank you to Dr. Julie Silver, who laid the foundation for this book and took a chance on me, generously offering your time, advice, and help. To Linda Konner, my incredible agent, I am indebted to you for your perseverance and dedication in moving this book forward, and for your wonderful personality and kindness. To Denise Silvestro and the Berkley Publishing Group, I appreciate your diligent guidance. It's a pleasure and an honor to work with you. To Robin Westen, thank you for your teaching and the many lessons that you passed on to me; you stretched me as a writer and helped cultivate my voice. I really want to thank my buddies and my parents for all of their excited cheerleading, and for lovingly staying on my case to hang out and play. I know I needed a good kick in the butt from time to time! I also want to give a hearty, loving "WOOF!" to Romeo, the wonder writing companion; thank you for sharing Guille, teasing me, and being such a devoted writing assistant. We miss you. And Guille, I am infinitely grateful to you for your unending patience, love, support, and passion for me and for this book throughout the many long hours of writing . . . and the late-night glare of the computer monitor.

RESOURCES

This section is intended to help you if you're looking for additional places to turn. However, if you still can't find the resources you want here, I strongly encourage you to look further: Search engines, discussion boards, your primary-care provider, friends, clergy, and local psychotherapy offices are great places to start.

1. **To learn more about therapy, whether it is right for you, and how to find a therapist:**

"Psychology Help Center," American Psychological Association: www.apa.org /helpcenter/index.aspx

2. **To find workshops, books, and DVDs for couples:**

"Books, DVDs, Workshops," The Gottman Institute: www.gottman.com/shop
The International Centre for Excellence in Emotionally Focused Therapy: www .iceeft.com

3. **To get help if you are physically unsafe and are afraid of your partner:**

The National Domestic Violence Hotline: 1-800-799-7233 (SAFE) or www.the hotline.org

4. **To get help and information if you are being emotionally abused by your partner, or if you're wondering whether you are being abused:**

"Domestic Violence and Abuse," HelpGuide.org: www.helpguide.org/articles /abuse/domestic-violence-and-abuse.htm

Patricia Evans, *The Verbally Abusive Relationship: How to Recognize It and How to Respond* (Avon, MA: Adams Media, 2010)

5. **If you or your partner are active-duty military or veterans, and you're interested in mental health services, including help with your relationship:**

U.S. Department of Veterans Affairs: www.mentalhealth.va.gov/index.asp

"Strengthen Your Family with Marital Counseling," Real Warriors Campaign: www.realwarriors.net/family/care/maritalcounseling.php

6. **If you're looking for ways to enhance your relationship with yourself and lift your self-esteem and self-acceptance:**

Brené Brown, *The Gifts of Imperfection: Let Go of Who You Think You're Supposed to Be and Embrace Who You Are* (Center City, MN: Hazelden, 2010)

Matthew McKay and Patrick Fanning, *Self-Esteem: A Proven Program of Cognitive Techniques for Assessing, Improving, and Maintaining Your Self-Esteem* (New York: MJF Books/Fine Communication, 2000)

7. **If you'd like to get better sleep and are looking for a range of information and resources:**

National Sleep Foundation: sleepfoundation.org

8. If you're interested in improving your nutrition habits:

The Nutrition Source, Harvard T. H. Chan School of Public Health: www.hsph .harvard.edu/nutritionsource

9. If you want to live a more active lifestyle or learn more about how physical activity can enhance your life:

"Physical Activity," Harvard Health Publications, Harvard Medical School: www.health.harvard.edu/topics/physical-activity

"Overcoming Barriers to Physical Activity," Centers for Disease Control and Prevention (February 16, 2011): www.cdc.gov/physicalactivity/everyone /getactive/barriers.html

"Tips for Getting Active," National Heart, Lung, and Blood Institute: www.nhlbi .nih.gov/health/educational/wecan/get-active/getting-active.htm

10. If you are searching for how to forgive, either your partner or yourself:

Desmond Tutu and Mpho Tutu, *The Book of Forgiving: The Fourfold Path for Healing Ourselves and Our World* (New York: Harper One, 2014)

Barton Goldsmith, "10 Simple Tools to Help You Find Forgiveness," *Psychology Today* (October 12, 2009): www.psychologytoday.com/blog/emotional -fitness/200910/10-simple-tools-help-you-find-forgiveness

Darlene Lancer, "How Do You Forgive Yourself?" PsychCentral (June 26, 2013): psychcentral.com/lib/how-do-you-forgive-yourself/00016908

Jean Lawrence, "Learning to Forgive Yourself," WebMD: www.webmd.com /balance/features/learning-to-forgive-yourself

11. For help with anxiety in relationships:

Carolyn Daitch and Lissah Lorberbaum, *Anxious in Love: How to Manage Your Anxiety, Reduce Conflict, and Reconnect with Your Partner* (Oakland, CA: New Harbinger, 2013)

Susan Heitler, "Worrying in Relationships: 3 Habits That Invite Anxiety," *Psychology Today* (April 27, 2012): www.psychologytoday.com/blog/re solution-not-conflict/201204/worrying-in-relationships-3-habits-invite- anxiety

12. For help with managing anxiety in general:

Edmund J. Bourne, *The Anxiety and Phobia Workbook* (Oakland, CA: New Harbinger, 2010)

Tamar E. Chansky, *Freeing Yourself from Anxiety: 4 Simple Steps to Overcome Worry and Create the Life You Want* (Ashland, OR: Blackstone Audio, 2012)

"Tips to Manage Anxiety and Stress," Anxiety and Depression Association of America: www.adaa.org/living-with-anxiety/managing-anxiety/tips

13. For help with managing depression:

Mark Williams, John Teasdale, Zindel Segal, and Jon Kabat-Zinn, *The Mindful Way Through Depression: Freeing Yourself from Chronic Unhappiness* (New York: Guilford Press, 2007)

William J. Knaus, *The Cognitive Behavioral Workbook for Depression: A Step-by-Step Program* (Oakland, CA: New Harbinger, 2006)

Diana Rodriguez, "10 Ways to Cope with Depression," Everyday Health: www .everydayhealth.com/depression-photos/ways-to-cope-with-depression .aspx#/slide-1

"Dealing with Depression," HelpGuide.org: www.helpguide.org/articles/depres sion/dealing-with-depression.htm

14. To help your partner who is struggling with anxiety:

"Spouse or Partner," Anxiety and Depression Association of America: www.adaa .org/finding-help/helping-others/spouse-or-partner

15. To help your partner who is struggling with depression:

"Helping a Depressed Person," HelpGuide.org: www.helpguide.org/articles /depression/helping-a-depressed-person.htm

16. If you want help with decreasing criticism toward your partner:

Susan Heitler, "Want Marriage Problems? Expect Your Spouse to Be Perfect," *Psychology Today* (May 29, 2013): www.psychologytoday.com/blog/resolu tion-not-conflict/201305/want-marriage-problems-expect-your -spouse-be-perfect

17. For help with skills to manage your emotions:

Alice Boyes, "10 Essential Emotion Regulation Skills for Adults," *Psychology Today* (April 8, 2013): www.psychologytoday.com/blog/in-practice/201304 /10-essential-emotion-regulation-skills-adults

18. For information on understanding post-traumatic stress disorder (PTSD) or helping a partner with PTSD or who survived trauma:

Aphrodite T. Matsakis, *Loving Someone with PTSD: A Practical Guide to Understanding and Connecting with Your Partner After Trauma* (Oakland, CA: New Harbinger, 2014)

National Institute of Mental Health, "Post-Traumatic Stress Disorder (PTSD)": www.nimh.nih.gov/health/topics/post-traumatic-stress-disorder-ptsd/index .shtml

19. Information on attachment:

Sue Johnson, *Hold Me Tight: Seven Conversations for a Lifetime of Love* (New York: Little, Brown, 2008)

Amir Levine and Rachel Heller, *Attached: Create Your Perfect Relationship with the Help of the Three Attachment Styles* (New York: Jeremy Tarcher, 2010)

Kendra Cherry, "Attachment Styles," About Health (March 29, 2015): psychology .about.com/od/loveandattraction/ss/attachmentstyle.htm

Kendra Cherry, "What Is Attachment Theory?" About Health (December 20, 2014): psychology.about.com/od/loveandattraction/a/attachment01.htm

20. For help with understanding and overcoming defensiveness in your relationship:

John M. Gottman, *The Relationship Cure: A Five-Step Guide to Strengthening Your Marriage, Family, and Friendships* (New York: Crown, 2002)

Heidi Grant Halvorson, "Stop Being So Defensive!" *Psychology Today* (August 17, 2010): www.psychologytoday.com/blog/the-science-success/201008/stop -being-so-defensive

Danielle B. Grossman, "In Relationships, the Worst Offense Is a Good Defense," PsychCentral: psychcentral.com/lib/in-relationships-the-worst-offense -is-a-good-defense/00013995

21. **For information and help with managing insecurity or neediness in a relationship:**

Leslie Becker-Phelps, *Insecure in Love: How Anxious Attachment Can Make You Feel Jealous, Needy, and Worried and What You Can Do About It* (Oakland, CA: New Harbinger, 2014)

Heidi Grant Halvorson, "Never Look Insecure Again," *Psychology Today* (December 11, 2012): www.psychologytoday.com/blog/the-science-success/201212/never-look-insecure-again

22. **To manage negative thoughts and resist getting hijacked by them:**

Shad Helmstetter, *What to Say When You Talk to Yourself: The Major New Breakthrough to Managing People, Yourself, and Success* (Scottsdale, AZ: Grindle Press, 1986)

Christopher K. Germer, *The Mindful Path to Self-Compassion: Freeing Yourself from Destructive Thoughts and Emotions* (New York: Guilford Press, 2009)

23. **For information on expectations in relationships:**

Mark D. White, "Expectations in Relationships: The Flip Side of Obligations," *Psychology Today* (August 26, 2010): www.psychologytoday.com/blog/maybe-its-just-me/201008/expectations-in-relationships-the-flip-side-obligations

24. **For help with tuning in to your partner's perspective:**

Andra Brosh, "Seeing Is Believing: How to Improve Your Relationships Through Perception," Intent Blog (May 31, 2013): intentblog.com/seeing-is-believing-how-to-improve-your-relationships-through-perception

25. **To increase acts of love in your relationship and make more time for each other:**

Susan Page, *Why Talking Is Not Enough: Eight Loving Actions That Will Transform Your Marriage* (San Francisco: Jossey-Bass, 2006)

Barton Goldsmith, "10 Ways to Make Your Relationship Magically Romantic," *Psychology Today* (October 30, 2010): www.psychologytoday.com/blog/emotional-fitness/201010/10-ways-make-your-relationship-magically-romantic

"Relationship Help," HelpGuide.org: www.helpguide.org/articles/relationships
/relationship-help.htm

The Ninja Wife, "50 Ways to Strengthen Your Relationship," Your Tango:
www.yourtango.com/experts/the-ninja-wife/71-ways-love-your-partner
-better

26. For help with identifying what you're feeling, and managing emotions:

Keely Savoie, "Are You Angry—or Guilty?" *Prevention* (September 27, 2012):
www.prevention.com/mind-body/emotional-health/when-you-cant
-identify-your-emotions

"Emotional Intelligence (EQ)," HelpGuide.org: www.helpguide.org/articles/
emotional-health/emotional-intelligence-eq.htm

27. For information on mindfulness and how to cultivate it, as well as mindfulness products:

Bhante Gunaratana, *Mindfulness in Plain English*, 20th Anniversary Ed. (Boston:
Wisdom Publications, 2011)

Jon Kabat-Zinn, *Wherever You Go, There You Are* (New York: Hyperion, 2005)

"Mindfulness," *Psychology Today*: www.psychologytoday.com/basics/mind
fulness

Alice Boyes, "6 Mindfulness Exercises That Each Take Less Than 1 Minute,"
Psychology Today (February 12, 2013): www.psychologytoday.com/blog/
in-practice/201302/6-mindfulness-exercises-each-take-less-1-minute

Mayo Clinic Staff, "Mindfulness Exercises," Mayo Clinic (November 10, 2015):
www.mayoclinic.org/healthy-lifestyle/consumer-health/in-depth/mindful
ness-exercises/art-20046356?reDate=23042015

28. To improve communication skills:

Jonathan Robinson, *Communication Miracles for Couples: Easy and Effective Tools
to Create More Love and Less Conflict* (Berkeley: Conari Press, 2012)

Michael P. Nichols, *Lost Art of Listening: How Learning to Listen Can Improve
Relationships*, 2nd ed. (New York: Guilford, 2009)

Matthew McKay, Patrick Fanning, and Kim Paleg, *Couple Skills: Making Your
Relationship Work* (Oakland, CA: New Harbinger, 2006)

29. For help with reducing stress:

Martha Davis, Elizabeth Robbins Eshelman, and Matthew McKay, *The Relaxation & Stress Reduction Workbook* (Oakland, CA: New Harbinger, 2008)

Jeannette Moninger, "How to Reduce Stress: 10 Relaxation Techniques to Reduce Stress on the Spot," WebMD: www.webmd.com/balance/guide /blissing-out-10-relaxation-techniques-reduce-stress-spot

30. To improve sex with your partner:

Lauren Gelman, "14 Days to Better Sex," *Prevention* (November 21, 2013): www .prevention.com/sex/better-sex/improve-your-sex-life-14-days

31. To bring more positivity and optimism into your outlook and your life:

Sonja Lyubomirsky, *The How of Happiness: A New Approach to Getting the Life You Want* (New York: Penguin, 2008)

Martin E. P. Seligman, *Learned Optimism: How to Change Your Mind and Your Life* (New York: Vintage, 2006)

Mayo Clinic Staff, "Positive Thinking: Stop Negative Self-Talk to Reduce Stress," Mayo Clinic (March 4, 2014): www.mayoclinic.org/healthy-lifestyle/stress -management/in-depth/positive-thinking/art-20043950?reDate=23042015

REFERENCES

Adams, R. D., & Baptist, J. A. (2012). Relationship maintenance behavior and adult attachment: An analysis of the actor-partner interdependence model. *The American Journal of Family Therapy, 40*, 230–244.

Ainsworth, M. D. S., Blehar, M. C., Waters, E., & Wall, S. N. (2015). *Patterns of Attachment: A Psychological Study of the Strange Situation* (Classic Ed.). New York: Psychology Press.

Ainsworth, M. D. S., & Bel, S. M. (1970). Attachment, exploration, and separation: Illustrated by the behavior of one-year-olds in a strange situation. *Child Development, 41*, 49–67.

Algoe, S. B., Fredrickson, B. L., & Gable, S. L. (2013). The social functions of the emotion of gratitude via expression. *Emotion, 13*, 605–609.

Appleton, A. A., Buka, S. L., Loucks, E. B., Gilman, S. E., & Kubzansky, L. D. (2013). Divergent associations of adaptive and maladaptive emotion regulation strategies with inflammation. *Health Psychology, 32*, 748–756.

Arens, E. A., Balkir, N., & Barnow, S. (2013). Ethnic variation in emotion regulation: Do cultural differences end where psychopathology begins? *Journal of Cross-Cultural Psychology, 44*, 335–351.

Aron, A., Norman, C. C., Aron, E. N., McKenna, C., & Heyman, R. E. (2000). Couples' shared participation in novel and arousing activities and experienced relationship quality. *Journal of Personality and Social Psychology, 78,* 273–284.

Balderrama-Durbin, C., Snyder, D. K., Cigrang, J., et al. (2013). Combat disclosure in intimate relationships: Mediating the impact of partner support on posttraumatic stress. *Journal of Family Psychology, 27,* 560–586.

Bardeen, J. R., Fergus, T. A., & Orcutt, H. K. (2014). The moderating role of experiential avoidance in the prospective relationship between anxiety sensitivity and anxiety. *Cognitive Therapy and Research, 38,* 465–471.

Bartlett, M. Y., Condon, P., Cruz, J., Baumann, J., & Desteno, D. (2012). Gratitude: Prompting behaviours that build relationships. *Cognition and Emotion, 26,* 2–13.

Baucom, B. R., Weusthoff, S., Atkins, D. C., & Hahlweg, K. (2012). Greater emotional arousal predicts poor long-term memory of communication skills in couples. *Behaviour Research and Therapy, 50,* 442–447.

Belanger, C., Laughrea, K., & Lafontaine, M.F. (2001). The impact of anger on sexual satisfaction in marriage. *The Canadian Journal of Human Sexuality, 10,* 91–99.

Bhatia, V., Davila, J., Eubanks-Carter, C., & Burckell, L. A. (2013). Appraisals of daily romantic relationship experiences in individuals with borderline personality disorder features. *Journal of Family Psychology, 27,* 518–524.

Biljstra, G., Holland, R. W., Dotsch, R., Hugenberg, K., & Wigboldus, D. H. J. (2014). Stereotype associations and emotion recognition. *Personality and Social Psychology Bulletin, 40,* 567–577.

Birditt, K. S., Brown, E., Orbuch, T. L., & McIlvane, J. M. (2010). Marital conflict behaviors and implications for divorce over 16 years. *Journal of Marriage and Family, 72,* 1188–1204.

Birnbaum, G. E., Mikulincer, M., & Austerlitz, M. (2013). A fiery conflict: Attachment orientations and the effects of relational conflict on sexual motivation. *Personal Relationships, 20,* 294–310.

Birnie, C., McClure, M. J., Lydon, J. E., & Holmberg, D. (2009). Attachment avoidance and commitment aversion: A script for relationship failure. *Personal Relationships, 16,* 79–97.

Blanchflower, D. G., Oswald, A. J., & Stewart-Brown, S. (2013). Is psychological well-being linked to the consumption of fruit and vegetables? *Social Indicators Research, 114,* 785–801.

Brassard, A., Shaver, P. R., & Lussier, Y. (2007). Attachment, sexual experience, and sexual pressure in romantic relationships: A dyadic approach. *Personal Relationships, 14*, 475–493.

Brenning, K. M., & Braet, C. (2013). The emotion regulation model of attachment: An emotion-specific approach. *Personal Relationships, 20*, 107–123.

Brody, S. (2010). The relative health benefits of different sexual activities. *The Journal of Sexual Medicine, 7*, 1336–1361.

Brunell, A. B., Kernis, M. H., Goldman, B. M., et al. (2010). Dispositional authenticity and romantic relationship functioning. *Personality and Individual Differences, 48*, 900–905.

Buck, A. A., & Neff, L. A. (2012). Stress spillover in early marriage: The role of self-regulatory depletion. *Journal of Family Psychology, 26*, 698–708.

Buyukcan-Tetik, A., Finkenauer, C., Kuppens, S., & Vohs, K. D. (2013). Both trust and self-control are necessary to prevent intrusive behaviors: Evidence from a longitudinal study of married couples. *Journal of Family Psychology, 27*, 671–676.

Campbell, L., Overall, N. C., Rubin, H., & Lackenbauer, S. D. (2013). Inferring a partner's ideal discrepancies: Accuracy, projection, and the communicative role of interpersonal behavior. *Journal of Personality and Social Psychology, 105*, 217–233.

Carissoli, C., Villani, D., & Riva, G. (2015). Does a meditation protocol supported by a mobile application help people reduce stress? Suggestions from a controlled pragmatic trial. *Cyberpsychology, Behavior, and Social Networking, 18*, 46–53.

Carson, J. W., Keefe, F. J., Goli, V., Fras, A. M., Lynch, T. R., Thorp, S. R., & Buechler, J. L. (2005). Forgiveness and chronic low back pain: A preliminary study examining the relationship of forgiveness to pain, anger, and psychological distress. *The Journal of Pain, 6*, 84–91.

Cassidy, J., & Berlin, L. J. (1994). The insecure/ambivalent pattern of attachment: Theory and research. *Child Development, 65*, 971–991.

Cattran, C., Oddy, M., & Wood, R. (2011). The development of a measure of emotional regulation following acquired brain injury. *Journal of Clinical Experimental Neuropsychology, 33*, 672–679.

Centers for Disease Control and Prevention (CDC). (2010). Health, United States 2010 with special feature on death and dying. Retrieved from http://www.cdc.gov/nchs/data/hus/hus10.pdf.

Centers for Disease Control and Prevention (CDC). (2011, March 31). An estimated 1 in 10 U.S. adults report depression. Retrieved from http://www.cdc.gov/features/dsdepression.

Charles, S. T., Piazza, J. R., Mogle, J., Sliwinski, M. J., & Almeida, D. M. (2013). The wear and tear of daily stressors on mental health. *Psychological Science, 24*, 733–741.

Cheung, W.Y., Wildschut, T., Sedikides, C., Hepper, E. G., Arndt, J., & Vingerhoets, A. J. J. M. (2013). Back to the future: Nostalgia increases optimism. *Personality and Social Psychology Bulletin, 39*, 1484–1496.

Chow, C. M., Buhrmester, D., & Tan, C. C. (2014). Interpersonal coping styles and couple relationship quality: Similarity versus complementarity hypotheses. *European Journal of Social Psychology, 44*, 175–186.

Christensen, A., Atkins, D. C., Baucom, B., & Yi, J. (2010). Marital status and satisfaction five years following a randomized clinical trial comparing traditional versus integrative behavioral couple therapy. *Journal of Consulting and Clinical Psychology, 78*, 225–235.

Cohen, S., Schulz, M. S., Weiss, E., & Waldinger, R. J. (2012). Eye of the beholder: The individual and dyadic contributions of empathic accuracy and perceived empathic effort to relationship satisfaction. *Journal of Family Psychology, 26*, 236–245.

Conger, R. D., Cui, M., Bryant, C. M., & Elder, G. H., Jr. (2000). Competence in early adult romantic relationships: A developmental perspective on family influences. *Journal of Personality and Social Psychology, 79*, 224–237.

Conty, L., Dezecache, G., Hugueville, L., & Grezes, J. (2012). Early binding of gaze, gesture, and emotion: Neural time course and correlates. *The Journal of Neuroscience, 32*, 4531–4539.

Coulter, K., & Malouff, J. M. (2013). Effects of an intervention designed to enhance romantic relationship excitement: A randomized-control trial. *Couple and Family Psychology: Research and Practice, 2*, 34–44.

Coy, A. E., Green, J. D., & Davis, J. L. (2012). With or without you: The impact of partner presence and attachment on exploration. *Journal of Experimental Social Psychology, 48*, 411–415.

Crum, A. J., Salovey, P., & Achor, S. (2013). Rethinking stress: The role of mindsets in determining the stress response. *Journal of Personality and Social Psychology, 104*, 716–733.

Cundiff, J. M., Smith, T. W., Butner, J., Critchfield, K. L., & Nealey-Moore, J. (2015). Affiliation and control in marital interaction: Interpersonal complementarity is present but is not associated with affect or relationship quality. *Personal and Social Psychology Bulletin, 41*, 35–51.

de Montigny-Malenfant, B., Santerre, M.E., Bouchard, S., Sabourin, S., Lazarides, A., & Belanger, C. (2013). Couples' negative interaction behaviors and borderline personality disorder. *The American Journal of Family Therapy, 41,* 259–271.

Derrick, J. L., Leonard, K. E., & Homish, G. G. (2012). Dependence regulation in newlywed couples: A prospective examination. *Personal Relationships, 19,* 644–662.

Dethier, M., Blairy, S., Rosenberg, H., & McDonald, S. (2013). Emotional regulation impairments following severe traumatic brain injury: An investigation of the body and facial feedback effects. *Journal of the International Neuropsychological Society, 19,* 367–379.

DeWall, C. N., Lambert, N. M., Slotter, E. B., et al. (2011). So far away from one's partner, yet so close to romantic alternatives: Avoidant attachment, interest in alternatives, and infidelity. *Journal of Personality and Social Psychology, 101,* 1302–1316.

Diamond, L. M., & Hicks, A. M. (2012). "It's the economy, honey!": Couples' blame attributions during the 2007–2009 economic crisis. *Personal Relationships, 19,* 586–600.

Ditzen, B., Schaer, M., Gabriel, B., Bodenmann, G., Ehlert, U., & Heinrichs, M. (2009). Intranasal oxytocin increases positive communication and reduces cortisol levels during couple conflict. *Biological Psychiatry, 65,* 728–731.

Edmondson, C. B., Conger, J. C., & Conger, A. J. (2007). Social skills in college students with high trait anger. *Journal of Social and Clinical Psychology, 26,* 575–594.

El-Sheikh, M., Kelly, R., & Rauer, A. (2013). Quick to berate, slow to sleep: Interpartner psychological conflict, mental health, and sleep. *Health Psychology, 32,* 1057–1066.

Epley, N., & Schroeder, J. (2014). Mistakenly seeking solitude. *Journal of Experimental Psychology: General, 143,* 1980–1999.

Feeney, B. C., & Lemay, E. P. (2012). Surviving relationship threats: The role of emotional capital. *Personality and Social Psychology Bulletin, 38,* 1004–1017.

Felmlee, D. H. (2001). From appealing to appalling: Disenchantment with a romantic partner. *Sociological Perspectives, 44,* 263–280.

Ferguson, Y. L., & Sheldon, K. M. (2013). Trying to be happier really can work: Two experimental studies. *The Journal of Positive Psychology, 8,* 23–33.

Flora, J., & Segrin, C. (2000). Affect and behavioral involvement in spousal complaints and compliments. *Journal of Family Psychology, 14,* 641–657.

Floyd, K., Pauley, P. M., & Hesse, C. (2010). State and trait affectionate communication buffer adults' stress reactions. *Communication Monographs, 77,* 618–636.

Franiuk, R., Pomerantz, E. M., & Cohen, D. (2004). The causal role of theories of relationships: Consequences for satisfaction and cognitive strategies. *Personality and Social Psychology Bulletin, 30*, 1494–1507.

Fraley, R. C., Roisman, G. I., Booth-LaForce, C., Owen, M. T., & Holland, A. S. (2013). Interpersonal and genetic origins of adult attachment styles: A longitudinal study from infancy to early adulthood. *Journal of Personality and Social Psychology, 104*, 817–838.

Frye-Cox, N. E., & Hesse, C. R. (2013). Alexithymia and marital quality: The mediating roles of loneliness and intimate communication. *Journal of Family Psychology, 27*, 203–211.

Gable, S. L., Gosnell, C. L., Maisel, N. C., & Strachman, A. (2012). Safely testing the alarm: Close others' responses to personal positive events. *Journal of Personality and Social Psychology, 103*, 963–981.

Gable, S. L., Gonzaga, G. C., & Strachman, A. (2006). Will you be there for me when things go right? Supportive responses to positive event disclosures. *Journal of Personality and Social Psychology, 91*, 904–917.

Gardner, B. C., Busby, D. M., & Brimhall, A. S. (2007). Putting emotional reactivity in its place? Exploring family-of-origin influences on emotional reactivity, conflict, and satisfaction in premarital couples. *Contemporary Family Therapy, 29*, 113–127.

Gere, J., & Schimmack, U. (2013). When romantic partners' goals conflict: Effects on relationship quality and subjective well-being. *Journal of Happiness Studies, 14*, 37–49.

Goldman, R. N., & Greenberg, L. (2013). Working with identity and self-soothing in emotion-focused therapy for couples. *Family Process, 52*, 62–82.

Gordon, A. M., & Chen, S. (2010). When you accept me for me: The relational benefits of intrinsic affirmations from one's relationship partner. *Personality and Social Psychology Bulletin, 36*, 1439–1453.

Gordon, A. M., & Chen, S. (2014). The role of sleep in interpersonal conflict: Do sleepless nights mean worse fights? *Social Psychological and Personality Science, 5*, 168–175.

Gordon, C. L., Arnette, R. A. M., & Smith, R. E. (2011). Have you thanked your spouse today?: Felt and expressed gratitude among married couples. *Personality and Individual Differences, 50*, 339–343.

Goto, S. G., Yee, A., Lowenberg, K., & Lewis, R. S. (2013). Cultural differences in sensitivity to social context: Detecting affective incongruity using the N400. *Social Neuroscience, 8*, 63–74.

Grace, J., & Grace, L. G. (1998). *The Art of Spooning: A Cuddler's Handbook*. Philadelphia, PA: Running Press.

Gratz, K. L., Dixon-Gordon, K. L., Breetz, A., & Tull, M. (2013). A laboratory-based examination of responses to social rejection in borderline personality disorder: The mediating role of emotion dysregulation. *Journal of Personality Disorders, 27*, 157–171.

Green, J. D., Davis, J. L., Luchies, L. B., et al. (2013). Victims versus perpetrators: Affective and empathic forecasting regarding transgressions in romantic relationships. *Journal of Experimental Social Psychology, 49*, 329–333.

Green, M., DeCourville, N., & Sadava, S. (2012). Positive affect, negative affect, stress, and social support as mediators of the forgiveness-health relationship. *The Journal of Social Psychology, 152*, 288–307.

Grewen, K. M., Girdler, S. S., Amico, J., & Light, K. C. (2005). Effects of partner support on resting oxytocin, cortisol, norepinephrine, and blood pressure before and after warm partner contact. *Psychosomatic Medicine, 67*, 531–538.

Gross, J.J. (2002). Emotion regulation: Affective, cognitive, and social consequences. *Psychophysiology, 39*, 281–291.

Gustavson, K., Røysamb, E., von Soest, T., Helland, M. J., Karevold, E., & Mathiesen, K. S. (2012). Reciprocal longitudinal associations between depressive symptoms and romantic partners' synchronized view of relationship quality. *Journal of Social and Personal Relationships, 29*, 776–794.

Hannon, P. A., Finkel, E. J., Kumashiro, M., & Rusbult, C. E. (2012). The soothing effects of forgiveness on victims' and perpetrators' blood pressure. *Personal Relationships, 19*, 279–289.

Hart, W. (2013). Unlocking past emotion: Verb use affects mood and happiness. *Psychological Science, 24*, 19–26.

Hawk, S. T., Fischer, A. H., & Van Kleef, G. A. (2012). Face the noise: Embodied responses to nonverbal vocalizations of discrete emotions. *Journal of Personality and Social Psychology, 102*, 796–814.

Hazan, C., & Shaver, P. (1987). Romantic love conceptualized as an attachment process. *Journal of Personality and Social Psychology, 52*, 511–524.

Helmich, I., Latini, A., Sigwalt, A., et al. (2010). Neurobiological alterations induced by exercise and their impact on depressive disorders. *Clinical Practice and Epidemiology in Mental Health, 6*, 115–125.

HelpGuide.org. (2014, October). Helping someone with PTSD. Retrieved from http://www.helpguide.org/articles/ptsd-trauma/ptsd-in-the-family.htm.

Herbenick, D., Reece, M., Schick, V., Sanders, S.A., Dodge, B., & Fortenberry, J.D. (2010). Sexual behaviors, relationships, and perceived health status among adult women in the United States: Results from a national probability sample. *The Journal of Sexual Medicine, 7,* 277–290.

Hess, U., & Fischer, A. (2013). Emotional mimicry as social regulation. *Personality and Social Psychology Review, 17,* 142–157.

Hill, C. L. M., & Updegraff, J. A. (2012). Mindfulness and its relationship to emotional regulation. *Emotion, 12,* 81–90.

Hira, S. N., & Overall, N. C. (2011). Improving intimate relationships: Targeting the partner versus changing the self. *Journal of Social and Personal Relationships, 28,* 610–633.

Holt-Lunstad, J., Birmingham, W. A., & Light, K. C. (2008). Influence of a "warm touch" support enhancement intervention among married couples on ambulatory blood pressure, oxytocin, alpha amylase, and cortisol. *Psychosomatic Medicine, 70,* 976–985.

Hrapczynski, K. M., Epstein, N. B., Werlinich, C. A., & LaTaillade, J. J. (2012). Changes in negative attributions during couple therapy for abusive behavior: Relations to changes in satisfaction and behavior. *Journal of Marital and Family Therapy, 38,* 117–132.

Hudson, N. W., Fraley, R. C., Brumbaugh, C. C., & Vicary, A. M. (2014). Coregulation in romantic partners' attachment styles: A longitudinal investigation. *Personality and Social Psychology Bulletin, 40,* 845–857.

Ijzerman, H., Karremans, J. C., Thomsen, L., & Schubert, T. W. (2013). Caring for sharing: How attachment styles modulate communal cues of physical warmth. *Social Psychology, 44,* 160–166.

Impett, E. A., Gordon, A. M., Kogan, A., Oveis, C., Gable, S. L., & Keltner, D. (2010). Moving toward more perfect unions: Daily and long-term consequences of approach and avoidance goals in romantic relationships. *Journal of Personality and Social Psychology, 99,* 948–963.

Impett, E. A., Kogan, A., English, T., et al. (2012). Suppression sours sacrifice: Emotional and relational costs of suppressing emotions in romantic relationships. *Personality and Social Psychology Bulletin, 38,* 707–720.

Inbar, Y., Pizarro, D. A., Gilovich, T., & Ariely, D. (2013). Moral masochism: On the connection between guilt and self-punishment. *Emotion, 13,* 14–18.

Inflammation: Causes, symptoms, and treatment. (2015, May 25). Medical News Today. Retrieved from http://www.medicalnewstoday.com/articles/248423.php.

Jaremka, L. M., Glaser, R., Loving, T. J., Malarkey, W. B., Stowell, J. R., & Kiecolt-Glaser, J. K. (2013). Attachment anxiety is linked to alterations in cortisol production and cellular immunity. *Psychological Science, 24,* 272–279.

Jarnecke, A. M., & South, S. C. (2013). Attachment orientations as mediators in the intergenerational transmission of marital satisfaction. *Journal of Family Psychology, 27,* 550–559.

Kar, H. L., & O'Leary, K. D. (2013). Patterns of psychological aggression, dominance, and jealousy within marriage. *Journal of Family Violence, 28,* 109–119.

Knippenberg, S., Damoiseaux, J., Bol, Y., et al. (2014). Higher levels of reported sun exposure, and not vitamin D status, are associated with less depressive symptoms and fatigue in multiple sclerosis. *Acta Neurologica Scandinavica, 129,* 123–131.

Kogan, A., Impett, E.A., Oveis, C., Hui, B., Gordon, A. M., & Keltner, D. (2010). When giving feels good: The intrinsic benefits of sacrifice in romantic relationships for the communally motivated. *Psychological Science, 21,* 1918–1924.

Kouvonen, A., Stafford, M., De Vogli, R., et al. (2011). Negative aspects of close relationships as a predictor of increased body mass index and waist circumference: The Whitehall II study. *American Journal of Public Health, 101,* 1474–1480.

Klonsky, E. D. (2008). What is emptiness? Clarifying the 7th criterion for borderline personality disorder. *Journal of Personality Disorders, 22,* 418–426.

Laak, J. J. F. T., Olthof, T., & Aleva, E. (2003). Sources of annoyance in close relationships: Sex-related differences in annoyance with partner behaviors. *The Journal of Psychology, 137,* 545–559.

Lambert, N. L., Gwinn, A. M., Baumeister, R. F., et al. (2013). A boost of positive affect: The perks of sharing positive experiences. *Journal of Social and Personal Relationships, 30,* 24–43.

Lamont, A., & Van Horn, M. L. (2013). Heterogeneity in parent-reported social skill development in early elementary school children. *Social Development, 22,* 384–405.

Lane, J. D., & Wegner, D. M. (1995). The cognitive consequences of secrecy. *Journal of Personality and Social Psychology, 69,* 237–253.

Lavner, J. A., & Bradbury, T. N. (2012). Why do even satisfied newlyweds eventually go on to divorce? *Journal of Family Psychology, 26,* 1–10.

Lavner, J. A., Bradbury, T. N., & Karney, B. R. (2012). Incremental change or initial differences? Testing two models of marital deterioration. *Journal of Family Psychology, 26*, 606–616.

Lavner, J. A., Karney, B. R., & Bradbury, T. N. (2012). Do cold feet warn of trouble ahead? Premarital uncertainty and four-year marital outcomes. *Journal of Family Psychology, 26*, 1012–1017.

Lawler-Row, K. A., Younger, J. W., Piferi, R. L., & Jones, W. H. (2006). The role of adult attachment style in forgiveness following an interpersonal offense. *Journal of Counseling and Development, 84*, 493–502.

Le, B. M., & Impett, E. A. (2013). When holding back helps: Suppressing negative emotions during sacrifice feels authentic and is beneficial for highly interdependent people. *Psychological Science, 24*, 1809–1815.

Lebow, J. L., Chambers, A. L., Christensen, A., & Johnson, S. M. (2012). Research on the treatment of couple distress. *Journal of Marital and Family Therapy, 38*, 145–168.

Leist, A. J., & Muller, D. (2013). Humor types show different patterns of self-regulation, self-esteem, and well-being. *Journal of Happiness Studies, 14*, 551–569.

Lemay, E. P., Jr., & Melville, M. C. (2014). Diminishing self-disclosure to maintain security in partners' care. *Journal of Personality and Social Psychology, 106*, 37–57.

Li, T., & Chan, D. K. (2012). How anxious and avoidant attachment affect romantic relationship quality differently: A meta-analytic review. *European Journal of Social Psychology, 42*, 406–419.

Little, K. C., McNulty, J. K., & Russell, V. M. (2010). Sex buffers intimates against the negative implications of attachment insecurity. *Personality and Social Psychology Bulletin, 36*, 484–498.

Lovett, E. (2012). Three stories of extraordinary forgiveness. *ABC News*. Retrieved from http://abcnews.go.com/US/cases-extraordinary-forgiveness/story?id=16065270.

Lynch, M. F. (2013). Attachment, autonomy, and emotional reliance: A multi-level model. *Journal of Counseling and Development, 91*, 301–312.

Martini, T. S., & Busseri, M. A. (2012). Emotion regulation and relationship quality in mother-young adult child dyads. *Journal of Social and Personal Relationships, 29*, 185–205.

Maisel, N. C., Gable, S. L., & Strachman, A. (2008). Responsive behaviors in good times and in bad. *Personal Relationships, 15*, 317–338.

Marganska, A., Gallagher, M., & Miranda, R. (2013). Adult attachment, emotion dysregulation, and symptoms of depression and generalized anxiety disorder. *American Journal of Orthopsychiatry, 83*, 131–141.

Martin, D., Slessor, G., Allen, R., Phillips, L. H., & Darling, S. (2012). Processing orientation and emotion recognition. *Emotion, 12*, 39–43.

Mauss, I. B., Troy, A. S., & LeBourgeois, M. K. (2013). Poorer sleep quality is associated with lower emotion-regulation ability in a laboratory paradigm. *Cognition and Emotion, 27*, 567–576.

McAllister, S., Thornock, C. M., Hammond, J. R., Holmes, E. K., & Hill, E. J. (2012). The influence of couple emotional intimacy on job perceptions and work-family conflict. *Family and Consumer Sciences Research Journal, 40*, 330–347.

McIntosh, D. N. (1996). Facial feedback hypotheses: Evidence, implications, and directions. *Motivation and Emotion, 20*, 121–147.

McMartin, S. E., Jacka, F. N., & Colman, I. (2013). The association between fruit and vegetable consumption and mental health disorders: Evidence from five waves of a national survey of Canadians. *Preventive Medicine, 56*, 225–230.

McNulty, J. K., & Karney, B. R. (2004). Positive expectations in the early years of marriage: Should couples expect the best or brace for the worst? *Journal of Personality and Social Psychology, 86*, 729–743.

Miller, M. W., Wolf, E. J., Reardon, A. F., et al. (2013). PTSD and conflict behavior between veterans and their intimate partners. *Journal of Anxiety Disorders, 27*, 240–251.

Miller, A. J., & Worthington, E. L., Jr. (2010). Sex differences in forgiveness and mental health in recently married couples. *The Journal of Positive Psychology, 5*, 12–23.

Miller, S. C., Kennedy, C., DeVoe, D., Hickey, M., Nelson, T., & Kogan, L. (2009). An examination of changes in oxytocin levels in men and women before and after interaction with a bonded dog. *Anthrozoos, 22*, 31–42.

Millisecond. (n.d.). Retrieved March 30, 2014, from http://en.wikipedia.org/wiki/Millisecond.

Montesi, J. L., Fauber, R. L., Gordon, E. A., & Heimberg, R. G. (2011). The specific importance of communicating about sex to couples' sexual and overall relationship satisfaction. *Journal of Social and Personal Relationships, 28*, 591–609.

Murray, S. L., Pinkus, R. T., Holmes, J. G., et al. (2011). Signaling when (and when not) to be cautious and self-protective: Impulsive and reflective trust in close relationships. *Journal of Personality and Social Psychology, 101*, 485–502.

Nagasawa, M., Mogi, K., & Kikusui, T. (2009). Attachment between humans and dogs. *Japanese Psychological Research, 51*, 209–221.

Nagurney, A. (2013). The effects of emotional writing on psychological well-being. *North American Journal of Psychology, 15*, 195–206.

National Institute of Mental Health. (n.d.). What is depression? Retrieved from http://www.nimh.nih.gov/health/topics/depression/index.shtml.

National Institute of Mental Health. (n.d.). What is post-traumatic stress disorder (PTSD)? Retrieved from http://www.nimh.nih.gov/health/topics/post-traumatic-stress-disorder-ptsd/index.shtml.

Neff, L. A., & Geers, A. L. (2013). Optimistic expectations in early marriage: A resource or vulnerability for adaptive relationship functioning? *Journal of Personality and Social Psychology, 105*, 38–60.

Nightingale, J., & Williams, R. M. (2000). Attitudes to emotional expression and personality in predicting post-traumatic stress disorder. *British Journal of Clinical Psychology, 39*, 243–254.

Nilsson, U. (2009). Soothing music can increase oxytocin levels during bed rest after open-heart surgery: A randomised control trial. *Journal of Clinical Nursing, 18*, 2153–2161.

Odendaal, J.S.J., & Meintjes, R. A. (2003). Neurophysiological correlates of affiliative behaviour between humans and dogs. *The Veterinary Journal, 165*, 296–301.

Orth, U., Robins, R. W., & Widaman, K. F. (2012). Life-span development of self-esteem and its effects on important life outcomes. *Journal of Personality and Social Psychology, 102*, 1271–1288.

Ossewaarde, L., van Wingen, G. A., Rijpkema, M., Backstrom, T., Hermans, E. J., & Fernandez, G. (2013). Menstrual cycle–related changes in amygdala morphology are associated with changes in stress sensitivity. *Human Brain Mapping, 34*, 1187–1193.

Overall, N. C., Simpson, J. A., & Struthers, H. (2013). Buffering attachment-related avoidance: Softening emotional and behavioral defenses during conflict discussions. *Journal of Personality and Social Psychology, 104*, 854–871.

Papp, L. M., Goeke-Morey, M. C., & Cummings, E. M. (2013). Let's talk about sex: A diary investigation of couples' intimacy conflicts in the home. *Couple and Family Psychology: Research and Practice, 2*, 60–72.

Pasipanodya, E. C., Parrish, B. P., Laurenceau, J. P., et al. (2012). Social constraints on disclosure predict daily well-being in couples coping with early-stage breast cancer. *Journal of Family Psychology, 26*, 661–667.

Patterson, J., Gardner, B. C., Burr, B. K., Hubler, D. S., & Roberts, K. M. (2012). Nonverbal behavioral indicators of negative affect in couple interaction. *Contemporary Family Therapy, 34*, 11–28.

Pelucchi, S., Paleari, F. G., Regalia, C., & Fincham, F. D. (2013). Self-forgiveness in romantic relationships: It matters to both of us. *Journal of Family Psychology, 27*, 541–549.

Pennebaker, J. W., & Beall, S.K. (1986). Confronting a traumatic event: Toward an understanding of inhibition and disease. *Journal of Abnormal Psychology, 95*, 274–281.

Peters, M. L., Flink, I. K., Boersma, K., & Linton, S. J. (2010). Manipulating optimism: Can imagining a best possible self be used to increase positive future expectancies? *Journal of Positive Psychology, 5*, 204–211.

Peterson, J. L., & DeHart, T. (2013). Regulating connection: Implicit self-esteem predicts positive non-verbal behavior during romantic relationship threat. *Journal of Experimental Social Psychology, 49*, 99–105.

Philippe, F. L., Koestner, R., & Lekes, N. (2013). On the directive function of episodic memories in people's lives: A look at romantic relationships. *Journal of Personality and Social Psychology, 104*, 164–179.

Reece, M., Herbenick, D., Schick, V., Sanders, S.A., Dodge, B., & Fortenberry, J.D. (2010). Sexual behaviors, relationships, and perceived health among adult men in the United States: Results from a national probability sample. *The Journal of Sexual Medicine, 7*, 291–304.

Rholes, W. S., Simpson, J. A., Tran, S., Martin, M. A., III, & Friedman, M. (2007). Attachment and information seeking in romantic relationships. *Personality and Social Psychology Bulletin, 33*, 422–438.

Ribeiro, J. D., Pease, J. L., Gutierrez, P. M., et al. (2012). Sleep problems outperform depression and hopelessness as cross-sectional and longitudinal predictors of suicidal ideation and behavior in young adults in the military. *Journal of Affective Disorders, 136*, 743–750.

Ricard, N. C., Beaudry, S. G., & Pelletier, L. G. (2012). Lovers with happy feet: The interdependence of relationship and activity factors for individuals dancing with a romantic partner. *Journal of Applied Social Psychology, 42*, 939–963.

Richards, J. M., Butler, E. A., & Gross, J. J. (2003). Emotion regulation in romantic relationships: The cognitive consequences of concealing feelings. *Journal of Social and Personal Relationships, 20*, 599–620.

Rim, S., Hansen, J., & Trope, Y. (2013). What happens why? Psychological distance and focusing on causes versus consequences of events. *Journal of Personality and Social Psychology, 104*, 457–472.

Robinson, K. J., & Cameron, J. J. (2012). Self-esteem is a shared relationship resource: Additive effects of dating partners' self-esteem levels predict relationship quality. *Journal of Research in Personality, 46*, 227–230.

Robinson, O. J., Charney, D. R., Overstreet, C., Vytal, K., & Grillon, C. (2012). The adaptive threat bias in anxiety: Amygdala-dorsomedial prefrontal cortex coupling and aversive amplification. *NeuroImage, 60*, 523–529.

Rodriguez, L. M., Knee, C. R., & Neighbors, C. (2014). Relationships can drive some to drink: Relationship-contingent self-esteem and drinking problems. *Journal of Social and Personal Relationships, 31*, 270–290.

Sadikaj, G., Moskowitz, D. S., Russell, J. J., Zuroff, D. C., & Paris, J. (2013). Quarrelsome behavior in borderline personality disorder: Influence of behavioral and affective reactivity to perceptions of others. *Journal of Abnormal Psychology, 122*, 195–207.

Saffrey, C., Bartholomew, K., Scharfe, E., Henderson, A.J.Z., & Koopman, R. (2003). Self- and partner-perceptions of interpersonal problems and relationship functioning. *Journal of Social and Personal Relationships, 20*, 117–139.

Sanford, K. (2012). The communication of emotion during conflict in married couples. *Journal of Family Psychology, 26*, 297–307.

Sato, W., Fujimura, T., Kochiyama, T., & Suzuki, N. (2013). Relationships among facial mimicry, emotional experience, and emotion regulation. *Plos One, 8(3)*, e57889.

Saunders, T. S., & Buehner, M. J. (2013). The gut chooses faster than the mind: A latency advantage of affective over cognitive decisions. *The Quarterly Journal of Experimental Psychology, 66*, 381–388.

Schmid, P. C., & Mast, M. S. (2010). Mood effects on emotion recognition. *Motivation and Emotion, 34*, 288–292.

Schueller, S. M., & Parks, A. C. (2014). The science of self-help: Translating positive psychology research into increased individual happiness. *European Psychologist, 19*, 145–155.

Schumann, K. (2012). Does love mean never having to say you're sorry? Associations between relationship satisfaction, perceived apology sincerity, and forgiveness. *Journal of Social and Personal Relationships, 29*, 997–1010.

Sherry, S. B., Mackinnon, S. P., Macneil, M. A., & Fitzpatrick, S. (2013). Discrepancies confer vulnerability to depressive symptoms: A three-wave longitudinal study. *Journal of Counseling Psychology, 60*, 112–126.

Seidman, G. (2012). Positive and negative: Partner derogation and enhancement differentially related to relationship satisfaction. *Personal Relationships, 19*, 51–71.

Seih, Y.T., Chung, C. K., & Pennebaker, J. W. (2011). Experimental manipulations of perspective taking and perspective switching in expressive writing. *Cognition and Emotion, 25,* 926–938.

Seikkula, J., Aaltonen, K., Kalla, O., Saarinen, P., & Tolvanen, A. (2013). Couple therapy for depression in a naturalistic setting in Finland: A 2-year randomized trial. *Journal of Family Therapy, 35,* 281–302.

Simmons, R. A., Gordon, P. C., & Chambless, D. L. (2005). Pronouns in marital interaction: What do "you" and "I" say about marital health? *Psychological Science, 16,* 932–936.

Slatcher, R. B. (2010). When Harry and Sally met Dick and Jane: Creating closeness between couples. *Personal Relationships, 17,* 279–297.

Slatcher, R. B., & Pennebaker, J. W. (2006). How do I love thee? Let me count the words: The social effects of expressive writing. *Psychological Science, 17,* 660–664.

Slotter, E. B., & Luchies, L. B. (2014). Relationship quality promotes the desire for closeness among distressed avoidantly attached individuals. *Personal Relationships, 21,* 22–34.

Smith, A., Lyons, A., Ferris, J., et al. (2011). Sexual and relationship satisfaction among heterosexual men and women: The importance of desired frequency of sex. *Journal of Sex and Marital Therapy, 37,* 104–115.

Smith, J. C. S., Vogel, D. L., Madon, S., & Edwards, S. R. (2011). The power of touch: Nonverbal communication within married dyads. *The Counseling Psychologist, 39,* 764–787.

Song, L., Northouse, L. L., Zhang, L., et al. (2012). Study of dyadic communication in couples managing prostate cancer: A longitudinal perspective. *Psycho-Oncology, 21,* 72–81.

Spielmann, S. S., Maxwell, J. A., MacDonald, G., & Baratta, P. L. (2013). Don't get your hopes up: Avoidantly attached individuals perceive lower social reward when there is potential for intimacy. *Personality and Social Psychology Bulletin, 39,* 219–236.

Sprecher, S., Treger, S., Wondra, J. D., Hilaire, N., & Wallpe, K. (2013). Taking turns: Reciprocal self-disclosure promotes liking in initial interactions. *Journal of Experimental Social Psychology, 49,* 860–866.

Sripada, C. S., Phan, K. L., Labuschagne, I., Welsh, R., Nathan, P. J., & Wood, A. G. (2013). Oxytocin enhances resting-state connectivity between amygdala and medial frontal cortex. *International Journal of Neuropsychopharmacology, 16,* 255–260.

Striepens, N., Scheele, D., Kendrick, K. M., et al. (2012). Oxytocin facilitates protective responses to aversive social stimuli in males. *PNAS Proceedings of the National Academy of Sciences of the United States of America, 109*, 18144–18149.

Survelum Public Data Bank. Love and relationships survey statistics. (n.d.). Retrieved from http://www.survelum.com/survey-results/kia_durham.

Sweeny, T. D., Suzuki, S., Grabowecky, M., & Paller, K. A. (2013). Detecting and categorizing fleeting emotions in faces. *Emotion, 13*, 76–91.

Szczygiel, D., Buczny, J., & Bazinska, R. (2012). Emotion regulation and emotional information processing: The moderating effect of emotional awareness. *Personality and Individual Differences, 52*, 433–437.

Szpunar, K. K., & Schacter, D. L. (2013). Get real: Effects of repeated simulation and emotion on the perceived plausibility of future experiences. *Journal of Experimental Psychology: General, 142*, 323–327.

Tan, R., Overall, N. C., & Taylor, J. K. (2012). Let's talk about us: Attachment, relationship-focused disclosure, and relationship quality. *Personal Relationships, 19*, 521–534.

Tangney, J. P., & Dearing, R. L. (2003). *Shame and guilt.* New York: Guilford Press.

Totenhagen, C. J., Curran, M. A., Serido, J., & Butler, E. A. (2013). Good days, bad days: Do sacrifices improve relationship quality? *Journal of Social and Personal Relationships, 30*, 881–900.

Uysal, A., Lin, H. L., & Bush, A. L. (2012). The reciprocal cycle of self-concealment and trust in romantic relationships. *European Journal of Social Psychology, 42*, 844–851.

Uysal, A., Lin, H. L., Knee, C. R., & Bush, A. L. (2012). The association between self-concealment from one's partner and relationship well-being. *Personality and Social Psychology Bulletin, 38*, 39–51.

U.S. Department of Veterans Affairs. (n.d.). Helping a family member who has PTSD. Retrieved from http://www.ptsd.va.gov/public/family/helping-family-member.asp.

U.S. Department of Veterans Affairs. (n.d.). PTSD: National Center for PTSD. Retrieved from http://www.ptsd.va.gov.

Uziel, L. (2012). Asymmetry in self-other agreement on attachment style among romantic partners. *Journal of Research in Personality, 46*, 223–226.

van der Horst, M., & Coffe, H. (2012). How friendship network characteristics influence subjective well-being. *Social Indicators Research, 107*, 509–529.

Vinkers, C. D. W., Finkenauer, C., & Hawk, S. T. (2011). Why do close partners snoop? Predictors of intrusive behavior in newlywed couples. *Personal Relationships, 18*, 110–124.

Wachs, K., & Cordova, J. V. (2007). Mindful relating: Exploring mindfulness and emotion repertoires in intimate relationships. *Journal of Marital and Family Therapy, 33*, 464–481.

Walsh, R. (2011). Lifestyle and mental health. *American Psychologist, 66*, 579–592.

Warren, H. K., & Stifter, C. A. (2008). Maternal emotion-related socialization and preschoolers' developing emotion self-awareness. *Social Development, 17*, 239–258.

Wastell, C. A., & Taylor, A. J. (2002). Alexithymic mentalising: Theory of mind and social adaptation. *Social Behavior and Personality: An International Journal, 30*, 141–148.

Weusthoff, S., Baucom, B. R., & Hahlweg, K. (2013). Fundamental frequency during couple conflict: An analysis of physiological, behavioral, and sex-linked information encoded in vocal expression. *Journal of Family Psychology, 27*, 212–220.

Whisman, M. A., & Uebelacker, L. A. (2006). Impairment and distress associated with relationship discord in a national sample of married or cohabitating adults. *Journal of Family Psychology, 20*, 369–377.

Wile, D. B. (2013). Opening the circle of pursuit and distance. *Family Process, 52*, 19–32.

Wiltermuth, S. S., & Gino, F. (2013). "I'll have one of each": How separating rewards into (meaningless) categories increases motivation. *Journal of Personality and Social Psychology, 104*, 1–13.

World Health Organization (WHO). (2012, October). Depression. Retrieved from http://www.who.int/mediacentre/factsheets/fs369/en.

Yeh, H. C., Lorenz, F. O., Wickrama, K. A. S., Conger, R. D., & Elder, G. H., Jr. (2006). Relationships among sexual satisfaction, marital quality, and marital instability at midlife. *Journal of Family Psychology, 20*, 339–343.

Yoon, J. E., & Lawrence, E. (2013). Psychological victimization as a risk factor for the developmental course of marriage. *Journal of Family Psychology, 27*, 53–64.

Young, V., Curran, M., & Totenhagen, C. (2013). A daily diary study: Working to change the relationship and relational uncertainty in understanding positive relationship quality. *Journal of Social and Personal Relationships, 30*, 132–148.

Yuan, J. W., McCarthy, M., Holley, S. R., & Levenson, R. W. (2010). Physiological down-regulation and positive emotion in marital interaction. *Emotion, 10*, 467–474.